P9-BYB-662

The PaineWebber Art Collection

ThePain
ArtCol

aWebber
llection

Introduction by *Jack Flam*

Commentaries on the plates by
Monique Beudert and Jennifer Wells

Foreword by Donald B. Marron

RIZZOLI
NEW YORK

First published in the United States of America in 1995 by
Rizzoli International Publications, Inc.
300 Park Avenue South, New York, NY 10010

Copyright © 1995 by Rizzoli International Publications, Inc., and PaineWebber, Inc.
Photo Essay © 1995 by Louise Lawler
Introduction © 1995 by Jack Flam
Illustrations © as credited to individual artists, except
page 64: © 1995 ARS, New York/VG Bild-Kunst
page 70: © 1995 Louise Bourgeois/VAGA, New York
pages 86, 88: © 1995 ARS, New York/Willem de Kooning
page 259h: © 1995 ARS, New York/VG Bild-Kunst
page 264h: © 1995 ARS, New York/ADAGP Paris

All rights reserved.
No part of this publication may be reproduced in any
manner whatsoever without permission in writing from
Rizzoli International Publications, Inc.

Library of Congress Cataloging-in-Publication Data

The PaineWebber Art Collection / introduction by Jack Flam ;
commentaries on the plates by Monique Beudert and Jennifer Wells ;
foreword by Donald B. Marron.
       p.   cm.
       ISBN 0-8478-1791-1
1. Art, Modern—20th century—Catalogs. 2. Art—New York (N.Y.)—Catalogs.
3. PaineWebber Inc.—Art collections—Catalogs. 4. Art—Private collections—
New York (N.Y.)—Catalogs. I. Flam, Jack D. II. Beudert, Monique.
III. Wells, Jennifer. IV. Title: PaineWebber Art Collection.
N6488.5.P35A78 1995   93-40324
709'.04'50747471—dc20   CIP

Book Design: Pentagram Design, Inc.
Consulting Designer: Brenna Garratt
Compositor: Rose Scarpetis
Editor: Charles Miers

Printed in Japan

Contents

Foreword

Foreword

Twenty-five years ago, the PaineWebber art collection began from the combination of my appreciation for art and the need to fill a sizable amount of wall space. It originated with the conviction that good contemporary art reflects contemporary trends in society, and truly outstanding works might even suggest the future—a particular benefit to us since our business tries each day to anticipate tomorrow.

Our first acquisitions were prints, followed by drawings, paintings, and an occasional piece of sculpture we could not resist. Among these early purchases were works by Jasper Johns, Robert Rauschenberg, Roy Lichtenstein, Frank Stella, and Ed Ruscha. These were followed by a combination of younger, emerging artists and established figures, including David Salle, Anselm Kiefer, Susan Rothenberg, Lucian Freud, and Cy Twombly.

Assembling any collection is complicated and takes time, but building a contemporary collection is even more complex. There is neither wisdom of the ages to define taste and style for new art, nor extensive reference material; there is only evolving scholarship and one's personal response to the work. That, of course, is one of the most exciting aspects of collecting contemporary art—it is the art of one's own era. Seeing as much work as possible is crucial. Learning about the artists and their various periods is essential in making decisions. This is no easy task, although it was much easier in the 1970s, when the most exciting work was being created in New York City by a relatively small number of artists.

To those artists, and to all whose works provide a continuing source of enlightenment and inspiration in our collection, I would like to convey my appreciation. Indeed, their art plays a vital role in our organization, inspiring communication and creativity, inviting us all to think beyond that which is apparent. It enhances the corporation and the workforce by providing a focus for thought and consideration each day. Moreover, it is a source of pride for admirer and critic alike.

I am also thankful to the many art dealers who helped to bring this collection together. They shared their enthusiasm, knowledge, and time, educating and enlightening a growing collector. They offered access to their files so that we could see the range of works of a given artist, and they helpfully discussed other artists, assisting us to build the collection. I would like to thank all those who worked with us on Saturday visits to their galleries and artists' studios, but particularly those who were encouraging and supportive in the collection's early years: Leo Castelli, Arne Glimcher, Angela Westwater, Brooke Alexander, Ken Tyler, and the late Nick Wilder.

Until 1985, we had part-time assistants to help with the collection. We then determined that the collection required more intensive administration, and brought in Monique Beudert as curator. Monique's impact was significant, combining an art historian's point of view with extensive experience on the curatorial staff at the Museum of Modern Art, New York. When Monique left us in 1990, we subsequently found Jennifer Wells, an art historian and curator from the Museum of Modern Art's Department of Painting and Sculpture. Jennifer's innate talent and her focus on younger artists had a lively impact on the collection.

10

During these twenty-five years, I have been closely associated with the Museum of Modern Art, first as a committee member, later as a trustee, as president in the late 1980s and early 1990s, and now as a vice-chairman. Within the Museum, informal talks with fellow trustees and with the curators combined with the influence of the extraordinary collection, have given me an unparalleled backdrop for collecting art. I want to thank all my friends and associates at the Museum for expanding my love of art. I should note that while I have benefited greatly from the Museum's integrity of decision-making and from its unstinting focus on quality, the PaineWebber art collection has, of course, been compiled in an independent manner.

I am grateful to the members of the PaineWebber board of directors for their support of our vision and goals as well as their endorsement of the collection's growth. In addition, I would like to thank the senior managers of our company, who have participated in the process, recognizing that our collection complements the character and identity of the company. Finally, for the sensitivity of their responses to works that are sometimes challenging to understand, I want to thank our employees. They make PaineWebber the outstanding company that it is.

11

Donald B. Marron
Chairman and Chief Executive Officer
PaineWebber Group Inc.

Louise Lawler: An Arrangement of Pictures

PaineWebber
120 Broadway, 1982

PaineWebber Building
1285 Avenue of the Americas, 1993

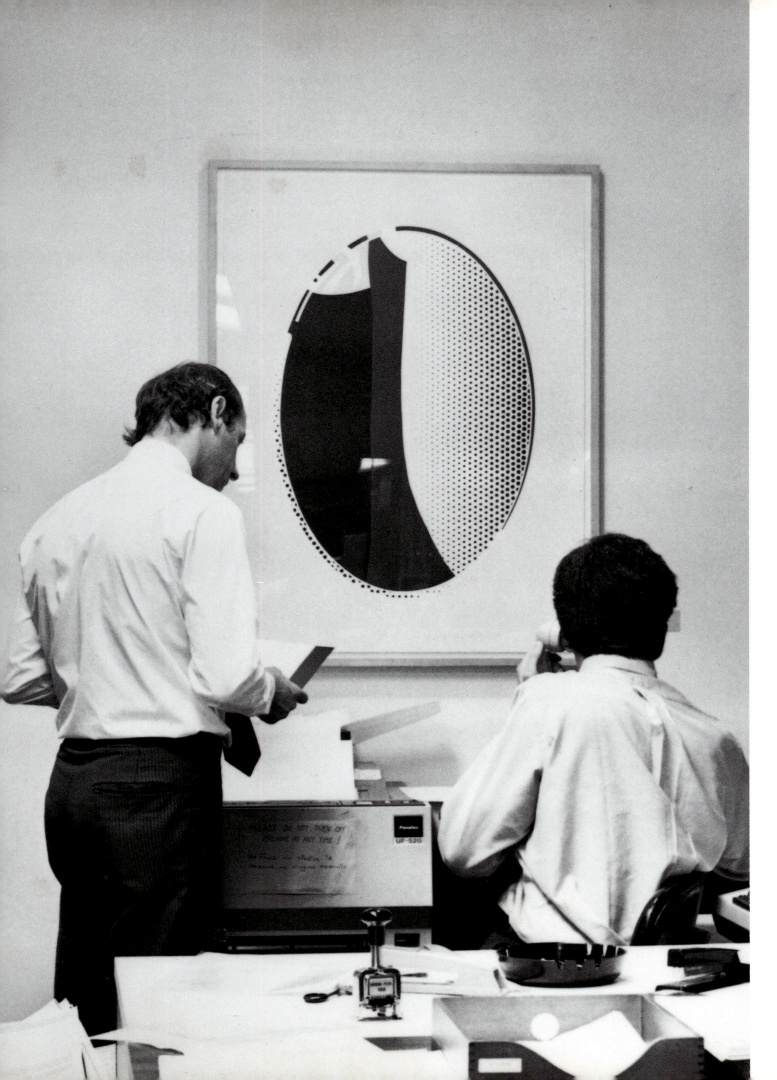

*Arranged by
Donald Marron,
Susan Brundage,
Cheryl Bishop
at PaineWebber,
Inc., NYC, 1982.*
Black-and-white
photograph.

Arranged by
Donald Marron,
Susan Brundage,
Cheryl Bishop
at PaineWebber, Inc.,
NYC, 1982.
Cibachrome.

*Arranged by
Donald Marron,
Susan Brundage,
Cheryl Bishop
at PaineWebber,
Inc., NYC, 1982.*
Black-and-white
photograph.

Untitled, 1993.
Cibachrome.

15th Floor, 1993.
Black-and-white
photograph.

Introduction

The PaineWebber Art Collection

Jack Flam

One of the most striking qualities of contemporary art is its ability to shock, outrage, and provoke its audience. Since these are characteristics that seem to be in direct opposition to the kind of public image that a large corporation seeks, it might seem anomalous for a corporation such as PaineWebber to be collecting contemporary art at all.

This anomaly is especially apparent in the way that PaineWebber's collection is displayed. As a matter of policy, the company keeps virtually all its art constantly on view in the hallways, corridors, conference rooms, and workspaces of its world headquarters in midtown Manhattan. The collection, in a sense, provides a kind of counterpoint to the company's activities as a financial services firm. Across from desks covered with banks of telephones, computers, and fax machines hang such paintings as Susan Rothenberg's lyrically violent *Dogs Killing a Rabbit* and Philip Guston's large, sullen interior called *In the Studio*.

What, you might ask, are these kinds of images doing in a brokerage house? How did they come to be there? And how do the people who see these works on a regular basis react to them?

❖　❖　❖

The PaineWebber Group's art program breaks many of the rules that are supposed to define corporate enterprise, and yet it remains very much a corporate program. This contradiction gives the collection, which has been correctly characterized as "strikingly avant-garde,"[1] a dimension of interest that goes beyond its high quality as a discriminating selection of contemporary art. And because the collection exists as an integral part of the environment at the company's New York headquarters, it also tells us something important about contemporary patronage and about how the art of our time is actually used and responded to by people who spend time living with it.

Perhaps I should begin by saying that I have been familiar with the PaineWebber art collection since 1985, and that I consider it to be one of the finest collections of contemporary art in America. It consists of paintings, drawings, prints, photographs, and sculptures by a wide range of contemporary and recent artists, American and foreign. Although the collection represents a broad spectrum of styles, it is not meant to provide a survey of contemporary art; the

Susan Rothenberg
(American,
born 1945)

Dogs Killing a Rabbit.
1991–92
Oil on canvas
87 × 141"
(221 × 358.1 cm)
1992.14

24

Philip Guston
(American, born
Canada. 1913–1980)

In the Studio. 1975
Oil on canvas
82 × 79"
(208.3 × 200.7 cm)
1989.41

primary basis for the selection of individual works is quality rather than comprehensiveness. And although a number of well-established artists are included—such as Georg Baselitz, Chuck Close, Lucian Freud, Jasper Johns, Anselm Kiefer, Roy Lichtenstein, Elizabeth Murray, Susan Rothenberg, and Frank Stella—a good deal of attention is given to younger, less well-known artists, such as Carroll Dunham, Günther Förg, Damien Hirst, Jim Shaw, Lorna Simpson, and Kiki Smith. The collection has clearly been put together with a relish for making discriminating judgments about what will hold up well over time, rather than simply following established reputations.

The PaineWebber collection is especially strong in works on paper, both prints and unique images. The prints include important concentrations of works by Jasper Johns, Roy Lichtenstein, and Frank Stella, along with a suite of monotypes from Eric Fischl's recent Scenes and Sequences series. One of the highlights among the prints is the group of works by Lucian Freud, which includes all the etchings he has made since he resumed printmaking in 1982. At present, most of these are gathered together in a small conference and dining room on the top floor of the PaineWebber Building; seen together there in a relatively intimate space, they create a moving and powerful effect.

The collection also includes an especially strong group of drawings and paintings on paper from the 1950s and 1960s by such artists as Joseph Beuys, Richard Diebenkorn, Helen Frankenthaler, Franz Kline, Willem de Kooning, Robert Motherwell, Claes Oldenburg, and Robert Rauschenberg. These provide a good historical foundation for the broad selection of more recent drawings by Francesco Clemente, Robert Longo, Brice Marden, Bruce Nauman, Cy Twombly, and others, and works on paper that include photographic imagery by such artists as Lothar Baumgarten, Cindy Sherman, and Yasumasa Morimura.

Like most corporate collections, one of its functions is to enhance the prestige of the company, and this it seems to do quite effectively—although, as we shall see, not in as uncomplicated a way as one might think. At the same time, the PaineWebber art collection is rather unusual. The selection of objects has been made almost entirely by Donald B. Marron, the

25

firm's chairman and chief executive officer, and one of its primary purposes is to embellish the workplace. At any given time, most of the collection is hung along the corridors and in the offices of PaineWebber's corporate headquarters in New York City; both the size of the collection, and to some degree the dimensions of the works in it, have been determined by this pragmatic function.

In many ways, it is also a rather daring collection, especially within the sensitive world of corporate image-making. As has been widely remarked, corporate collections frequently aim for a certain neutrality, what has been characterized as a form of visual Muzak or "white noise."[2] They tend to focus on reassuring forms of representational art, such as landscapes and still lifes, or on rather cool and impersonal abstract art that avoids the expression of strong emotions.[3] Indeed, corporate curators frequently explain that they avoid anything overtly political or controversial, especially images of nudes, religious subject matter, or anything they consider to be "too abstract or crazy."[4]

The PaineWebber collection, by contrast, seems to override virtually all these taboos. It is not confined to a single school or style, such as realist landscapes or "cool," geometrical abstractions. Rather it is more like a private collection, driven by a desire for quality and remaining unapologetically personal in many of its choices. As a reflection of Marron's personal taste, for example, it contains virtually no Minimalist or Conceptual art, and it stays clear of funky assemblages and installations.

Nor is the PaineWebber collection confined to a specific sort of subject matter or imagery that is supposed to be a direct reflection of the company's activities and interests. That sort of collecting marked some of the earliest art-related activities of American corporations, such as the rosy depictions of the American West commissioned by the Atchison, Topeka and Santa Fe Railroad at the end of the last century, or Nabisco's collection of prints that showed Victorian children eating biscuits.[5] That kind of collecting still exists, especially among product-oriented companies and in smaller, regional firms with a narrowly defined clientele. But because PaineWebber is a large, international, service-oriented company with a broad

26

Georg Baselitz
(German, born 1938)

Die Wendin (from the series *Die Dresdner Frauen {The Women of Dresden}*). 1990
Maple painted with oil and egg tempera
46 × 26 × 13¼"
(116.8 × 66 × 33.7 cm)
1990.50

base of clients, its collection can relate to the company's business in a broader, more general, more indirect way. As a result, the PaineWebber collection is full of the kinds of imagery that people say corporations should avoid, such as nudes and violent or "controversial" subjects. In its aim to represent the best art of our time, it has remained surprisingly free of self-censorship.

This is apparent the moment we arrive on the executive floor at PaineWebber headquarters. (Although the placement of individual works is periodically changed, the effect of the collection on its surroundings remains pretty much the same as it was during the recent visit I am about to describe.) The architectural setting is cool and elegant: deep mahogany paneling and an expanse of pale green carpeting punctuated by polished steel columns create a sleek, assured ambience. But moments after we enter this coolly elegant space we run smack into Georg Baselitz's rough-hewn wooden sculpture *Die Wendin*. This unsettling, primitivistic image of an anguished face with its features oddly turned back on themselves in a concave hollow suggests both introversion and agony. Its head tilted upward as if in a kind of silent cry, the sculpture looks almost perversely crude and individualistic—especially in the context of the tasteful "corporate" surroundings.

No less surprising, as we look beyond the reception desk, is Eric Fischl's *The Chester's Gambit*, a large oil painting that is like an ironic takeoff on the conventions of the family snapshot. In it, the members of the family—mom, dad, baby, babysitter—stand behind a leather couch and look out at us from the middle distance of a sleekly appointed room, not at all unlike the room that we ourselves are standing in as we stare back at them. The foreground of the picture is constructed like a kind of barricade comprised of depictions of other works of art: the crowned visage of a gothic king, a female nude torso, the head and mane of a Greek horse. After a moment, we realize that the carpet in that painted room is almost exactly the same color as the one we are standing on, and that the blurred rendering of everyone in the painting suggests not so much the action of the figures themselves as it does our own sense of movement, even though we are standing still, as if anticipating that

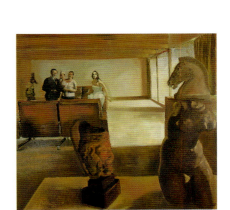

Eric Fischl
(American,
born 1948)

The Chester's Gambit.
1991
Oil on linen
86 × 98"
(218.4 × 249 cm)
1991.48

any second we will begin to move. Only the woman's head in this picture seems fixed, as she examines us with an appraising, discomfiting gaze.

Here, as elsewhere in the collection, you feel almost as if the pictures are meant not only to decorate the offices but to ruffle the surface of daily life at PaineWebber—to provoke people. And in doing so, the collection also sends out another, rather subtle signal, to the effect that "we understand that life is complex, and that human nature is quirky and unpredictable." (In a curious way, the toughness of the collection seems to reinforce the firm's image as having a broad, comprehensive view of human nature—exactly the sort of savvy attitude that you might seek in a financial services company.) A good deal of contemporary art takes this kind of tension for granted, and the works in the PaineWebber collection seem constantly to welcome rather than deny it.

For example, one of the most inviting public spaces on the executive floor is a small sitting room furnished with a tastefully upholstered beige sofa and side chairs. This is the place where you wait to be greeted by the person you have come to see, the waiting room meant to set you at your ease. But above the sofa is Lucian Freud's *Double Portrait*, an oddly incongruous painting of a thoughtful, somewhat mannish woman cuddling a sleeping dog. This is a curious image, full of contradictory implications. Seen historically, it is a variant of a subject that has traditionally been treated in a sexual, even perverse way by such artists as Fragonard and Courbet. Here, however, the image seems to have been made into something rather more innocent—or almost so—at once touchingly domestic and charged with a kind of feral unpredictability.

But more to the point, this particular painting has an especially odd effect in this particular corporate waiting room. For it reminds you very clearly of the part of yourself that you, by necessity, have to leave at home in the morning when you leave for work, in preparation for sitting in a room like this one. Paradoxically, the painting on the wall in this public space is intensely private; and the paradox is made all the more striking by the way that this painting

Lucian Freud
(British, born
Germany 1922)

Double Portrait.
(1988–90)
Oil on canvas
44½ × 53"
(113 × 134.6 cm)
1991.19

Francesco Clemente
(Italian, born 1953)

Perseverance. (1982)
Oil on canvas
78 × 93"
(198.1 × 236.2 cm)
1982.5

about the tame and untameable aspects of human love is as civilized and subdued in color as the buff and beige room that you are sitting in when you see it—on the executive floor of an international financial services company.

I do not mean to say, of course, that the works in the PaineWebber collection were purposely chosen to be provocative, but rather that the collection seems to have been put together in a remarkably open-minded and freewheeling way. And I find this policy especially appealing because it runs counter to so much public-relations activity, which seems to treat the public—that is, us—as if we are incapable of dealing with the ambiguities and contradictions of real life, as if we really believed the Pollyannaish values that are espoused—or in any case, paid lip service to—by corporate image-makers and mass-communications strategists.

A painting such as Francesco Clemente's *Perseverance,* for example, in which a roughly painted striding figure grasps a small building that resembles the Pantheon in Rome, seems to suggest simultaneously a number of contradictory interpretations (in addition to the dream narrative that the picture was based on). On the one hand, given the title, there is the suggested optimism of "Rome wasn't built in a day," mixed in with a whole range of rather sinister associations, including theft, ransacking, and physical attack, which evoke an undermining of traditional cultural values. As to which of these is the primary reading of the painting, it is hard to say. We are left to draw our own, perhaps unsettling conclusions. Unlike business transactions, which are based on definitive answers, this picture reminds us that in art as in life there are relatively few definitive answers.

Disquiet is expressed in a different way in Georg Baselitz's *Fünfmal Meise,* in which the lyrical turns melancholy by the way color and subject are set in counterpoint to each other. The gentle poetry of the blue-and-yellow color harmony is belied by the way the birdlike forms are trapped within the netlike yellow grid that surrounds them, creating an ominous note of discord and menace. Jannis Kounellis's *Untitled* is no more reassuring; it aggressively

29

sets severed heads against childlike drawings of faces and pieces of broken glass, evoking a terrible sense of loss and ruin.

In some cases the collection includes very different kinds of works by the same artist. Philip Guston's abstract style of the mid-1950s is represented by a wonderfully rhythmic brush and ink drawing, while his late figurative style is very well illustrated by the powerful 1975 interior *In the Studio*. Here the artist, smoking a cigarette, sits among a number of his own works, contemplating a painting of a truncated foot. The picture sets up an arresting contrast between antic, deadpan irony and a poignant sense of emotional nakedness, which in turn is perfectly matched by the simplified, rather awkward manner of rendering.

Richard Diebenkorn is also nicely represented both by his figurative and abstract modes. The 1964 drawing *Table and Chair* is a wonderfully fresh example of the way this artist was able to balance the depiction of actual objects with a strong sense of abstract composition, while his 1983 *Untitled (Ocean Park #13)* is a small but powerful example of the metaphysical overtones characteristic of his abstract Ocean Park series, in which atmospheric light and suggestions of landscape are condensed within an austere geometrical scaffolding. This painting on paper is also an excellent example of the discrimination and restraint that guides PaineWebber's collecting policy. Although it is considerably smaller than the oil paintings in the Ocean Park series, the work is nonetheless a very fine example of this aspect of the artist's work, presumably acquired at a relatively advantageous price.[6] A similar discrimination is also apparent in the collection's inclusion of works on paper by other older American masters, including Kline, Motherwell, and David Smith.

There are stimulating instances of call and response between works made by different artists several decades apart. An untitled drawing of 1987 by Richard Long provides a fascinating complement to a David Smith untitled 1952 brush and ink drawing, which employs the same kind of allover abstract formal vocabulary. The Long drawing, which is made out of river mud rather than ink, also provides an especially vivid reminder of "nature," which is

30

Richard Diebenkorn
(American,
1922–1993)

*Untitled (Ocean Park
#13)*. 1983
Gouache and acrylic
on paper
25 × 36"
(63.5 × 91.4 cm)
1984.19

Table and Chair.
1964
Ink wash and
graphite on paper
12 × 17¾"
(30.5 × 45.1 cm)
1989.56

quite poignant within the denatured setting of an office. In an abstract fashion it evokes the distant outdoors in a way that landscape painting functioned in the nineteenth century, bringing reminders of nature into urban interiors. In a very different vein, Alex Katz's *Good Morning I*, with its placid canoers paddling toward us on the glassy surface of a lake, also evokes a wry sense of not being *here*, in an office—a sense of there being other ways to live. Or in any case, within the office setting, it is a reminder of the rewards of escape that can be earned by working.

Jasper Johns is represented by a number of prints as well as by a wonderfully lyrical abstract work on paper, rendered in paintstick. The abstract painting, though small in size, packs an enormous amount of pictorial incident and emotional force into its relatively small format. A suite of Johns lithographs based on the numbers zero through nine is equally arresting and has a particular resonance within the context of a collection like PaineWebber's. In fact, while seeing this collection in this setting surely tells us something about the PaineWebber Group, it also makes us think about how such a setting affects our view of the art. For seeing these works in this context does bring to the fore particular characteristics of individual works that we might not have otherwise remarked; it puts a different spin on them.

Although I do not mean to suggest that the specific context of the collection does, or should, redefine the nature of individual works, one cannot help but feel that certain works do take on a different sort of edge when they are seen in an office setting. This is especially apparent in works that appropriate popular imagery or that are clearly based on arbitrary codes and sign systems, such as Ashley Bickerton's *Catalog: Terra Firma Nineteen Hundred Eighty Nine #2*, John Baldessari's *If This Then That*, Alexis Smith's *Seven Wonders*, or Christopher Wool's *Untitled,* 1988.

But this phenomenon is also evident, and in a more interesting way, in works that can be only indirectly related to the office environment. Paintings such as Cy Twombly's *Untitled, 1972*, with its rush of scribbled numbers and scrawled, barely legible words, have often seemed to me like extended metaphors for the fragmentary jumble of existence in general. The scribbles function somewhat like the notations you might find on a bedside pad—

31

words scrawled in the middle of the night, which seem to bear some deep psychic significance, but which you are unable to decipher the next morning. This mysterious evocation of fragmentary glimpses into feelings and thoughts takes on a particular resonance when seen cheek by jowl with the PaineWebber computers, telephones, and copy machines. The Twombly painting becomes, among other things, a kind of metaphor for the process of thinking, figuring, and refiguring that is constantly going on at the desks around it. Similarly, the Jasper Johns *0–9* lithographs take on an edge of deadpan irony when seen within the context of a financial services firm. And even the irregular geometry of Sean Scully's *Us* is contextualized in a very particular way when seen next to the complex geometric grids of multiple windows and doors characteristic of an office interior. In this environment, Scully's own geometric network seems not only to insist on the handmade nature of the artist's geometry but also on the ubiquitousness in our contemporary world of the rectangle, bar, and stripe.

David Salle's *My Subjectivity* takes on an especially odd flavor as a result of the office context. In any setting, this painting would evoke a rather unsettling series of ambiguous reactions. But within the office setting, the contrast between the vulnerabililty of the naked girl and the impersonality of the black Masonite panel—itself a standard feature in much office architecture—is given an especially disquieting emphasis by the fact that the girl is seated on what looks very much like an office chair.

The office environment also adds a dimension of whimsy to other works. Tony Cragg's *Grey Moon*, with its provocative array of found objects, evokes the paradoxical nature of the relationship between artworks and urban detritus. And in Gerhard Richter's *Helen*, the woman in the party dress seems to smile at us as if the picture were a company photograph from an office party, lending it an especially droll subtext.

The experience of viewing works in an office environment is quite different from the experience of a museum. In terms of space and lighting, the conditions for viewing the paintings at PaineWebber are not as controlled or focused as they would be in a museum setting. But at the same time, seeing these pictures within a workaday environment gives them a

Tony Cragg
(British, born 1949)

Grey Moon. (1985)
Grey and white
plastic found objects
86⅝ × 52" overall
(irreg.)
(220 × 132 cm)
1987.13

32

Jannis Kounellis
(Greek, born 1936)

Untitled. (1980)
Glass, ink on paper,
and two painted
plaster heads on steel
shelves
46 × 29½ × 8" overall
(116.8 × 74.9 ×
20.3 cm)
1987.4

more direct relationship to real life, and even a sharper urgency. The variable states of mind and mood that you can bring to a picture in this kind of setting are not so easily available in a museum, where you tend to come and stare, concentrate briefly, and then walk away.

At the PaineWebber offices you see the works in a setting that lies somewhere between domestic environment and museum—in a space that is semipublic but not primarily an exhibition space. (Yet since most people cannot afford to have contemporary art of this quality in their homes, a setting such as PaineWebber's affords one of the few alternatives to museum viewing.) As you move through the corridors in which the art is seen, you are constantly struck by your changing physical relationship to the pictures and by the wide variety of viewing experiences that you have over the course of a day. These range from the closeup views you have from a desk—virtually face to face with a large painting—to the casual experience of walking past several pictures on your way to somewhere else to the fairly extensive vistas that are offered as you move down a hallway and look at the pictures at the other end. Moreover, after you have been in this kind of space for a while, you become aware of the way that the corridor walls tend to "separate" from the desks and machinery opposite them and produce a curious sort of gallery effect.

In a very real way, viewing pictures under these circumstances provides a kind of test that museum viewing does not. For here, as in a domestic setting, the pictures are seen when we are in different moods; and they have a constant presence, sometimes at the center of our attention, sometimes only at the edge of our consciousness, that forces us to confront them on several different levels. Among other things, this kind of setting provides one of the few instances in which large numbers of works of art can be brought together in a single place and allowed to exert themselves full force on their immediate environment. And since, unlike museum installations, such a presentation is not inherently iconlike, the works of art must assert their merit within a less focused setting that does not necessarily valorize them. An enterprise like PaineWebber's art collection not only puts to test public views about contemporary art, it also puts contemporary art itself to a particular kind of test.

❖   ❖   ❖

33

If the PaineWebber collection seems more like a large and ambitious personal art collection than a corporate program, this is because it bears so much of Donald Marron's personal stamp.

Marron, a native New Yorker, began to collect art in the early 1960s, initially acquiring a modest collection of nineteenth-century American landscape paintings, especially of the Hudson River School. In the mid-1960s Marron became especially interested in prints, and this interest led to his involvement with contemporary American art. "I started out collecting painting," Marron later recalled, "and I stumbled across prints sort of inadvertently one day, and I realized I was into an exciting art form, one about which I knew very little, although I knew [about] the artists—I'm thinking about late nineteenth and early twentieth century— who made the prints."[7] The work that first caught Marron's eye came from the beginning of what is frequently referred to as the American Print Renaissance. Shortly afterwards, Marron became especially interested in the work that he saw at Gemini G.E.L., the California print workshop that was publishing prints by some of the most renowned contemporary American avant-garde artists, and at Tatyana Grosman's Universal Limited Art Editions on Long Island. Among Marron's earliest acquisitions were works by Jasper Johns, Roy Lichtenstein, Robert Rauschenberg, Ed Ruscha, and Frank Stella.

At about this time, Marron joined the board of the California Institute of Arts and became a member of the prints acquisition committee of the Museum of Modern Art. (Marron developed especially close ties to the museum; he served as president of the board of trustees from 1986 to 1991 and guided the museum through its major expansion program.) By the late 1960s Marron had become a systematic collector of contemporary American prints, and in 1968, as an extension of this enthusiasm, he decided to begin a corporate collection at Mitchell Hutchins, a privately held financial services and securities company of which he was president.[8] "We had a beautiful modern building," he later recalled, "and it seemed to me clear that if you could enjoy good artists, and expose people to them, instead of the posters and stuff you used to see as corporate art, that was the best thing to do."[9]

Alex Katz
(American, born
1927)

Good Morning I.
1974
Oil on canvas
96 × 72"
(243.8 × 182.9 cm)
1986.14

This approach would not only provide the basis for a first-rate corporate collection, he believed, it would also give direct support to contemporary American artists. Marron also felt that the presence of contemporary art in the workplace would introduce challenging recent art to people who might not otherwise see it and thereby provide for it a broader general base of appreciation and support. At the same time, it would also broaden the cultural background and general outlook of the firm's employees.

After PaineWebber acquired Mitchell Hutchins in 1977, it also acquired its art collection, which at that time consisted of about ninety works and which provided the core for the new PaineWebber collection. Under its new ownership the collection was broadened to include paintings, sculptures, and photographs as well as prints. Eventually the geographical scope of the collection was also expanded to include European as well as American art, partly as a reflection of the firm's international activities and partly as the result of the increased presence of contemporary European art in New York. And while the collection has remained focused on contemporary art, important works of the 1950s and 1960s were also acquired, including pictures by such artists as Diebenkorn, Kline, de Kooning, Motherwell, and Smith.

The way in which the PaineWebber art collection is used reflects an interesting combination of abstract idealism and pragmatic self-interest. What I would call the idealism is Donald Marron's insistence that living with contemporary art can have an inherently positive effect on people. The self-interest lies in the obvious fact that the art is meant to help promote an image of quality for the company, while at the same time also representing a substantial financial asset.

At the core of what I would characterize as the idealistic part of the company's program is what Marron has called "letting the art speak for itself." Although he is aware that, left to their own devices, most people would not become actively involved with contemporary art, he firmly believes that the presence of contemporary art in the workplace makes its physical accessibility translatable into aesthetic accessibility. If most people tend not to be very

35

interested in advanced contemporary art, he believes, it is in large measure because they do not have much exposure to it. Moreover, Marron feels that the company can benefit from the stimulating effect that the art has on its employees.

This is a belief that Marron has held for several years. "If you are in a contemporary business contemporary art is another link with society," Marron told an interviewer in 1986. "We are all looking for information, trying to understand how things work, why things work. It's a visceral thing. It's what's going on. Right next to the art in our offices we have the most sophisticated technological devices telling us about the most specific things going on in the world." The art, he asserted, "conditions you to accept change." And this he felt was especially important for the people who work at PaineWebber, who are in a "very rapidly changing business, and the more input people have, the more valuable it is."[10]

In a recent conversation, Marron reaffirmed this belief. "We're in a service business," he stated. "We're very much in a business where quality is a central element in everything we do and extends to every aspect of how we conduct the business. . . . And one way to get at quality is through exposure to contemporary art. I think good contemporary art reflects the society that creates it; and great contemporary art tends to anticipate things in that society. So you get a combination of quality and a relationship between your people and the world . . . both those things are possible through really first-rate contemporary art."[11]

The pragmatic aspect of the PaineWebber collection is also complex and interesting. On the one hand, on the most basic level, any large company has a certain amount of wall space to be decorated, and the PaineWebber collection certainly fulfills this function. Moreover, it fulfills this function in a way that is felt to be stimulating to the company's employees. But this, of course, is only part of the story, for the collection also represents a considerable public relations asset, as well as a financial investment that presumably is expected to maintain a certain rate of growth.[12]

Marron agrees that the collection has a real public relations function: "I think that people in the firm see it as another extension of the firm's image and method of communication. For

Ashley Bickerton
(British, born
West Indies 1959)

*Catalog: Terra
Firma Nineteen
Hundred Eighty
Nine #2.* 1989
Peppers, copper
sulfate, pebbles,
urban debris, metal
shavings, coral, sea-
weed and skate eggs,
cigarettes, raw pig-
ment, broken glass,
hay, cheese curls,
vacuum-cleaner
refuse, human hair,
sand, and lichen in
sixteen painted-steel
and safety-glass
elements
13½ dia. × 9½" each.
(34.3 × 24.1 cm)
88 × 88" overall
(223.5 × 223.5 cm)
1990.16

36

John Baldessari

(American,
born 1931)

If This Then That.
(1988)
Acrylic on two
black-and-white
photographs,
one framed
84 × 70" overall
(213.4 × 177.8 cm)
1989.33

example, many works of art are lent out to museums all over the country, I'd say continuously. Each of those works of art carries the firm's name and a kind of identification with a certain kind of quality. We have offices in every major city in the United States; every time a work of art is included in a show or travels, the firm is represented in a very positive way in that city. The second thing that happens, though this wasn't intentional, is that even those people who themselves are not terribly involved in art or perhaps don't even identify with the art—if they have the opportunity to come across someone that does, or knows of art, they usually get very good reinforcing comments. . . . Now is it as important as running the firm? No. But does it fit in with the idea of advertising, public relations, and responsibility in the community? Yes, because we in effect make available various artistic expressions all over the United States."[13]

During the period that the PaineWebber collection was being formed, American corporations were beginning to be sharply aware of the desirability of making some sort of social payback from the private sector to the public by allocating part of their profits to support various kinds of philanthropic endeavors. Increased emphasis was being given to the role that the private sector could play within the culture at large, and supporting the arts was seen as good for business in general. At a time when corporations were often seen as having increasingly impersonal relationships both toward their employees and toward the public at large, patronage for the arts gave companies an opportunity to communicate a sense of social responsibility and support for humanistic values.[14]

Like many chairmen of large corporations, Marron was very much aware of this need. And given his own history as a collector and his deep engagement with contemporary art, it was only natural that PaineWebber would concentrate on the visual arts. "I really believe that in a post-industrial society, art plays a more important role in our lives than we realize," Marron said in a 1983 interview. "Anything that can make art—or design—more accessible should be done. Corporations are businesses, but they are also where most people spend most of their lives; if corporations invest time and energy in the architecture of spaces, factories, office buildings, it is logical that what their people live with should be akin to the quality of the product, to the architecture, and to the people. . . . I believe that corporations can give a certain percentage of their profits to the arts—the only question is whether they should invest in art to hang on their walls or invest in the showing of art through sponsorship of shows, competitions, and various other things. The subject has not been well thought through, but there is growing awareness. One thing I notice is the direct relationship between the involvement of senior officers and the success of the collection—it's what makes the difference between a corporate collection and an art collection that hangs in a corporation. PaineWebber's is an art collection . . . . "[15]

When Marron became chairman of PaineWebber in 1981, plans were developed to move into a new world headquarters at what was then the Equitable Center in midtown Manhattan. This was an especially handsome space designed by the renowned architectural firm Skidmore, Owings and Merrill, and it provided an especially appropriate setting in which to show the art. As the collection grew, the need for a full-time curator also became apparent. This acknowledgment marked an important point in the development of the collection, representing as it did an increased level of commitment to the art. In 1984 Monique Beudert, who had been working in the Department of Painting and Sculpture at the Museum of Modern Art, was hired as curator. The following year, Beudert oversaw the installation of the collection at the company's new offices in what is now the PaineWebber Building at 1285 Avenue of the Americas. Although Marron continued to make the final decisions regarding most of the acquisitions, Beudert helped refine and shape the collection and provided a second eye in the selection of new works for it. As part of her curatorial duties, Beudert also oversaw the hanging of the collection and the logistics of caring for, as well as displaying, such a large body of works. In 1990 Jennifer Wells, who had worked at the Walker Art Center in Minneapolis and at the Museum of Modern Art, succeeded Beudert as curator. Beudert, now based in London, has remained an advisor to the collection.

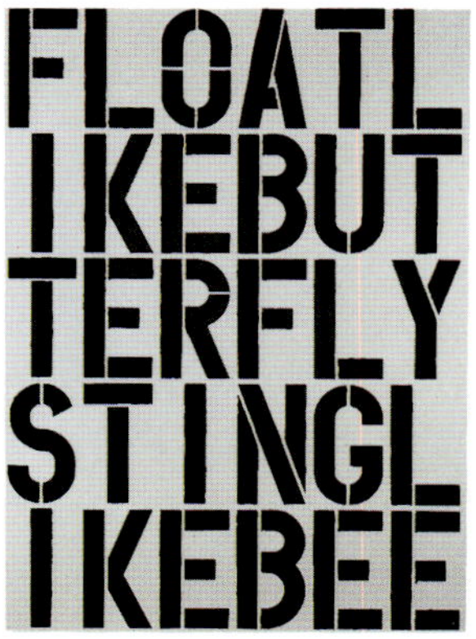

FLOATL
IKEBUT
TERFLY
STINGL
IKEBEE

Christopher Wool
(American,
born 1955)

Untitled.
1988
Alkyd and Flashe
on aluminum
84 × 60"
(213.4 × 152.4 cm)
1993.2

The new building also allowed the company to expand its art-related activities with a gallery space in the lobby that is used for temporary exhibitions. This space has been made available on a regular basis to a number of New York nonprofit arts institutions, such as the Studio in a School and the Museum of the City of New York, in order to provide them with a midtown showcase. Each institution is also given a generous sum of money to cover the expenses involved in mounting its exhibition, with the proviso that any excess funds can be kept by the institution for future projects. The lobby gallery has been very popular with PaineWebber employees and clients and has also drawn numerous visitors.

The role that art plays at PaineWebber is thus rather unusual among American corporations. Although the company collection grew out of the enthusiasm of a single person, Donald Marron, it is now an integral part of the PaineWebber company culture. At the same time, Marron has continued to guide it in a very personal way, overseeing the shape and feel of the collection, which has been supplemented by the ongoing exhibitions program within company headquarters. The full-time curatorial support has also been very advantageous for the collection; both Beudert and Wells have not only participated in decisions about acquisitions, but have also managed the complex logistics of keeping the collection optimally displayed at the company's headquarters and of arranging loans of works to museums across the country.

As has been noted, all works that are acquired for the company are meant to be displayed at PaineWebber headquarters. For conservation reasons, however, many works must be periodically "rested," away from light and in a controlled climate. Other works are loaned to museums for special exhibitions. The works that are on view in the company offices are frequently rotated, so that employees get to "live with" a good number of different works over a period of time. As Marron asked an interviewer shortly after PaineWebber moved into its new headquarters, "Where else can you see such a spectrum of recent work?"[16]

39

And indeed, because the best contemporary art is so expensive, a corporation such as PaineWebber is in a unique position to make it part of people's daily lives. The company both has the funds to acquire it and the space in which to show it. (This points to an interesting paradox. Although artists sometimes complain about their pictures ending up as the property of corporations, the pricing structure of contemporary art necessarily makes corporations—along with museums—the main collectors of the art.)

"What makes our situation different," Marron told me, "is that going to a museum is something which you may or may not choose to do, or buying art books is something that you may choose not to do. But art in a corporation is there, it's part of the life of the corporation and therefore in a way I think it's a very important test of its validity and its power to communicate, and in the end hopefully to provide enjoyment. Our experience is that most art, at least what we have, has met those tests."[17]

Contemporary art tends to shock and provoke its audience, and the employees of PaineWebber are no exception to this.[18] Although a number of employees felt that the art collection does in fact play an important role in relation to the company's image and in relation to the work environment, reservations were expressed about the company's philosophy with regard to the kind of art it has chosen—and about the validity and essential worth of contemporary art in general.

One thing that I found surprising, however, was that there were relatively few objections aimed directly at individual works of art. In speaking to PaineWebber employees, it became clear that despite the highly charged subject matter of many of the works, there had been very few requests to have pictures moved, despite the company's policy that "if a work is hanging in a public space and the people who are exposed to it every day object or don't like it or would prefer something else . . . we will simply change it."[19] In the few instances where such changes have been requested, the reasons have sometimes been unexpected. One person objected to Guston's *In the Studio* because it portrayed someone smoking. Another wanted Robert Longo's large painting of a man flying through the air in a business suit *(Untitled, 1981)*

Cy Twombly
(American,
born 1928)

Detail from
Untitled.
(1981)
Various dimensions
and mediums in
seven parts,
Paintstick, flat paint,
crayon and tempera
on paper
53½ × 59½"
(135.9 × 151.1 cm)
1985.32 a–g

40

Jasper Johns
(American,
born 1930)

Detail from *0–9*.
1960–63
Portfolio of ten
lithographs, 8/10
sheet: 20½ × 15¾"
(each approx.)
(52.1 × 40 cm)
1988.34 a–j

moved because it seemed to resemble a particular colleague. One employee told me that she thought John Ahearn's *Clyde (Black and White)* was "pretty creepy" to have near her work station, especially at night, but that she had not asked to have it moved because "it's art."

The area in which there seems to be greatest agreement among employees is that the collection makes the office a more interesting place to work. "Traveling throughout the building is an absolute joy," one employee noted. "There is a feast for my eyes at every turn and along every corridor."

"It makes the office look nicer," remarked another, "as if you're home, which makes people have a better attitude when they are in a better mood." One longtime employee listed the most positive aspects of the collection as follows: "Being able to appreciate it on a daily basis. Working for a company which places importance on culture. Positive public image as a backer of the arts." Even an employee who felt that most of the art that the company collects is "ridiculous" and that "some paintings should be burned" admitted that it was "better to look at art than white walls."

There also seems to be fairly widespread agreement about the way in which the art enhances the company's image. "Makes me more productive if I feel more comfortable in my work environment. The PW art collection adds to my comfort level," one employee noted, adding that the collection was good for the firm's image: "Large, bold, professional. Represents strength and power without being overwhelming." Another employee asserted that the collection "shows that PaineWebber can distinguish quality from decoration and that the collection is modern shows that PaineWebber believes in the future and in today." And another remarked that "it creates an aesthetic, cultural atmosphere in the workplace which, for me, is extremely satisfying and positive. The collection is diverse, thought-provoking, and helps to provide an environment that fosters creative thinking and imagination."

But in some cases, even employees who feel that the collection enhances the workspace expressed strong doubts about what the art does for the company's image, largely because of reservations about the kind of art the company collects. In fact, opinion about the validity

41

of the art itself—and by extension, about advanced contemporary art in general—varies quite widely. On the positive side, it was remarked that the collection is "fantastic and provocative, leading to creative thinking." One employee even went so far as to assert that "art and investing have a common theme—creativity (and both are not subject to scientific analysis)."

But the pleasure that some employees derive from the collection is not unalloyed. One employee noted that the "exposure to various styles of art is interesting. I enjoy anticipating changes in the collection." But the same person also remarked, "Sometimes art is depressing." Another stated that "there are a significant number of pictures that the employees do not like" and offered the suggestion that the company "show the most 'accessible' and 'attractive' 50% of the pictures and store the rest."

In sum, contemporary art's reception at PaineWebber is remarkably like its reception in other parts of society—except for the distinct advantage that PaineWebber employees have in being able to base their opinions on firsthand experience of the art. And this, I should think, is no surprise to anyone. When Marron first began seriously collecting contemporary art, many people in the corporate world thought that it was quite eccentric to do so. Such collecting may now be more widely accepted, but there are nonetheless strong pockets of resistance. It remains an uphill endeavor, even though many more people are now willing to concede that it is worth the effort.

In a larger sense, PaineWebber's experience seems to reflect attitudes toward the arts in the country as a whole. In good economic times, people are more willing to support the arts; but when the economy takes a downward turn, the arts come to be seen as a somewhat superfluous luxury. Many people also seem to feel that the arts should be "better behaved" than they are, as has been seen in the recent controversies over public funding.

But those who are committed to supporting the arts realize that they must sustain their support through thick and thin. They understand that support for the most profound expressions of our culture—the works by which our period will eventually come to be remembered—is no mere frill. Part of what I find so admirable about the PaineWebber art program

Gerhard Richter
(German, born 1932)

Helen.
1963
Oil and graphite
on canvas
42¾ × 39⅛"
(108.6 × 99.4 cm)
1987.7

is precisely what some of the company's employees complain about: that the company *does* give its art program a high enough priority to place it above the regular ups and downs of the business cycle; that the company sees the collection as a challenge to the people who are exposed to it and operates under the assumption that they are capable of rising to that challenge in the same way that they rise to the challenges of their jobs and their everyday lives. But most of all, I am impressed by the optimism inherent in the way that PaineWebber uses its collection: by the belief that people will rise to it, simply because of the quality of the art itself.

The notion that exposing the public to first-rate contemporary art would eventually result in people accepting the art and being improved by it goes back at least to the beginning of the century. Most of the early experiments that come to mind—such as Karl Ernst Osthaus's Museum Folkwang in Germany, Sergei Shchukin's Sunday open house for his collection in Moscow, or the educational programs of the Kröller-Müller collection in Holland—met with rather mixed results, at least in terms of convincing the general public about the validity of avant-garde art. But the continued efforts of successive generations created a tradition of collectors and collections acting as a bridge between advanced contemporary art and the public at large. In fact, this tradition has played an important role in the exhibition and educational programs of museums that show contemporary art and in determining many underlying assumptions of corporate collecting.

When I reviewed the broad range of responses from PaineWebber employees about the company's art collection, I was fascinated to see that a kind of longstanding cultural constant of resistance continues to be in effect. Even after years of exposure to the art, PaineWebber employees still had rather mixed feelings about it. Paradoxically, I believe that this is a healthy situation. If the art that the company collected were more readily acceptable, that might well indicate that PaineWebber was not really collecting the most vital art of our time—which has, almost by definition, the power to shock and outrage people.

❖　❖　❖

43

Because of the way artworks in the PaineWebber collection are shown, the acquisitions of the future will to some degree be determined by the physical limitations of available wall space. As the collection has grown, what once seemed like unlimited wall space now appears very much finite. Yet according to Donald Marron, the company will continue to collect and future plans include an exhibition tour of part of the collection, extended loans, and possibly even future gifts to museums.[20]

Aside from taking into account the physical limitations of the space in which it is shown, there is no systematic underlying program for what is included in the PaineWebber collection, other than a commitment to quality. This was the driving force behind Marron's own collecting and it has remained the top priority for the company's curatorial office. "In a time of pluralism and diversity," Monique Beudert stated a few years after she had been appointed curator, "we are forming a collection which is discriminating rather than reportorial. Our goal is to bring together the best art of our time."[21] To a remarkable degree, the PaineWebber collection has continued to do just that.

44

David Salle
(American,
born 1952)

My Subjectivity.
(1981)
Oil on canvas and
household paint
on Masonite in
two panels
86 × 112"
(218.4 × 284.5 cm)
1981.17

Notes

1. *Calvin Tomkins, "The Art World: Medicis Inc.,"* The New Yorker, *April 14, 1986, p. 88.*

2. *See Patrick Pacheco, "'Find Me the Next Picasso!'"* Art and Antiques *(April 1987), p. 126.*

3. *See Rosanne Martorella,* Corporate Art *(New Brunswick and London: Rutgers University Press, 1990), pp. 73–74.*

4. *Ibid., pp. 73–75.*

5. *Ibid., pp. 21–22.*

6. *In an interview with Donald Marron, he emphasized that price was sometimes a determining factor in the company's purchases: "If for example in some cases there were budgetary constraints, we would prefer to get a print by someone who we thought was the artist we wanted represented rather than go somewhere else where we could get a painting, but not by the artist that we wanted." Interview with Donald Marron, New York, July 6, 1993.*

7. *"Collecting Prints: The Buyers Meet the Sellers,"* Print Collector's Newsletter, *vol. 16, no. 1 (March–April 1985), p. 5.*

8. *Since Mitchell Hutchins was a privately held company, there is some question about the actual date at which the collection formally came to be considered the property of Mitchell Hutchins. In any case, it seems that Marron began to collect for Mitchell Hutchins in 1968, even though the formation of the company collection proper may date to 1971.*

9. *S{tuart} G{reenspan}, "Donald Marron,"* Art and Auction, *vol. 5, no. 6 (February 1983), p. 65.*

10. *Douglas C. McGill, "Art People,"* The New York Times, *December 26, 1986.*

11. *Interview with Donald Marron, July 6, 1993.*

12. *In this sense, the PaineWebber collection is very much in line with the reasoning behind corporate art collections in general: they function as an aspect of public relations and public image, as a benefit for employees, and also as a capital asset with real potential for increased value. See Martorella 1990, pp. 26–36.*

13. *Interview with Donald Marron, July 6, 1993.*

14. *"For emerging corporate elites in search of status, affiliation with artistic endeavors also proved an effective vehicle for cultural achievement, visibility, and prestige." Martorella 1990, p. 13. According to the American Council for the Arts, corporate philanthropic support for the arts reached about $500 million in 1987; about $40 million of this went to acquisitions. As a point of comparison, the budget for the National Endowment for the Arts peaked at $220 million in 1982; by 1990 it had leveled off to about $170 million. See Martorella 1990, pp. 11–19, for a discussion of various aspects of corporate patronage during the 1980s.*

15. *G{reenspan}, "Donald Marron," p. 65.*

16. *Tomkins, "Art World," p. 88.*

17. *Interview with Donald Marron, July 6, 1993.*

18. *The following employee opinions are quoted from responses to a questionnaire about the collection that was distributed at my request in August 1993, and from conversations with people who work at the firm.*

19. *Interview with Donald Marron, July 6, 1993.*

20. *Ibid.*

21. *Valerie F. Brooks, "Art & Business in the 80's: The Billion-Dollar Merger,"* Artnews, *vol. 86, no. 1 (January 1987), p. 21.*

Coll
ect
ion

John Ahearn
Clyde (Black and White). (1982)

(American,
born 1951)

Oil on
fiberglass

26 × 15 × 9"
(66 × 38.1 ×
22.9 cm)

1984.11

A decade of pluralism, the 1980s witnessed a plethora of movements, themes, and working processes in the visual arts. Set against this vast panorama of interpretation, John Ahearn's sculptures epitomize a tendency of artists in this period toward expressionistic, collaborative, and socially conscious work.

As a member of Colab (Collaborative Projects, Inc.), a New York artists' collective founded in the late 1970s, Ahearn was interested in work that addressed both social and artistic issues. Although a painter by training, he began casting sculpture from living subjects as a way to involve other people in his art making. Fascinated by mass-produced religious statuary and fueled by a desire to mesh fine art with the popular arts, Ahearn turned to the inexpensive and readily available medium of plaster. His first life-casts of other artists and friends were shown in 1980 at Fashion Moda, an alternative space in the South Bronx, a neighborhood where Ahearn later resided. Attempting to reclaim a place for art in the fabric of daily life and to renew the ancient role of the artist as portraitist, Ahearn focused on his working-class neighbors (of mostly African-American and Hispanic-American descent) as subjects.

Ahearn's work hovers between realism and expressionism. In the tradition of American Social Realism, much like Edward Hopper, he also is an observer of the American scene and the inhabitants of urban environments. However, unlike Hopper, who portrayed anonymous figures in these ordinary settings, Ahearn has chosen to portray actual individuals from particular places. And, more precisely, the artist selects people who also are not typically the subjects of portraits. Ahearn's casts embody the sitters' expressions, gestures, and personal idiosyncrasies, from tattoos to hairstyles. As Robert Storr has pointed out, "These portraits collectively project a specific social reality—life in the South Bronx—and by extension provide a glimpse of the life and vitality of the American urban underclass."[1]

From the start, Ahearn's art has been a collaboration with Rigoberto Torres. A native of Puerto Rico, Torres grew up in the South Bronx and, as Ahearn's apprentice, suggested that he cast his neighbors. Comparing himself to "an itinerant portrait painter," Ahearn does his casting on the sidewalk, involving the local community in the process. Although most of these works ultimately end up in museums and private art collections, many remain in the neighborhood, because each sitter is given a completed cast.

Ahearn's subjects are of all ages, ranging from young children to the neighborhood elders. *Clyde (Black and White)* portrays a local welder who has assisted Ahearn and Torres with large-scale projects and commissions. Like many of Ahearn's subjects, Clyde had three different sittings resulting in five total works; this cast is the second version of the second sitting. The plaster or, in this case, fiberglass, is rough and rugged, like the character of the subject's face. After the cast sets, Ahearn enlivens it by painting skin, hair, and garments. Clyde's direct downward glance seems at first tough and unsettling, but, as with all the people Ahearn portrays, the figure's underlying sensitivity is soon recognized.

JW

1. Quoted in Robert Storr, "John Ahearn and Rigoberto Torres at Brooke Alexander." Art in America, vol. 71, no. 110 (November 1983). p. 227.

49

Richard Artschwager
Seated Group. (1962)

(American,
born 1923)

Charcoal
and acrylic
on Celotex

42 × 60"
(106.7 ×
152.4 cm)

1986.42

By design, Richard Artschwager's work defies classification. Neither painting nor sculpture, abstract nor figurative, aesthetic nor functional, it paradoxically manages to be all of these. The components of Artschwager's art, his choice of materials and relocation of utilitarian forms into the realm of fine art, are unconventional and often unprecedented in art making and suggest affinities both with Pop and Conceptual art without firmly identifying with either movement. Continuing in the tradition both of Cubist collage and the iconoclasm of Marcel Duchamp, Artschwager uses found objects to comment on illusion and art, thereby challenging the viewer's own perceptions. In his use of such everyday materials as Formica for sculpture and Celotex, a building material with a textured surface, for painting, for example, Artschwager plays on the notion of trompe l'oeil, using it simultaneously to question and clarify the meaning of his objects as art. His intention is "to make art that has no boundaries."[1]

Artschwager studied with the Purist painter Amédée Ozenfant after leaving Cornell University, but in 1953 he abandoned painting to become a furniture maker and designer. In 1958 his workshop was destroyed by fire, an event that precipitated his return to making art. In about 1960, drawing on his background as a craftsman and stimulated in part by a commission he received from the Catholic Church to make portable altars for ships, Artschwager began fabricating a series of wall objects from Formica and wood. Formica attracted him because of its vulgar, artificial connotations and because, as he said in an interview in 1965, "it was a picture of a piece of wood. If you take that and make something out of it, then you have an object. But it's a picture of something at the same time it's an object."[2]

In this explanation of his choice of material, Artschwager articulates the basic premises of his art: the examination of the relationships between abstraction and reality, object and image. These concerns are evident in his early paintings, which are based on found images, executed in grisaille, and painted on Celotex. *Seated Group,* one of Artschwager's earliest paintings, is based on a photograph that appeared in the newspaper *El Diario* of a Puerto Rican ad hoc town meeting in New York City. In the painting, all specific information from the source has been suppressed in favor of general characteristics: the room is reduced to the basic components of floor, wall, table, chairs, and flag, while the photograph's nine figures are represented only by their clothing and hairstyles. This gives the painting the unsettling quality of being a deliberately anonymous portrait, thus rendering meaningless a long-established genre. Significantly, the table is now the centerpiece of the portrait. This horizontal form was later adopted as the basis for one of Artschwager's most important free-standing sculptures, *Long Table with Two Pictures* of 1964,[3] in which an interior is presented in the form of sculpture that looks like furniture. This recontextualization of medium, subject, meaning, and form is at the core of Artschwager's work.

MB

1. Quoted by Richard Armstrong in Artschwager, Richard, exhibition catalogue (New York: Whitney Museum and W.W. Norton & Company, 1988), p. 13.
2. Ibid., p. 17.
3. Private collection.

51

73,800 miles   69,500   78,100   228,200   1,612,000

John Baldessari
If This Then That. (1988)

(American,
born 1931)

Acrylic on
two black-
and-white
photographs,
one framed

84 × 70"
overall
(213.4 ×
177.8 cm)

1989.33

John Baldessari's work is concerned with issues of meaning and with how information is communicated. A native of California, where he taught from 1970 to 1989 at the California Institute of the Arts in Valencia, and where he continues to live, Baldessari has since the mid-1960s consistently challenged many of the standards and values inherited from the modernist tradition. His strong interest in relationships between text and image give his work a distinctive spirit. As he has described, "I try to get my work to resonate with my understanding of the world. It's paradoxical, full of ambiguities."

California culture has long been dominated by the film and television industries, whose influence on the visual arts became increasingly apparent during the 1980s. Among the first California-based artists to use appropriated pictures in his work, Baldessari mined the potential theatricality and artifice of media imagery, as well as the possible fragmentation of narrative and time in film.

In addition to images taken from movie stills, Baldessari also incorporates his original photographs into his work. He juxtaposes these fragments of found and unique images to trigger free associations and to challenge the supposed objectivity of photography, a medium that most people equate with truth. Although some direction is provided by the titles, the images are cropped and rearranged to conjure up a personal story for each viewer. Baldessari purposely exploits the power of media-based images to reflect on collective experience: "I guess I'm using images from movies, from newspapers, and so on, because

there lies the archpower of language. We can't sit down and talk in Sanskrit, we have to talk in a language we know."

In 1986 Baldessari began using white, black, and colored circles to mask people's faces in the photographs. The effect was to lessen the specificity, and therefore the authority of those depicted, while alluding to the media's control of visual information. The masking of the faces also shifted the focus from individuals to generic types, and from these types to other details in the picture. In most cases, the disk obliterates the photograph's most apparent salient focal point, ironically leaving the task of expression to the surrounding details and overall composition.

If This Then That could be interpreted as a comment on the relationship of the individual to the planet. The work features two distinctly different images: a film still from a musical with dancers and performers and a photographic image of various planets paired with (fictitious) mileage figures that make reference to the distance between the planets. Instead of obscuring the people's faces, Baldessari superimposed the color disks over their heads "coded to a personality type, emotional state."[1] This strange and puzzling juxtaposition immediately invites interpretation.

JW

1. Quoted by Coosje van Bruggen in John Baldessari, *exhibition catalogue (Los Angeles and New York: Museum of Contemporary Art and Rizzoli International Publications, 1990), p. 144.

53

Jennifer Bartlett
In the Garden #105. (1980)

(American,
born 1941)

Conté crayon
and oil pastel
on paper

19¾ × 26"
(50.2 × 66 cm)

1981.1

In the Garden #105 is one of a series of 197 drawings begun by Jennifer Bartlett in January 1980 in the South of France and finished fifteen months later in her New York studio. The complete cycle, shown in New York in 1981, affirmed Bartlett as an artist capable of reinvigorating the ideas of Conceptual art by employing figuration. Bartlett's reputation as technically innovative had been established in 1976 with the exhibition of *Rhapsody,* a monumental room installation executed in paint, silkscreen, and baked enamel on 988 steel plates, in which the concerns of process and series were explored. Her interest in a single image processed through a variety of artistic methods was evident in *Graceland Mansions* (of 1978–79; also in PaineWebber's collection), a five-part print in which a form based on Elvis Presley's home is repeated successively in drypoint, etching and aquatint, silkscreen, woodcut, and lithography.

The drawings that constitute the In the Garden series take as their subject the grounds of Bartlett's rented villa in Nice. Frustrated by lack of progress on a writing project and having recently seen the nearby chapel in Vence designed by Henri Matisse, whose brush drawings are translated there into large ceramic-tile murals, Bartlett decided to turn her hand to drawing. She focused on the nearest subject, her garden, and selected as the key compositional elements for the drawings a kitsch statue of a boy urinating, a pool, and the surrounding cypress trees and foliage. In all, Bartlett employed ten different mediums: pencil, color pencil, pen and ink, brush and ink, Conté crayon, charcoal, watercolor, oil pastel, gouache, and pastel.

Throughout the cycle, Bartlett exploited the full potential for markmaking and emotional expression that each technique embodies, often incorporating her knowledge of other artists' styles.

In the series, the standard image of a figure in a landscape is seen from several points of view, in different times of day, and under various conditions of light. In some drawings the forms are fractured or abstracted into shapes; in others certain elements are isolated and specific details made prominent. A range of marks, from descriptive to expressive, is employed, and the use of color is both representative and decorative, from the black and white of the pencil and charcoal drawings to the full color of the pastels and watercolors and the saturated blue of the final drawings in the series.

In the Garden #105 is one of a group (#74–#118) in the series in which the sheet is divided in two, with the image in each half rendered in a different medium. Here, Conté crayon is used on the left side to depict the garden in a lyrical mode, while on the right the pool becomes an ominous vortex, turbulently expressed in oil pastel. This juxtaposition of contrasting moods and styles is characteristic of the entire project. Viewed together, the drawings form a narrative that speaks not only of the interpretive properties of drawing as a medium but also of the emotional intensity and formal discipline of the artist's vision.

MB

55

Georg Baselitz
Fünfmal Meise [Five Times Titmouse].
1988–89

(German,
born 1938)

Oil on canvas
98⅜ × 98⅜"
(249.9 ×
249.9 cm)

1990.27

In his paintings and sculptures, Georg Baselitz has negotiated skillfully the territory between pure form and representation. Baselitz gained international recognition at the end of the 1970s when critical attention was focused on new forms of figurative art. Yet like other German artists of his generation, including Sigmar Polke (page 186) and Gerhard Richter (pages 190–93), his oeuvre is in fact a complex manifestation of one of the central themes of modern art— the often uneasy coexistence of abstraction and figuration.

Having grown up in postwar Germany, where French and American culture predominated, Baselitz initially was determined to discover his own native and unconventional strategy for making art (recognizing in this intent a German precedent in Dada, particularly in the work of Kurt Schwitters). Born Georg Kern in 1938, the artist later took the name Baselitz in 1961 from his birthplace, a town in Saxony. That year he also issued with Eugen Schönbeck, a fellow painter, the first of two *Pandemonium* manifestoes—texts influenced by the ideas of "outsider" art as expressed both in the subversive writings of Artaud and Lautreament (their extremism deliberately placing them beyond the bounds of both aesthetic and social propriety) and by the art of the insane, which the psychologist Hans Prinzhorn had collected and published in 1926. Intended as a statement for a new beginning, the manifestoes focus on eroticism, death, decay, and paranoia, and are charged with hallucinatory intensity.

These texts and the drawings that embellished them generated the new iconography of strange, fantastic creatures (see *Peitschenfrau*, 1964, page 258) that populate Baselitz's works of the early 1960s.

In 1965 and 1966 Baselitz made a celebrated series of "hero" paintings in which he invented a "new type." These were in fact representations of anti-heroes, rural figures (often shepherds) who seem powerless, repressed, or wounded (see *Untitled {Hero}*, 1966, page 258). At about this time, Baselitz also concluded that the figures in his paintings need not have specific meaning nor represent anything; they could be justified on purely pictorial grounds. He began to fracture or bisect the image, or leave it partly unfinished, or sometimes break it into parts or weave it into the ground of the painting. In 1969, resolving to empty his images of all narrative content, he inverted the figures. By then he had substituted standard academic subjects—landscapes, still lifes, portraits, and nudes—for his earlier, intensely personal iconography. In presenting the forms upside down, Baselitz freed his painting from literal interpretation, establishing it as autonomous, yet paradoxically retaining the force of association.

Baselitz began making sculpture in 1979, with his first sculptures bearing a strong resemblance to the crude figures and heads of his early 1960s paintings. Baselitz acknowledges his interest in tribal sculpture (especially that from Africa, which he collects), an influence that links him with early modern artists, particularly the German

Georg Baselitz

Die Wendin [from the series **Die Dresdner Frauen (The Women of Dresden)]. 1990**

(continued from previous page)
Expressionists Ernst Ludwig Kirchner and Karl Schmidt-Rotloff. Baselitz admires the consistency of form in tribal art; once the model for a sculpture of a figure or god is established, it is remade for centuries. The directness of the process of making sculpture (in contrast to painting) also appeals to Baselitz: "Sculpture is more primitive, more brutal, it lacks the reserve that you find in painting."[1] Baselitz's sculptural tools are those of a woodsman: he uses a saw, a chisel, and an ax to draw the form from a block of wood. He sees the sculptural process as aggressive and confrontational, and his figures bear the marks of these confrontations, appearing almost battle-scarred.

During 1989 and 1990 Baselitz worked on a group of ten monumental sculptures entitled Die Dresdner Frauen (The Women of Dresden). *Die Wendin* is one of these, a massive head gouged out of maple and painted cadmium yellow. "By working in wood," Baselitz said in 1987, "I want to avoid all manual dexterity, all artistic elegance, everything to do with construction. I don't want to construct anything."[2] His sculptural figures remain close in character to the tree trunks from which they are hewn, thus connecting the human form with nature and asserting the importance to the artist of material and process over representation. Doused in brilliant yellow, the ten female heads of The Women of Dresden declare themselves as contemporary totems.

Strong formal links connect the artist's paintings and drawings, as well as his sculpture and prints, with each process informing the other. Baselitz maintains separate studios for each process at his home in Dernberg, thereby facilitating his ongoing work in each medium. *Fünfmal Meise (Five Times Titmouse),* painted in 1989, shows the influence of sculpture, with the crude network of quick, energetic lines in the background recalling the roughly carved surface of his sculpture, and relating to the making of woodblock prints. The background grid has appeared in Baselitz's work since 1982 and is featured prominently in Ciao America, a series of nine large woodcuts and three paintings from 1988–1989, in which he also used birds as a motif.

In *Fünfmal Meise,* Baselitz boldly pushes the image to the point of abstraction. The painting is built up in layers, with a large form (perhaps that of a bird) lurking like a shadow beneath the painted surface. The five birds of the title and two oblong yellow shapes are captured in the grid, which unifies the surface and holds it together. The use of a grid and of an allover pattern, two standard devices of American abstract painting, tempt speculation on the meaning of the reference in the series title, Ciao America. Baselitz adopts these conventions for his own purposes, using them to structure a painting in which formal invention becomes meaning. The tension between the shape hovering below the surface and the composition on top (i.e., between the discarded composition and its replacement) charges the painting. This formal conflict is intensified by the electric blue and yellow palette—the natural colors of the birds themselves—that the artist uses.

MB

1. *Quoted in an interview with Jean Louis Froment and Jean Marc Poinsot in* Georg Baselitz: Sculpture and Early Woodcuts, *exhibition catalogue (London: Anthony d'Offay, 1987), pp. 9–10.*
2. *Ibid., p. 15.*

(German, born 1938)

Maple painted with oil and egg tempera

46 × 26 × 13¼" (116.8 × 66 × 33.7 cm)

1990.50

Jean-Michel Basquiat
Tobacco versus Red Chief. 1981

(American,
1960–1988)

Oil and oilstick
on canvas

78 × 70"
(198.1 ×
177.8 cm)

1985.18

Tobacco versus Red Chief is one of the first paintings made by Jean-Michel Basquiat during his brief but prolific career (he died in 1988, at twenty-seven). As the graffiti artist SAMO in the late 1970s, Basquiat gained attention for his scrawled phrases and pictograms of crowns and copyright signs that he wrote on walls in New York's Soho district. By 1981 he had abandoned the walls of buildings for canvas. His paintings included distinctively different images—stick figures, abstract marks, skulls and bones (many of which came from *Gray's Anatomy*)—that revealed not only his street style but an awareness of modernism as well.

Born in Brooklyn, New York, into a middle-class family, Basquiat never received formal artistic training. He left home in his teens and fashioned himself as a primitive, romanticizing his origins and creating a sense of his independence. His style—like that of the French artist Jean Dubuffet, to whom Basquiat is often compared—was awkward, rough, and made use of imagery from the subconscious. Dubuffet's work, inspired by naive art and art of children and the insane, was exhibited at the Solomon R. Guggenheim Museum in 1981, a show that Basquiat probably saw.

Included in the 1981 group show *Public Address,* at the Annina Nosei gallery (Nosei first represented Basquiat), *Tobacco versus Red Chief* is one of several paintings concerned with stereotypes and is a biting, sardonic commentary on an American myth. The large and imposing figure is a Native American Indian chief, his arm raised, suggesting the television-Indian greeting "How!" Rendered in outline in a boxy, primitive manner, the figure is filled in with color and articulated by raw detail—like the wooden figures used to advertise tobacco stores. His masklike face has been painted black, linking him with another minority and demonstrating Basquiat's tendency—common among artists and historians—to impose in the process of image-making their own identity on creations. The Indian is framed within a coarse, spiked line that reads as barbed wire. Gestures of painted color and drawn line are added, giving the composition a sense of agitation.

Basquiat's own deep-rooted concerns about race, human rights, the accumulation of power and wealth, and the control of and respect for nature are evident in *Tobacco versus Red Chief.* He identified with the plight of Native Americans and the loss of their land to what the settlers regarded as industry and progress. For example, the tepees in this painting, which also appear in other works, are Basquiat's symbol for "subjugated peoples."[1] The scrawled letters in the lower left-hand corner appear to spell "hotel" (a temporary home, in this case within barbed wire), establishing a potent juxtaposition of word and image.

JW

1. Richard Marshall, Jean-Michel Basquiat, *exhibition catalogue* (New York: Whitney Museum of American Art, 1992), p. 18.

61

El Dorado

Lothar Baumgarten
El Dorado. (1985)

(German,
born 1944)

Three black-
and-white
photographs in
artist's frames

26¼ × 33¼"
each (66.7 ×
84.5 cm)

1989.3

Language, the most immediate form of exchange between cultures, is the essential tool in Lothar Baumgarten's art. Language provides us with a means to circumscribe and define cultures, and in his art Baumgarten examines the disciplines by which we chart the world (for example, ethnography, history, geography). The artist focuses on the interchange between two societies, most often European countries and indigenous populations affected by centuries of territorial expansion and colonialism. Baumgarten combines photographs, objects, words, typography, and paint to mount evocative installations that address the ways different cultures see each other. He also publishes books, writes texts, and produces films and photographs related to his extensive travels. The approach of Baumgarten's investigations is holistic; he restores or visualizes the situation from the experience of the other, the native culture. For example, in *Accès aux quais: Tableaux Parisiens,* a work completed in Paris in 1986, Baumgarten intervened in the official version of French history by relabeling the stops on a Metro line with references to French imperialism in South America, Africa, Asia, and the South Pacific that replaced the existing names commemorating Napoleonic victories.

Like Anselm Kiefer (pages 136–39) and Blinky Palermo (page 184), Baumgarten studied at the Kunstakademie in Düsseldorf with Joseph Beuys (pages 64, 259), who inculcated in his students the concept of art as a form of social action. Baumgarten's early work was based on information he obtained from books and historical accounts and culminated in *Origins of the Night,* a film inspired by the Amazon jungle that was actually shot in the forest of the Rhine River between 1973 and 1977. From October 1978 to March 1980, Baumgarten lived among the Yanomani Indians in the Orinoco Valley in southwestern Venezuela, an experience that profoundly affected his work. The photographs, audio recordings, films, drawings, oral histories, and records of myths that he accumulated while in Venezuela are the basis for many of his projects.

El Dorado is part of a series of photographs that Baumgarten took in 1978 of La Gran Sabana, an enormous grassy plain in southeast Venezuela and one of the putative locations of El Dorado, the legend that spurred the Spanish conquest of South America. Fabulous stories of gold mines, of a city made of gold, and of an Indian chieftain who was supposedly painted in gold, led the Spanish conquistadors into the interior of the continent. The environment of La Gran Sabana currently is threatened by a second wave of destruction through forestry and mining, a situation the artist compares with the earlier Spanish invasion, which also tore the continent apart in a search for wealth. In *El Dorado,* Baumgarten exploits the documentary nature of photography to record the landscape as it is. Nevertheless, it is difficult for the uninformed viewer, inspired by the deep vistas and panoramas, not to project notions of an exotic wilderness. The legend "El Dorado," printed under the center photograph in an earthy, sanguine red, cautions against this misplaced romance.

MB

63

Joseph Beuys
Gold Sculpture. (1956)

(German,
1921–1986)

Graphite and
gold paint on
six sheets of
paper mounted
on board and
framed together

30⅞ × 23"
overall
(78.4 ×
58.4 cm)

1988.19

Joseph Beuys is one of the most remarkable figures in twentieth-century art. Central to the German artist's work was his expanded concept of art, or "Social Sculpture," in which all human activity is art and everyone is an artist, in the sense that everyone has creative abilities that should be developed and used in the political restructuring of society. For Beuys, sculpture was the essential artistic process, but his definition of sculpture was all-encompassing, including history, language, and human thought. Thus in Beuys's theory, the traditional notions of art are replaced both by an anthropological concept of art and a utopian ideal of art as permeating the whole of life.

Beuys's activities took many forms. He was a performer, a controversial and influential professor of art at the Kunstakademie in Düsseldorf (among his students were Baumgarten, Kiefer, and Palermo, see pages 62, 136–39, 184), a politician, a sculptor, and a draftsman. His art can be divided into three categories: drawings, sculpture and objects, and conversations or actions. Throughout his life Beuys made thousands of drawings, which provided an immediate, expressive outlet and became a repository of his ideas. As such, they can be seen as a rich and continuous background for his other projects.

Beuys's presence formed an integral part of his art, and he traveled frequently in America and Europe, making installations

and actions. Because of the peripatetic nature of his life, the simplicity and diaristic quality of drawing must have appealed to him. Indeed, some of his drawings are executed on calendar pages and hotel stationery, forming a record of certain periods. Beuys's use of everyday materials underscores his intention to integrate art and life. Scrap paper, cardboard, cloth, sketchbooks, newspaper, and wrapping paper he marked with a wide range of materials, from the organic (blood, vegetable and fruit juices, tea, coffee, and chocolate) to the more traditional (pencil, oil paint, watercolor, wood stain, floor paint, and gold paint).

Gold Sculpture, an early work predating Beuys's political activities, dates from 1956, a period of personal crisis and intense drawing activity in Beuys's life. Executed on a variety of papers, some of which are torn, yellowed, and creased, *Gold Sculpture* is a glossary in gold paint of potential sculptural shapes—coils, flat sheets, a bar, a triangle wedged into a corner, a nugget, some forms resembling vessels, and what seems to be a bell clapper. Many of these images took three-dimensional form in Beuys's later work. Among these forms are dispersed handwritten notations, which range from the banal—appointments, names, and telephone numbers; to the practical—notes on the format of a catalogue; to the mystical—the Latin inscription *qua patet orbis.*[1] Art and nonart sources combine in *Gold Sculpture,* and the deliberate arrangement by the artist of the six sheets together in one frame anticipates his later assembling of objects in vitrines and room installations. The title invokes alchemy, the pursuit of turning base metal into gold, and thus affirms Beuys's idea of transformation as an important artistic process.

MB

1. *This Latin phrase, which means "as far as the globe extends," also has autobiographical and historical significance. It was inscribed by Moritz von Nassau on one of the columns for his monument to the union of love and war, erected in 1652 in Cleves, where Beuys was raised. The monument enthralled Beuys as a child, and he subsequently used it as the basis of his installation at the German Pavilion at the Venice Biennale in 1976. Two versions of that work, entitled* Strassenbahnhaltestelle (Tram Stop), *exist. One is in the collection of the Rejksmuseum Kröller-Müller, Otterlo; the other is in the Marx Collection, Berlin.*

65

Ashley Bickerton
Catalog: Terra Firma Nineteen Hundred Eighty Nine #2. 1989

(British,
born West
Indies 1959)

Peppers, copper
sulfate, pebbles,
urban debris,
metal shavings,
coral, seaweed
and skate eggs,
cigarettes, raw
pigment, bro-
ken glass, hay,
cheese curls,
vacuum-cleaner
refuse, human
hair, sand, and
lichen in sixteen
painted-steel
and safety-glass
elements

13½ dia. ×
9½" each
(34.3 ×
24.1 cm)
88 × 88"
overall
(223.5 ×
223.5 cm)

1990.16

The industrial materials, pristine fabrication techniques, and serial imagery of Ashley Bickerton's work reveal a strong awareness of Minimalist sculpture of the 1960s. The very format of his wall reliefs suggests an indebtedness to such artists as Donald Judd (page 132). Although these simple primary forms depend on sheer physical presence for their impact, Bickerton, who came to prominence in the 1980s, ultimately undermines their purity. Through adapting a high-tech approach to traditional subject matter, from portraiture to landscape, the artist lends a novel meaning to the genre with materials borrowed from the latest product design, sporting equipment, and automobile accessories. "Visually noisy, overly engineered and para-functional," as Richard Armstrong has noted, Bickerton's work "bristles with the hyperbole of consumerist perfection."[1]

Beginning in 1988 Bickerton extended his analysis beyond the relationship of art to culture to address the relationship of culture to nature. The bold confrontation between nature and technology achieves high-density resolution in *Catalog: Terra Firma Nineteen Hundred Eighty Nine #2.* The second of three versions, this update on the traditional genre of landscape not only provides a contemporary, unsentimental view, but summarizes and makes an aesthetic ideal of our complicity in the destruction of the environment.

In this work the sixteen circular steel containers, painted yellow and sealed with safety-glass covers, are oddly reminiscent of

a ship's portholes—perhaps alluding to Bickerton's enthusiasm for the open sea, as he grew up in the West Indies. Arranged in four rows of four, the units display contents visible through the glass covers; each is packed with an organic or synthetic material, such as seaweed, copper sulfate, cigarette butts, or cheese curls. Preserved in an airtight repository, the detritus remains on view for future contemplation or retrieval. Bickerton's encapsulation not only protects the various materials, but also conveys the techniques of display of a natural history museum, where specimens are preserved for future generations. "I almost think of my objects as existing sometime in the future, when the world has been completely reorchestrated in terms of the hegemony of Western culture, and existing as sort of strange artifacts from what was, when something else held the keys to control."[2] His use of debris, such as the vacuum-cleaner refuse, to create form is also similar to that of British sculptor Tony Cragg (page 82), as both artists share in their work a concern for the dichotomy of the natural versus the man-made.

JW

1. *Richard Armstrong in* Mind over Matter: Concept and Object, *exhibition catalogue (New York: Whitney Museum of American Art, 1991), p. 11.*
2. *Quoted by Dan Cameron in* NY Art Now: The Saatchi Collection *(London: The Saatchi Collection, 1987), p. 40.*

67

Jonathan Borofsky
Splithead at 2,783,798. (1974)–1982

(American,
born 1942)

Cast bronze
with metal
base, 2/3

67¾ × 14 × 15"
including base
(172.1 × 35.6
× 38.1 cm)

1983.9

Jonathan Borofsky's art focuses on the affir-
mation of his identity as an artist, which
he defines through his dreams and his subconscious life. The fears, expectations, desires,
and anxieties of human life are expressed, and
related sociopolitical themes such as oppres-
sion, violence, and inequality are raised. His
images, at once personal and universal, often
employ escapist imagery and titles, such as
I Want to Run Away or *I Dreamed I Could Fly.*
Borofsky is best known for his installations,
in which he uses sculpture, objects, machines,
drawings, paintings, and wall paintings, usually accompanied by written words, lights,
sounds, and movement, making a visually
complex and sensory-stimulating, if sometimes disorienting, experience for the viewer.
In 1980, when asked, "What do you think art
should be about?" Borofsky responded, "It's
about the maker and how the maker sees and
deals with him- or herself in the context of
the universe, the planet, the people who live
there. Art is for the spirit is as close as I've
been able to say it. . . . Art helps to make life
happen."[1] A unique screenprint from 1989
emblazoned with the slogan "ART IS FOR THE
SPIRIT" is in PaineWebber's collection.

Splithead is one of an edition of three
bronze casts based on a clay version of the
sculpture, which was included in Borofsky's
first exhibition at the Paula Cooper Gallery
in New York in 1975. The clay model was
cast in plaster in 1981, and in 1982 the
bronze cast was made. The image of a split
head, representing both the conscious and
the subconscious mind as well as the notion
of an internal and external life, recurs constantly in Borofsky's work as an emblem of
universal experience. This sculpture expresses
dichotomy, the state of splitting into two
distinct parts. A calm, masklike face of
almost classical serenity hides another bald,
skull-like human head. This hidden head
has the appearance both of a newly born
child, in the way it nestles into the curve of
the reverse of the mask, and of a death mask,
because of its peaceful air of resigned finality.
The two heads sit on top of an elongated,
twisted neck, which is cracked in two places,
as if the form had grown too fast for the
structure to accommodate it. Despite the static condition of cast bronze sculpture, meta-
morphosis is implied, as well as the division
of a whole into its parts and the emergence
of an interior, personal life from behind the
mask of polite behavior. Seen from the front,
the work has the appearance of a modernist
sculpture, perhaps one inspired by Brancusi.
The simple base on which the artist has
placed the work reinforces this perception. It
is only when the viewer circles the work that
the entire image, with its multiple meanings,
is revealed.

MB

1. Quoted by Kathy
Halbreich in Jonathan
Borofsky: An
Installation, *exhibi-
tion brochure (Cam-
bridge: Massachusetts
Institute of Technology,
Hayden Gallery,
1980), n.p.*

69

Louise Bourgeois
Untitled. (1949)

(American,
born France
1911)

Ink on paper

22 × 15"
(55.9 ×
38.1 cm)

1988.15

Louise Bourgeois was born in 1911 in France; in 1938 she emigrated to New York. In the past decade her highly personal yet formally rigorous work has received long-deserved recognition, culminating in her being selected as the representative for the United States at the 1993 Venice Biennale. For Bourgeois, making art is inextricably linked with her personal history and the exorcism of the past. "Every day you have to abandon your past or accept it," she has recently written, "and then, if you cannot accept it, you become a sculptor."[1] Art becomes an act of will, of control; a method of survival.

Her earliest sculptures, which date from the late 1940s and early 1950s, are totemic figures. They were exhibited in groups or clusters, defining each other and the space around them. Some of these are portraits of people, others are archetypes. While her forms are essentially abstract, they frequently bear reference to real things. Later pieces resemble appendages, genitalia, machines, and structures, and in the past ten years the artist has made a number of remarkable room installations. The materials she has used range from the flexible to the resistant, including latex, rubber, plaster, wood, marble, and bronze. Often the same forms are remade in different mediums, suggesting the artist's belief that a kind of accuracy can be achieved through repetition. Her sculptures have a substantial material presence, as if to annihilate the doubt and fear from which they are generated.

Bourgeois has made drawings throughout her career. They seem to be an instinctive activity, valuable for their immediacy of experience and ease of construction, unlike sculpture. Speaking in an interview about the relative freedom of drawing, she said: "You can work on the same drawing for days, it goes on forever. . . . I draw at night, for hours, and I don't feel the time passing by. I am completely unconscious of time passing by."[2]

In keeping with the reverie she describes, her drawings seem to depict dreamlike forms and landscapes, even having an affinity with the Surrealists' use of automatic drawing to unlock the unconscious mind.

Untitled, 1949, which dates from the same period as the early sculptures, shows two figures, one a cocoonlike form described in contour, the other a more volumetric rendering of hair or fibers. The form on the left, which seems to be suspended, relates directly to the artist's childhood. Her parents were tapestry restorers in Aubusson, and as a child Bourgeois was employed in their business working with skeins of yarn. "The skeins of wool are a friendly refuge, like a web or cocoon," the artist has written. "The caterpillar gets the silk from his mouth, builds his cocoon and when it is completed it dies. The cocoon has exhausted the animal. I am the cocoon. I have no ego. I am my work."[3] Thus the drawing, which shows both the skein and the cocoon, can be read as a visual metaphor for the artist's vital and consuming relationship to the artistic process.[4]

MB

1. *Quoted by Christiane Meyer-Thoss in* Louise Bourgeois: Designing for Free Fall *(Zurich: Ammann, 1992), p. 184.*
2. *Ibid., p. 136.*
3. *Ibid., p. 197.*
4. *In 1989 the artist returned to the skein-like image, using it as the source for a drypoint in* Anatomy, *a portfolio published by Peter Blum Edition, New York.*

Vija Celmins
Night Sky #5. 1992

(American,
born Latvia
1939)

Oil on canvas
mounted on
wood panel

31 × 37½"
(78.7 ×
95.3 cm)

1992.6

Vija Celmins's representational paintings, drawings, and prints have often been identified with contemporaneous styles, including Pop, Minimalism, Conceptual art, and Photo-Realism. A significant figure since her emergence in the early 1960s, Celmins's subjects and images, despite their familiarity to viewers, remain idiosyncratic and often mysterious.

In the early 1960s Celmins began her career in Los Angeles, where in her Venice studio she created paintings of ordinary household objects. Like Edward Ruscha (pages 204–9), another Los Angeles-based artist, Celmins painted Pop images on monochromatic fields of color. Toward the end of the decade, she increasingly used photographs as source material, inspired primarily by those of the moon's surface taken by satellite in 1969. At this time she was engaged with her own photographic documentation of the Pacific Ocean.

The transformation from Pop to more Conceptual art imagery represented a general trend seen among artists in the early 1970s. Within a short period, Celmins's subjects shifted from material objects to forms of nature that incarnate patterns of energy—the ocean, the galaxies, and the desert floor. This close observation of the natural world would form the core of her art.

In 1973 Celmins began a series of small graphite drawings based on scientific photographs of galaxies. Translating the image

from photography into drawing, she made thousands of graphite marks, with the small white areas of the page remaining untouched by graphite forming illusions of stars. Among these works are *Galaxy #1 (Coma Berenices)*, *Galaxy #2 (Coma Berenices)*, and *Galaxy #4 (Coma Berenices)* (all page 261), three of four drawings of quadrants of the Coma Berenices galaxy.

After a twenty-year hiatus, Celmins returned to painting (and New York) in the mid-1980s. "I went back to painting because I wanted more form, I wanted the work to carry more weight. . . ."[1] *Night Sky #5*, included in her second exhibition of paintings at McKee Gallery in New York, is one of a group of works that portrays an open, crystalline sky saturated with an infinite number of pulsating stars dispersed across the matte blackness. The sensation is mesmerizing: viewed closely it appears as a clear night sky filled with stars, some faint, others bright, that visually pulls the viewer deeper into the galaxy. Despite its relatively small and condensed scale, this is nonetheless one of Celmins's largest paintings to date, with its illusion of cosmic expansiveness seeming even greater than that of her drawings. The stars in the drawings are represented by the absence of graphite; in the later paintings, however, Celmins covers the entire surface with layers of black and white paint—sanding down the surface and repeatedly adding more layers—until the surface, the image, and the paint are one.

JW

1. *Quoted by Chuck Close in* Vija Celmins, *edited by William S. Bartman (Los Angeles: A.R.T. Press, 1992), p. 38.*

Sandro Chia
Three Boys on a Raft. 1983

(Italian,
born 1946)

Oil on canvas

97 × 111"
(246.4 ×
282 cm)

1983.12

Sandro Chia is among the group of Italian artists who came to prominence in the early 1980s and were loosely associated by the Roman critic Achille Bonito Oliva under the term *transavangardia (transavantgarde)*. A fundamental premise of this movement as articulated by Oliva was the antimodernist notion that art need not move continually forward in a linear history, but could evolve in many parallel directions at once. In several respects, the movement is similar to the classical revival that took place in Europe after the First World War. Although their work is not always related stylistically, the Transavantgarde artists share an interest in reviving the art of the past as the foundation for a new art. Borrowing freely from various cultural and artistic sources, they consider the imagery of the past to be at their disposal. Their work, appearing to represent a complete departure from the Minimalist and Conceptual art dominant in the 1970s, was considered to mark a "return" to painting.

In addition to Chia, this group included the artists Francesco Clemente (pages 76–79, 262), Enzo Cucchi (pages 84, 263), Nicola de Maria, and Mimmo Paladino (pages 182, 275). Their art was often figurative and composed in such traditional mediums as oil on canvas, fresco, and cast bronze. Chia's work from this period is exuberantly figurative and draws on a range of art historical sources, particularly Italian Mannerist painting, the art of Alberto Savinio, and the late works of Savinio's brother Giorgio de Chirico. Although Chia's figures often appear as larger than life, they seem buoyant, unfettered by their size and weight, and are depicted in vivid colors and painted with lively brushstrokes. Chia draws on the past irreverently and with a sense of humor, much in the spirit of *opera buffa,* in which the subjects, often classical in origin, are treated farcically. This light touch is evident in Chia's large drawing *Free Elaboration* (page 261) from 1981.

Chia received classical training in art at the Istituto d'Arte in Florence, where he was raised. His ability to merge his technical facility with an ironic sensibility is clear in a series of large paintings of figures, including *Three Boys on a Raft,* executed in 1983. In their size and mock-heroic subjects, these works are reminiscent of tapestries. Closely related to a work entitled *Zattere Temeraria (Audacious Raft),*[1] which had been exhibited at the international exhibition *Zeitgeist* in 1982, *Three Boys on a Raft* shows three figures, two large and one small, drifting at sea and waving languorously to unseen figures on the shore. Although the painting is festive, there is a slightly ominous mood, as if the three men are moving unawares towards danger. The title of the painting invokes the innocence of the nursery rhyme "Three Men in a Tub" while its composition caricatures the splendid horror of one of the icons of nineteenth-century Romanticism, *The Raft of the Medusa* by Théodore Géricault.[2]

MB

1. *Private collection.*
2. *Musée du Louvre, Paris.*

75

Francesco Clemente
Perseverance. (1982)

(Italian,
born 1953)

Oil on canvas

78 × 93"
(198.1 ×
236.2 cm)

1982.5

Francesco Clemente came to prominence in the early 1980s at a moment when critical attention was focused on new figure painting, dubbed Neo-Expressionism. Clemente was associated with a group of Italian artists, including Sandro Chia (pages 74, 261), Enzo Cucchi (pages 84, 263), and Mimmo Paladino (pages 182, 275), who frequently exhibited work together. Although Clemente had been exhibiting since 1971, he began painting in oil only in 1980. He had previously been known for installations that incorporated frescoes and drawings. Works on paper, particularly pastel and watercolor, have been an important means of expression for the artist throughout his career (page 262). He also has produced prints in a variety of techniques, including woodblock printing done in Japan. The contemporary artists whom Clemente cites as influences are Cy Twombly and Alighiero Boetti, although his work combines a range of art historical and cultural sources, from the Renaissance and Surrealism to Indian and ancient art.

Born in Naples in 1952, Clemente made his first trip to India in 1973. Since then, he has spent time in Madras, Naples, and New York, absorbed in three cultures—East, West, and the New World. The experience of

displacement is evident in his work, which is marked by a sense of transition and impermanence, self-analysis, a lack of interest in absolutes, and an interest in metaphysical systems, including alchemy, mythology (both Christian and Classical), and astrology. Clemente's exploration of self includes both the psychological and the physical. The human body (frequently the artist's own) is often used symbolically in his art, as he has said, to represent his "interest in these two spaces, the space inside and the space outside, and the weights those two spaces have . . . there is a landscape of the world and there is also an inner landscape of the world."[1] Clemente's images are both cosmic and specific, showing the cycle of human life from birth to death and including explicit sexual and scatological activities.

In the winter of 1981–82, Clemente completed a series of paintings entitled The Fourteen Stations. This group, which was shown at the Whitechapel Art Gallery in London in 1983, is central to the artist's oeuvre and his depiction of the human condition. It includes twelve Stations, numbered I–XII, and two related canvases, entitled *Fortune* and *Perseverance.* While based on a Christian subject, the journey of Christ to the Crucifixion, the twelve Stations present a

77

Francesco Clemente
Salvation (previously titled **Boat**). 1987

(continued from previous page)
personal and apocalyptic vision of the world, fusing Christianity with cultural history and contemporary life. The paintings are richly colored and thickly painted and are dense with dreamlike figures placed in lurid scenes.

Perseverance, one of the two companion paintings to the cycle, is less complex in its imagery and lighter in tone than the twelve Stations, which were completed before *Perseverance* was finished. However, the painting is deeply symbolic and directly related to a dream that the artist had shortly after moving to New York. In it, he was wandering around the streets of the city, naked, while excrement poured down on him from the sky. "Diffused through every part of the dream," wrote Henry Geldzahler in the Whitechapel exhibition catalogue, "was the artist's overwhelming awareness of the fragility of the human body, a small and delicate pantheon . . . amidst the machinery of the world."[2]

The dream is vividly transcribed in the painting, in which Clemente stands, footless, cradling the Pantheon in his arms while fistfuls of ocher paint are hurled down on him. The painting speaks of physical and cultural dislocation, as does the dream. The Pantheon, a temple dedicated to the gods, can be read as a symbol of Clemente's cultural past, which he must both confront and protect in a new environment. It can also be understood as a weight he has carried with him and which he struggles to elevate. The quick and ferocious manner in which the paint is applied to the primed canvas reinforces the idea of physical and emotional conflict.

In *Salvation,* painted five years after *Perseverance,* Clemente's dreams take the form of a vision. The title suggests deliverance or protection, and the painting seems to portray a cosmic journey undertaken by boat. Clemente combines sacred and pagan themes: salvation is the Christian route to heaven, while the Greeks took the ferry across the River Styx to Hades. The painting is composed with three very thinly painted horizontal fields that overlap, adding to the sense of an illusion. The outer area depicts ocean liners in a style reminiscent of Art Deco fabric or wallpaper. This frames the next zone, a body of water surrounding the center, where a stylized bark hovers in deep space. Although painted at the same time as a somber group of nonfigurative works entitled The Funerary Paintings, the emotional tone of *Salvation* is very different. The dark, horizontal canvases of The Funerary Paintings suggest death and entombment, while *Salvation* celebrates the voyage beyond.

MB

(Italian, born 1953)

Pigment on linen

76 × 183 3/4" (193 × 466.7 cm)

1990.4

1. Statement made in an interview with Rainer Crone and Georgia Marsh in Clemente *(New York: Vintage Books, 1987), pp. 46-47.*
2. Henry Geldzahler *in* Francesco Clemente: The Fourteen Stations, *exhibition catalogue (London: Whitechapel Art Gallery, 1983), p. 36.*

78

Chuck Close
Self-Portrait. 1991

(American,
born 1940)

Oil on canvas

100 × 84"
(254 ×
213.4 cm)

1991.34

Since 1968, when he was initially described as either a realist painter or a Photo-Realist (indicating the delicate balance between painting and photography inherent in his work), Chuck Close has been painting larger-than-life portraits that have a startling, seemingly animated likeness. With a grid as an armature, thousands of painted or drawn marks coalesce into a single recognizable likeness.

Not significantly changed since his first painting, in which the grid clearly derived from Minimalism, his technique is similar to that of the Post-Impressionists Georges Seurat and Paul Signac, who composed images organized by individual dots of color. Working from a close-up frontal photograph of the sitter (as in *Large Mark Pastel*, page 262), Close first overlays a grid and then transfers the image in pencil square by square before applying paint. As one critic has noted, "Ironically, by limiting himself to recording only that information contained within the photograph, he found he was actually making shapes and patterns that were totally new, unlike any he had invented as an abstractionist."[1] In this sense, Close's monumental paintings have been described as an attempt to close the gap between figuration and abstraction in twentieth-century art.

Self-Portrait, painted in a palette of black, white, and gray, is among the first paintings Close completed following a spinal injury in 1989 that left him partially paralyzed and in a wheelchair. Unable to grasp a paintbrush, he must strap an orthotic device to his wrist to hold a brush. He is acutely aware that his existing system of painting allowed him to continue to create powerful portraits and it is interesting to note that at a time when he most needs his system of grids, he has undermined them with a new sense of urgency and painterly energy. Whereas earlier marks were tightly and meticulously laid down, his recent works are more loosely and expressionistically painted; viewed from a distance, they appear almost abstract. The monumental scale of the painting also allows the viewer to be enveloped in the process of the image's solution and dissolution.

Close, as fascinated by the process as by the image, has stated: "All the work I've done has that building-block, incremental nature. I've always been overwhelmed by problems of the whole—'How am I going to make this thing?' Not only that, I'm plagued by indecision, so it's liberating to turn this formidable series of decisions into little yes/no choices. For me, the real joy is in putting coveys of these silly little marks together. Some of them look like hot dogs, some of them look like doughnuts, but they're pictorial syntax: I build a painting by putting those marks together, just the way a writer makes a novel by slamming words together."[2]

JW

1. Lisa Lyons in Lisa Lyons and Robert Storr. Chuck Close (New York: Rizzoli International Publications, 1987), p. 28.
2. Quoted in Edith Newhall, "Close to the Edge," New York, April 15, 1991, p. 39.

81

Tony Cragg
Grey Moon. (1985)

(British,
born 1949)

Gray and
white plastic
found objects

86 5/8 × 52"
overall (irreg.)
(220 × 132 cm)

1987.13

British sculptor Tony Cragg's original and thought-provoking use of materials unifies his kaleidoscopic body of work. The artist employs a range of both traditional and unconventional mediums—from marble, plaster, bronze, and wood to plastic, rubber, glass and Cor-ten steel—to link the natural and man-made worlds.

Mass-produced items, such as containers and furniture, and discarded materials, the flotsam and jetsam of industrial culture, are not merely relocated into an aesthetic realm, but are transformed and used in ways that the artist deems of consequence. Natural materials, for example stone or metal, are shaped to assume the form of man-made items, such as tools, test tubes, and portable stereos. To Cragg, natural and artificial are potentially equal: both are suitable for making art, and art is a proposition for locating mankind in the world. "To live in a world that has become predominantly artificial and man-made," he has said, "that I can accept as long as the man-made world is providing images and meanings which are just as deep and meaningful as those which are found in naturally occurring things."[1]

The tone of his art varies from the celebratory to the sinister. In the early 1980s Cragg began the series for which he is best-known: wall pieces made from discarded plastic. In these works, plastic fragments collected from industrial sites, roadsides, and riverbanks are mounted on the wall to form a diagram of an object. The scale of the work and the accumulation of material force the viewer to contemplate the sheer quantity of things that are fabricated in the world, that each thing has a function, and that these items are enduring fragments of our culture. His use of found and ready-made objects to express scientific and environmental concerns is distinctly of its own time, but the method belongs to a twentieth-century tradition, which includes work by Picasso, Schwitters, Smith, Rauschenberg, and Chamberlain.

Grey Moon is one of four wall pieces in the shape of a crescent moon. In this piece Cragg depicts a natural object, the moon, in salvaged plastic pieces, which range from dirty white to dark gray. The moon, a source of wonder, information, and myth since ancient times, became the focus of intense scientific discovery and exploration in the mid-twentieth century, culminating in the historic moon walk in 1969 (an event wittily alluded to by Cragg through his inclusion of a toy plastic spaceman). The space program, originally geared toward landing a man on the moon, resulted in an explosion of technological invention and information. The image presented by Cragg suggests our complex relationship to the natural world and is both poetic and mundane: a silver crescent of discarded plastic objects, ranging from a disposable lighter to a film canister.

MB

1. *Quoted by Lynn Cooke in "Tony Cragg: Thinking Models,"* Tony Cragg, *exhibition catalogue (London: Arts Council of Great Britain, 1986), p. 53.*

83

Enzo Cucchi
Vitebsk-Harar. (1984)

(Italian,
born 1950)

Oil on canvas
and iron
element

92 × 216"
overall
(233.7 ×
548.6 cm)

1985.16

The Museum
of Modern
Art, New York.
Fractional
gift of
PaineWebber
Group, Inc.

Associated with the Transavantgarde movement, Enzo Cucchi came to international prominence in the early 1980s with a series of brightly colored figurative paintings and large charcoal drawings representing ritual, fable, and natural forces. In *Leone dei Mari Mediterranea (Lion of the Mediterranean Sea)*, 1979–80 (page 263), for example, a green lion is tossed in a rowboat on an orange red sea beneath a hovering yellow head. A conflict among the elements—water, air, and fire— is invoked in the painting, with the hot colors and grinning face of the balloonlike head mitigating a sense of impending disaster.

In his more recent work Cucchi has been influenced by the Italian artist Alberto Burri's eloquent use of rough materials, particularly burlap, tar, and scorched steel and wood, as emblems of decay. The expressive use of materials can be seen in *Vitebsk-Harar,* a large two-part work consisting of an eighteen-foot-long painting above which hangs an iron element of similar length. This component is made of welded iron, which was left outdoors with salt on its surface, causing it to rust and to begin to disintegrate.

The title of the work, one of a series on the theme of Vitebsk and Harar that Cucchi exhibited in 1984, refers to two geographical locations, one in Europe and the other in Africa. Vitebsk is the city in Belarus that was the center, between 1919 and 1922, of Russian Constructivist revolutionary activity. Thus for Cucchi, the city stands for a utopian, social ambition for art. Located in Ethiopia, Harar was the French Symbolist writer Arthur Rimbaud's final destination. Rimbaud's great contribution to modern literature is his use of poetry for intense, wild, fragmentary expressions of the subconscious. It is the capability of art to express powerful, hallucinatory, and destructive forces that Harar exemplifies in Cucchi's work. Vitebsk and Harar, then, represent opposite impulses in art. One is edifying, ordered, and rational; the other mad, negative, and destructive.

The work itself seems closer to Rimbaud's vision of art than to Malevich's. The painting recalls a line from Rimbaud's celebrated poem *Le Bâteau ivre (The Drunken Boat),* written when the author was seventeen: "I have come to know the skies splitting with lightnings, and the waterspouts, and the breakers and currents."[1] Rather than describing a coherent narrative, Cucchi's work provokes a series of associations. The embryonic image sailing over the two geometric slabs in the painting seems to refer to a primordial state of creativity. The podlike form of the metal element can be identified with nature and a process of growth, or it can be read as a shroud, carrying implications of death. The sense of catastrophe is reinforced by the violent, stormy atmosphere in which the scene takes place. This gives another, more literal meaning to the metal element, which could be seen as a cloud from which the foul weather descends. Thus the cycles of birth and death and destruction and regeneration are established in the work.

MB

1. Arthur Rimbaud. Collected Poems, translated by Oliver Bernard (London: Penguin Books, Ltd., 1962), p. 167.

85

Willem de Kooning
Untitled. (c. 1950)

(American, born
The Nether-
lands 1904)

Pastel and char-
coal on paper

19 × 24¼"
(48.3 × 61.6
cm)

1986.27

One of the leaders of the Abstract Expressionist movement, Willem de Kooning occupies
a central role in American art and in the art
of this century. Born in The Netherlands in
1904, the artist emigrated to New York
in 1926. He has produced a body of work remarkable for its continuing inquiry and
invention. In his paintings, drawings, and
sculptures created during the course of this
century, de Kooning's synthesis of abstraction and figuration stands as his most important achievement. For most of his career,
de Kooning's art has flourished from the inherent contradiction of his approach.

The process of drawing is fundamental
to de Kooning's art. This is especially true
of his work from the late 1940s and early
1950s, when he made his first important
abstract paintings and simultaneously began
his famous Women series. Educated for eight
years at the Rotterdam Academy of Fine
Arts, it was necessary for de Kooning to over-
come his classical training in order to use
drawing to integrate figure and ground, rather
than rendering them distinct from one
another. In the early 1950s, as the importance
of improvisation and process grew in de
Kooning's paintings, working with drawing
became an essential way to try new shapes
and resolve relationships between forms in a
composition.

Untitled, c. 1950, is executed on the back
of chart paper that de Kooning's friend the
sculptor Philip Pavia had obtained as surplus
from the United States Customs House in
1950. The drawing is unusual in its use of
pastel and charcoal rather than the black
enamel that de Kooning employed in a series
of well-known works drawn on the gridded
side of chart paper. Although a work in its
own right and not simply a study for a painting, *Untitled,* c. 1950, seems related to the
series of great "white" paintings that the
artist made in 1949–50, in which he integrated form and line, surface and ground, and
color and black-and-white in complex, interlocking compositions.[1] Often in these paintings, as in *Untitled,* c. 1950, black line outlines and defines some shapes, while in other
areas, color alone performs this function. In
Attic and *Excavation,* white paint is used as
both surface and ground, unifying and flat-
tening the painting. De Kooning achieved
the same effect in *Untitled,* c. 1950, with his
liberal use of an eraser to remove pastel and
thus restore the ground while leaving a transparent veil of the erased color. Pastel is also
used to add white to the composition.

It seems likely that in *Untitled,* c. 1950,
as in many of his works on paper, de Kooning
was rehearsing ideas for paintings that he was
currently finishing. The voluptuous forms
and pink tones of the drawing suggest the
female body and remind us that de Kooning
began *Woman I* in June 1950, within days of
completing *Excavation.*

MB

1. *Among these are*
Asheville, *The
Phillips Collection;*
Attic, *Muriel Kallis
Newman and The
Metropolitan Museum
of Art, New York;
and* Excavation,
*The Art Institute of
Chicago.*

87

Willem de Kooning
Untitled III. (1982)

(American, born
The Nether-
lands 1904)

Oil on canvas

80 × 70"
(203.2 × 177.8
cm)

1991.10

In 1975, after spending the early part of the decade concentrating on sculpture, Willem de Kooning turned his attention to painting once again. Upon completing an important series of landscape paintings in New York City in 1963, the artist had moved permanently to Long Island, drawn to its proximity to water and by the golden natural light, frequently compared to the light of his native Holland. However, de Kooning's late paintings are not so much landscapes as evocations of the artist's reaction to and intimate knowledge of a place. In an interview with Harold Rosenberg in 1972, de Kooning described his sense of intimacy with his surroundings: "I got into painting the atmosphere I wanted to be in. It was like the reflection of light. I reflected upon the reflections on the water, like the fishermen do. They stand there fishing. They seldom catch any fish, but they like to be by themselves for an hour. And I do that almost every day."[1]

The artist's late paintings can be divided chronologically into two groups—those done between 1975 and 1979 and those executed from the early to mid-1980s. The earlier works are thickly painted, robust, and often turbulent with a startling sense of physical immediacy and sensuousness. The later paintings, although still lively, are calmer, more reductive, and imbued with a transcendental

light. Drawing, which always has been critical to de Kooning's work, appears not only as line but as the essence of form in these paintings. In *Untitled III*, 1982, from this period, the white background is tinged with color, and undulating ribbons of rosy hues evoke both human form and landscape. The water, sky, and dunes of eastern Long Island are suggested as well as human presence; together they are merged into one vibrant, celebratory expression.

De Kooning's hand is in complete control, balancing colors and white, shape and line, while retaining the sense of invention and spontaneity that was the basis of Abstract Expressionist art. The composition is divided diagonally by free-flowing forms snaking down the canvas from the upper left. This is de Kooning's art in its purest, most elemental form. In some passages of *Untitled III*, the color has been scraped back with a palette knife, a technique that parallels the artist's earlier innovative use of pastel and eraser (evident in *Untitled*, c. 1950, page 86), and adds to the essential, bare-bones quality of the work. The shimmering incandescence of the painting suggests transparency and physical dissolution, but this is contradicted by the vigorous authority of line that springs from seven decades of making art.

MB

1. Interview with Harold Rosenberg in Artnews, *no. 71 (September 1972), p. 56.*

89

Richard Diebenkorn
Table and Chair. 1964

(American,
1922–1993)

Ink wash and
graphite on
paper

12 × 17¾"
(30.5 × 45.1
cm)

1989.56

Richard Diebenkorn's art is closely associated with the light and landscape of California, where he worked for most of his life, but his extraordinary oeuvre extends the development of modernist painting in the tradition of Cézanne, Mondrian, and Matisse. His career can be separated into three stylistic phases: his first maturity as an abstract painter from 1948 to 1955; his representational period from 1956 to 1967; and his return to abstraction, which began in 1967 with the Ocean Park series—named after the Santa Monica district where Diebenkorn's studio was located—and ended with his move from Southern to Northern California in 1988. Yet the artist's body of work would be more accurately characterized not as a series of different styles, but rather as a continuous development with changes of emphasis. Speaking of his shift from representational to abstract art in the late 1960s, Diebenkorn said, "I didn't start seeing things differently. I simply saw different things."[1] In all Diebenkorn's art the affinities and distinctions between abstraction and representation are made evident. Diebenkorn's working process incorporated uncertainty and discovery, and the effect of his effort to "get all the elements right"[2] was cumulative and progressive. It is the resolution of this struggle that finally is seen.

Diebenkorn is known as a colorist, but drawing, as well as color, is intrinsic to his art, with both playing key structural roles in the work. His use of vibrant color is sensuous and seemingly instinctive, yet it is as critical as line in the ordering of space. This is especially true in the Ocean Park series, where blocks of color are employed to build the compositions, while drawing supplies the scaffold and facilitates the negotiation between the parts of the composition. The artist considered his highly developed works on paper a separate body of work that satisfies "my need to do relatively small works, independent of others and complete in themselves. But a small canvas usually becomes for me an unfeasible miniature. Paper, however, I find is something else, lending itself to the different scale of the small size. It's almost as though if I can call my work a large drawing instead of a small canvas, it becomes possible."[3]

Table and Chair is from 1964, a year in which the artist did not complete any paintings, instead focusing his attention on drawings and making his first etchings and drypoints. In this drawing, one of several still lifes and interiors completed that year, the artist has concentrated on the furniture in the foreground. The horizontal planes of the chair seat, table-top, and cushion beyond are juxtaposed with the vertical walls and window in a

91

Richard Diebenkorn
Untitled (Ocean Park #13). 1983

(American,
1922–1993)

Gouache and
acrylic on paper

25 × 36"
(63.5 × 91.4
cm)

1984.19

(continued from previous page)
carefully selected view of observed reality.
Diebenkorn demonstrates his virtuoso control
over a difficult medium, ink wash, which
covers the sheet in tones ranging from pale
gray to deep black, like the ground of an
etching plate into which the artist has drawn.
These modulated tones function in the place
of color in the structure of the drawing. The
composition is opened in the center by the
clear white area of the sheet, which is left
exposed. Light also seeps in at the interstices
between the objects in the room. These glim-
mers and the lines defining the edges of
the furniture and wall provide a network that
locks together the surface of the drawing.
The readily identifiable subject is expressed
both by blocks of shadow and light and by
the ordering linear structure. In balancing
abstraction and representation, drawings such
as *Table and Chair* presage Diebenkorn's later
abstract work.

Untitled (Ocean Park #13), executed
nearly twenty years after *Table and Chair*, is a
characteristic work of the Ocean Park series.
Although these untitled works are not
descriptions of the views from or around the
studio, their translucent character and color
relationships recall the bright sun, sky, and
pastel light of Southern California. Landscape
and architecture (most often walls, arches,
doors, and windows) are alluded to in this
group of works, but not described. For example, the forms in the upper right of *Untitled
(Ocean Park #13)* could be read as architectural elements, but their importance to the composition is the role they play in opening up

an abstract sense of the space, suggesting a
shift in internal scale, and acting as a foil to
the large areas of color. This section recalls a
similar zone in the upper right corner of the
monumental Matisse painting of 1916 *The
Moroccans*,[4] as does Diebenkorn's use of green
and ocher, the same colors that Matisse
employed to depict the melons and leaves
occupying the lower left quadrant of his
painting. The elongated arch at the bottom
of *Untitled (Ocean Park #13)* is a vestige of a
playing-card spade, an iconic form recurring
in Diebenkorn's work for about a year and a
half beginning in 1981. Its appearance signaled a change in the absolute rectilinearity
of the Ocean Park series. In *Untitled (Ocean
Park #13)* the opaque colors and their relationship to each other are balanced against
the network of drawing and the geometric
elements. The irregular, brushed expanse of
ocher is composed of interlocking rectangular
segments articulated by ruled lines and
changes in the direction of the brushstrokes
and activated by pentimenti. The rich,
worked surface and the resonant, high-keyed
colors in this drawing declare the artist's
hard-won satisfaction in working with paint.[5]

MB

1. *Quoted by John
Elderfield in* The
Drawings of Richard
Diebenkorn, *exhibi-
tion catalogue (New
York and Houston:
The Museum of Mod-
ern Art and Houston
Fine Art Press,
1988), p. 41.*
2. *Ibid., p. 22.*
3. *Quoted in* Draw-
ings since 1974,
*exhibition catalogue
(Washington, D.C.:
Hirshhorn Museum
and Sculpture Garden,
Smithsonian Institu-
tion, 1984), p. 77.*
4. *Collection of The
Museum of Modern
Art, New York.*
5. *In 1983
Diebenkorn used*
Untitled (Ocean
Park #13) *as the basis
for a woodblock print
entitled* Ochre, *which
was published by
Crown Point Press.*

92

Carroll Dunham
Purple and Blue. 1986

(American, born
1949)

Casein, dry pig-
ment, shellac,
and graphite on
elm veneer

28¾ × 24"
(73 × 61 cm)

1992.5

Carroll Dunham's abstract paintings, developed in the early 1980s, share with those of his
contemporaries Bill Jensen (pages 126, 269)
and Terry Winters (pages 252, 283) a very personal, eclectic form of abstraction inspired by
the organic world. Unlike Winters, however,
who refers to a preexisting vocabulary of
images, Dunham immerses himself in a
process from which he spontaneously creates
color-and-form relationships. As he has stated,
"Things that come up in my paintings tend to
be much more an expression of an attitude
about process than they do [sic] the expression
of an attitude about subject matter."[1]

Dunham's method combines intuition
with conscious choice and recalls automatic
drawing, a technique practiced by the Surrealists to counter the constraints of the rational mind. Adopting the psychoanalytic model
of free association, Surrealist artists let chance
determine their compositions, sometimes
drawing with closed eyes, searching for compositions in random scribbles, or passing the
same drawing from artist to artist for collective input. Despite this link to Surrealist and
Expressionist tradition, Dunham is very
much an artist of his time, and his work, like
that of Jean-Michel Basquiat (page 60), shows
the influence of such "low" sources as graffiti,
Saturday morning cartoons, and bathroom
humor.

Despite its spontaneity and exuberance
of forms, the layered composition *Purple and
Blue* resulted from a labor-intensive creative
process. Dunham builds his works slowly,
beginning with biomorphic shapes that
divide and multiply at a dizzying rate like
organisms. He then adds charcoal drawings of
cartoonlike billowy amoebas and clouds that
appear on the verge of turning into body
parts. Bands of painted colors and white and
black paint that has been allowed to drip
interrupt and complicate the composition.
The entire surface is profusely activated by
pentimenti and a variety of doodles, from
small, carefully drawn organic shapes to
impulsively gestured expressionistic marks.
As part of the creative process, he casually
inscribes a drawing with dates during which
he worked on it as well as his previous choices
for the title.

Purple and Blue is one of a suite of twelve
drawings collectively titled Drawings in Col-
or that were made on elm veneer on the occasion of Dunham's 1986 solo exhibition at
Barbara Krakow Gallery in Boston. He began
working on various wood veneers in 1982,
employing the material for its physical attrib-
utes as well as its strong reference to Cubist
collages (which used veneer and remnants of
wallpaper to evoke a particular place or setting). Drawing improvisationally, he enhanced the grain pattern by playing off the
rippling irregularities of the veneer, which
reflect the organic quality of his marks.

JW

1. Quoted in "An
Interview with Carroll
Dunham by Betsy
Sussler," Carroll
Dunham, *exhibition
catalogue (Cologne,
Germany, and New
York: Jablonka
Galerie and Sonnabend
Gallery, 1990), n.p.*

95

Eric Fischl
Untitled #8 and **Untitled #10.** 1986

(American,
born 1948)

Two monotypes

25¼ × 22½"
each sheet
(64.1 × 57.2
cm)

1988.33q–r

Eric Fischl began making monotypes at the suggestion of the publisher Peter Blum in the New York studio of printer Maurice Sanchez in March 1986. Fischl continued print-making throughout the rest of the year, pro-ducing a group of 144 monotypes—one of the most ambitious printmaking projects known of by a contemporary artist. With an accompanying text by the writer E. L. Doc-torow, fifty-eight of the prints were published in facsimile in the book *Scenes and Sequences* (1989).[1] Of these prints, twenty-two were acquired by PaineWebber. As poetically artic-ulated by Doctorow's text, the theme of this project is desire and its companion activities and experiences of looking, longing, and loss. The events depicted occur in bedrooms, back-yards, and at the beach (all of which are potential sexual playgrounds), in situations suggesting both knowledge and innocence. Within this arena, Fischl establishes con-frontations between male and female, black and white, youth and old age, and tribal and modern cultures.

The images that Fischl created, many of which are derived from his own and others' photographs, are evocative: they are dreams, fantasies, and exercises of the unconscious. The title of the book suggests episodes rather than complete stories and indicates observa-tion as the primary activity of the project. Through the act of looking, the viewer becomes a participant in each episode.

Fischl had already realized the narrative potential of the portfolio format in his earlier prints. For example, in *Year of the Drowned Dog,* 1983, the six color etchings in the port-folio can be rearranged and layered to develop the story, while in *Floating Islands,* 1985 (also in PaineWebber's collection), one vertical sheet portrays a dreamer and the four accom-panying horizontal sheets depict the dreams. Particularly well-suited to Fischl's art, the process of monotype further allows for the appearance, disappearance, and reappearance of figures in changing juxtapositions. In monotype the medium (here lithographic ink) is applied directly on the plate and then without the intervention of a fixing process is transferred to the paper, thereby producing a unique image, like a drawing in reverse. Most of the ink (and therefore the image) is trans-mitted, but sometimes ghostly afterimages remain that can be used as the basis for the next composition. Transformation and meta-morphosis, integral to the monotype process, are qualities Fischl used as components of the narrative as well. In the two plates illustrated here from the *Dream* section of the book, a naked girl sunbathing on a mat outdoors becomes a nude lying on a bed indoors, with the presence of the window reinforcing atten-dant associations of voyeurism. The fluid sur-face of the image, the manipulation of light and dark, and the luminous colors become emblems of the emotionally and psychologi-cally loaded situations the artist portrays.

MB

1. *Scenes and Sequences is orga-nized into thirteen sec-tions titled by the artist. In order of their appearance in the book, these are:* Stroll, Voodoo, Vision, Dance, Companion, Specter, Dream, Girl, Backyard, Man, Fable, Beach, *and* Boy.

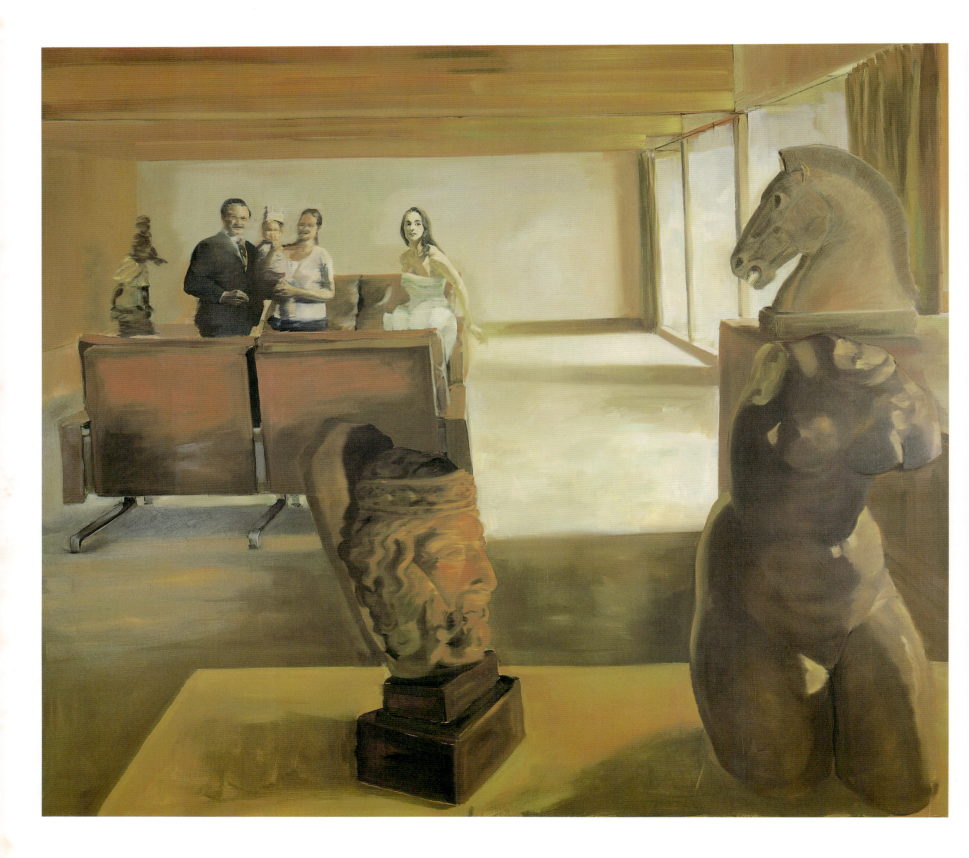

Eric Fischl
The Chester's Gambit. 1991

(American,
born 1948)

Oil on linen

86 × 98"
(218.4 × 249
cm)

1991.48

Eric Fischl asserts the narrative voice of painting. The work that established him in the early 1980s as a painter of psychological tableaux depicted adolescent boys in suburban homes and addressed such social taboos as masturbation, violence, alcoholism, and incest. Since the mid-1980s Fischl's work has taken as one of its themes the spiritually empty, leisured existence of the middle and upper classes. He often has been linked with the great French painters of bourgeois domestic scenes and with the American realists Eakins, Homer, and, of course, Hopper. While his images can recall the lonely isolation of Hopper's figures, the psychological thrust of his work places him nearer to Munch, Beckmann, and Balthus.

For the viewer, looking at Fischl's art involves recognition either from first-hand experience or familiarity with the images from popular media, magazines, and films that Fischl uses. Presented with a narrative moment rather than a complete story, we are left to fill in the details from our own imaginations, much like the experience provoked by seeing a film still outside a movie theater. This use of the narrative fragment links the artist with Cindy Sherman (pages 220, 279–80) and David Salle (pages 212, 279). However, rather than employing staged photographs (like Sherman) or densely layered images (like Salle), Fischl has opted for the illusionary unity that traditional painting provides. His skillful use of oil painting technique to portray strikingly contemporary images contributes to the impact of his art.

Given the furnishings of the room and the people depicted in *The Chester's Gambit,* it is easy to date the painting to the end of the twentieth century, although the work belongs to the history of family portraiture that includes paintings by Velázquez and Degas. While both Velázquez's *Las Meninas*[1] and Degas's *La Famille Bellelli*[2] can be read as images of isolation placed within splendid settings, the estrangement of the family group in *The Chester's Gambit* seems less poignant from our contemporary perspective. The gap in age between the husband and wife, her stylish beauty, and his middle-aged suavity, the displacement of the mother by a nanny holding the child (ironically wearing a crown), the distance between the mother and the rest of the figures all speak of brittle, superficial attachments. The perfection of the modern interior suggests emotional sterility, and the collection of sculptures from various cultures stands like a group of fetishes, primarily functioning to gratify the narcissism of their owner. A classic compositional device is enacted by the sculptural figure in the background who, arm extended, points toward the family, grouped in the back of the room with their gazes directed outward. The mother/wife holds a pose. Luxurious golden light pours in from the windows on the right and illuminates the room. The surface of the painting is smooth, almost glassy, as if it were a mirror reflecting the family portrait back to its subjects in a perfect image of self-absorption.

MB

1. *Collection Museo del Prado, Madrid.*
2. *Collection Musée d'Orsay, Paris.*

99

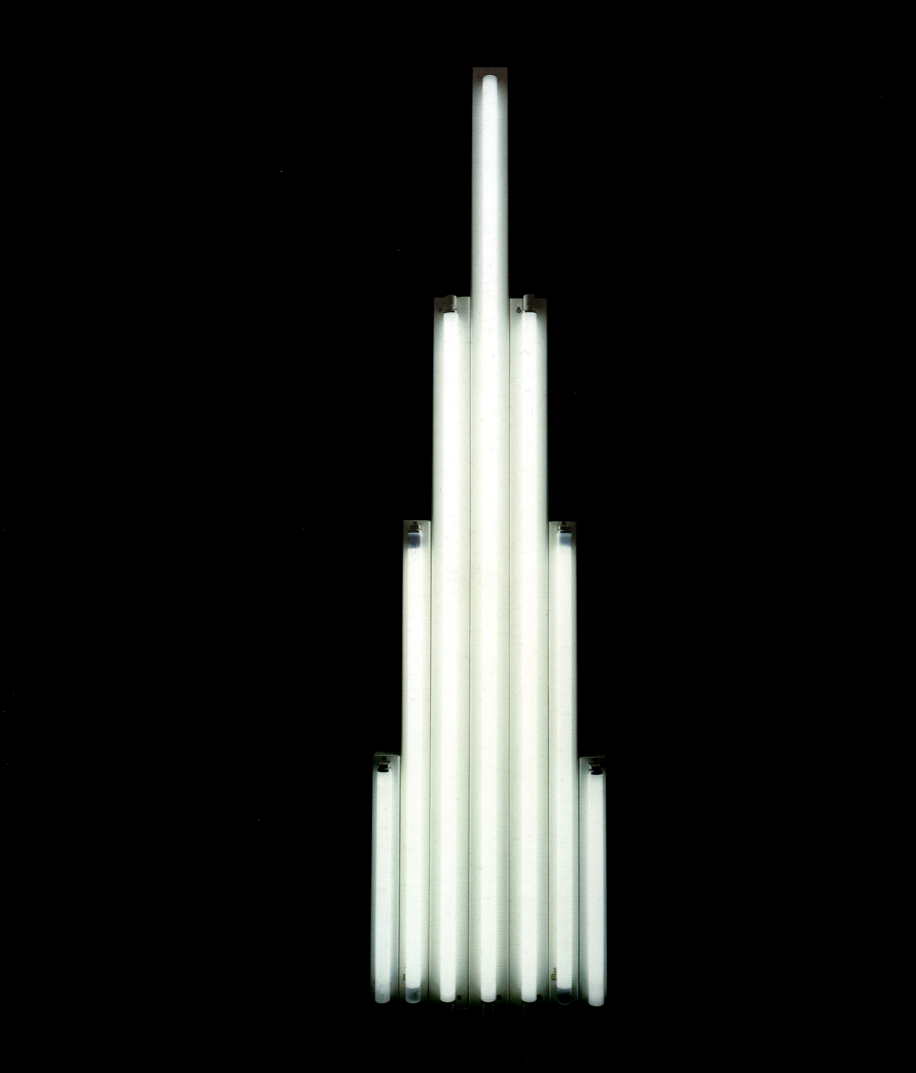

Dan Flavin
"monument" 1 for V. Tatlin. (1964)

(American,
born 1933)

Fluorescent
light bulbs and
metal fixtures

96 × 23⅛ ×
4¼"
(243.8 × 58.7
× 10.8 cm)

1988.18

The Museum
of Modern Art,
New York.
Fractional
gift of
PaineWebber
Group, Inc.

Dan Flavin's first works of art using electric light were a series of eight nearly square "icons," which combined rectangles of painted canvas with light fixtures. Flavin, like his Minimalist contemporaries Carl Andre, Donald Judd, Sol LeWitt, and Robert Morris, was trying to formulate an art that had lightness and clarity of structure as its foremost qualities. At first the solution seemed grounded in painting, but in 1963 the artist realized that "the radiant tube and the shadow cast by its supporting pan seemed ironic enough to hold alone,"[1] and he abandoned the canvas for the light fixture.

Not only did the formal simplicity and industrial source of the fluorescent tube appeal to Flavin, he was also drawn to the fact that light placed in a room activated the surface it was mounted on as well as the space of the entire room. His first fluorescent light piece, *Diagonal of May 25, 1963,* took form in a diagram. Flavin systematically has used drawings and diagrams as a "record of thought however to whatever use whenever."[2] On August 1, 1964, Flavin made the first of his drawings for a series that eventually included thirty-nine realized sculptures, the "monuments" for V. Tatlin, which occupied the artist on and off until 1982 and form the most comprehensive series in his work to date.

Flavin has stated that the series memorializes Vladimir Tatlin, the "great revolutionary who dreamed of art as science."[3] Tatlin was an important Russian Constructivist who in 1918 headed the Moscow section of the new communist government's Department of Fine Arts, which commissioned his project for a memorial to the Third International. Tatlin's proposal, a vertical spiral containing a hemisphere, a pyramid, and two cylinders of glass, was exhibited in November and December 1920. Although the building was never built and the original model exists only in photographs, the work is considered one of the great designs of utopian architecture.

The term "monument" in Flavin's series is used ironically, although the homage is meant sincerely. Initially, he referred to the works as "pseudo-monuments" because, unlike traditional commemorative sculptures, they were not carved from marble or cast in bronze, but manufactured from common fluorescent light with a life span of only twenty-one hours of illumination.

Although the diagram for *"monument" 1 for V. Tatlin* was the first drawing to be executed in the series, the work itself was not fabricated until 1969, on the occasion of an exhibition of Flavin's work entitled *Fluorescent Light, etc.* at the National Gallery of Canada, Ottawa. The vertical form of the piece echoes Tatlin's dynamic, thrusting model, but the brilliance of the seven tubes of cool white fluorescent light and the simplicity of its form identify it as an icon of a later period.

MB

1. *From a text by the artist in* Fluorescent Light, etc. from Dan Flavin, *exhibition catalogue (Ottawa: National Gallery of Canada, 1969).* p. 18.
2. *Quoted in "Some Artist's Remarks," in* "monuments" for V. Tatlin from Dan Flavin, 1964–1982 *(Chicago: Donald Young Gallery, 1989), p. 3.*
3. *Quoted in* Dan Flavin: Three Installations in Fluorescent Light, *exhibition catalogue (Cologne: Wallraf Richartz Museums and Kunsthalle, 1973), p. 18.*

101

Günther Förg
Lead Painting. 1988

(German, born
1952)

Acrylic on lead
on wood, four
parts each in
two panels

70⅞ × 47¼"
each
(180 × 120 cm)

1988.16

Günther Förg's interest in the ordering and perception of space informs all his work. In his exhibitions the artist often combines several of the many forms he uses—painted walls, bronze reliefs, freestanding sculpture, paintings, photographs of people and architecture, and works on paper—to make finely tuned installations in which the constituent parts interact to form an integrated whole. The emphasis on the articulation of space in Förg's work and his construction of paintings in solid blocks of color recall the work of a slightly older German artist, Blinky Palermo (page 184), who died in 1977.

One of the motifs Förg uses to explore concrete spatial relationships is the window, a device employed symbolically in Western art from the Renaissance to the twentieth century. Over time, the form of the window as both metaphor and a means of organizing composition has been identified with such disparate artists as Caspar David Friedrich, Henri Matisse, and Marcel Duchamp. In the Renaissance model, the painting itself is conceived of as a framed window into another world, which exists separately from the viewer. In deliberate contrast to this illusionistic tradition, Förg often uses painting as an architect would a window: to dematerialize walls and penetrate the surrounding real space. Fascinated by the form, Förg has done blocks of watercolors on the theme of windows and has made them a feature of his photographs of architecture (page 266).

Lead Painting is comprised of four panels, each consisting of two parts. The paintings are on lead mounted over wood, a combination of mediums that Förg began using in 1986. The use of lead, a heavy substance, underscores the materiality of the paintings, and the wrinkles and creases that form on the surface add to the sense of physicality. Although for the most part the ground is solidly covered with paint, the tonality of lead tinges the vibrant colors that the artist used, giving them a somber, velvety intensity. In one panel, however, the colors are applied lightly, revealing the lead through translucent coats of orange and pale blue and imparting to the panel a metallic sheen and a lightness that balances the density of the other elements. While Förg uses color to establish internal rhythms in the work, when installed the panels also interact structurally and spatially with each other, with nearby objects, and with the room that contains them. Unlike many of Förg's paintings, this group is human-scale (each panel is just under six feet tall), which reinforces their association with windows and doors. The artist does not stipulate the sequence in which the panels should be hung nor their relationship to each other, but requests that the distances between them are uneven, thus ensuring an infinitely variable work that changes each time it is installed.

MB

103

Helen Frankenthaler
Untitled. 1961

(American, born
1928)

Oil and colored
crayons on
paper

14⅛ × 22½"
(35.9 × 57.2
cm)

1993.8

Helen Frankenthaler established her reputation in the early 1950s as one of the "second generation" of Abstract Expressionist artists. Her approach to painting and the soak-stain technique that she worked out in 1952 while painting *Mountains and Sea*[1] substantially influenced the development of the art of the New York School, as Abstract Expressionism was known. By using thinned-down oil paint soaked into raw canvas to make luminous, airy paintings, Frankenthaler indicated the direction towards color field painting, the dominant style of abstraction in the 1960s. This approach, which influenced the painters Kenneth Noland and Morris Louis, was built on Pollock's idea of "allover" space but eliminated the spatial illusionism inherent in the application of paint on the surface of canvas. The spontaneity and immediacy of Frankenthaler's painting method resembled the use of watercolor or gouache, and drawing with color became the basis of her style. In unifying color and line, she was able to define pictorial space by establishing a balance between color, line, and area. The expressive quality of her gestural drawing gives her work a sense of intimacy on a large scale. For over four decades, she has produced a body of work remarkable for its pictorial richness, invention, and lyrical expression.

The graphic impulse in Frankenthaler's art is evident in *Untitled,* 1961, a complex drawing of apparently simple parts. Drawn in oil and colored crayons, line is used both as contour and form to establish the frame of the composition and the incident within it. The bare sheet acts both as the ground and as part of the composition, thereby denying the standard relationship between medium and support and creating spatial unity. In the early 1960s Frankenthaler's paintings became more symmetrical and static. Often, as in this work, the composition is centered around a square that structures the expressive gestures. Accidents such as drips, stains, and stray marks are incorporated into the composition, which swirls around the central core. The line is taut and vigorous, slightly awkward but also elegant, and the drawing seems charged with an emotional intensity springing from the artist's direct personal expression. In *Untitled,* 1961, and in large paintings from the same year, such as *Swan Lake I* and *Swan Lake II,* the symmetrical form of the composition amplifies the artist's use of abstract imagery.

The dedication on this drawing is to Tatyana and Maurice Grosman, the pioneering print publishers who established Universal Limited Art Editions on Long Island, where many prominent contemporary American artists have made prints. Frankenthaler was beginning her work there in 1961, the year her first three lithographs were published.

MB

1. Collection of
the artist, on loan
to the National
Gallery of Art,
Washington, D.C.

105

Lucian Freud
Double Portrait. (1988–90)

(British, born
Germany 1922)

Oil on canvas

44 1/2 × 53"
(113 × 134.6
cm)

1991.19

Lucian Freud is one of a number of contemporary painters in England—others include Frank Auerbach, Francis Bacon, Howard Hodgkin, and R. B. Kitaj—who are loosely associated as the "School of London," a designation made in 1976 by Kitaj at the time of an exhibition that he organized entitled *The Human Clay.* Although stylistically diverse, these artists share a commitment to depicting the figure in their work. All these artists have painted portraits, a venerable tradition in British art. None, however, have attempted the startling realism characteristic of Freud's work. His sitters are people he has known well—his mother, his children, other artists, close friends, and patrons—a circumstance that makes idealization unnecessary, seeming to eliminate the need for the painter to take flattery into account when rendering his subjects. In Freud's portraits we become aware not only of the painter observing, but of the sitter's sense of being observed. The sessions appear to be physically and emotionally intense and are transmitted directly in paint without the use of metaphor or illusion. For example, Freud's subtle nuances of color are used naturalistically. "I would like my portraits to be of the people not like them," Freud has said. "As far as I am concerned, the paint is the person. I want it to work for me just as flesh does."[1] This stated objectivity is present in the paintings, which, despite their intensity, are often colored by a disconcerting sense of the artist's detachment.

Double Portrait is one of four paintings that Freud has made since 1985 of a dark-haired woman sitting or lying with one or two whippets. In this painting, the two figures lie nestled together, the dog's head resting in the crook of the woman's arm so that their faces are near to each other. The sense of gentle companionship, kinship, and intimacy between the human and the animal is deeply moving.

Freud usually begins painting by drawing directly onto the canvas, without working out the composition in advance. Often the figure runs off the edge of the completed canvas. In other instances, it becomes necessary to extend the stretched canvas as the painted figure takes form. In *Double Portrait,* additional canvas has been added twice on the left— first at the bend of the woman's right arm, and then slightly below her knees. The lengthened, serpentine body of the woman divides the painting diagonally, creating a form that cradles the dog, whose tawny coat is painted in heavy impasto. Behind the woman is a mound of painting rags that have accumulated on the floor of the artist's studio. The self-contained introspection of the sitter and the somber, tonal light of the painting recall Rembrandt's portraits, an influence Freud has acknowledged. In 1987 the artist wrote, "What do I ask of a painting? I ask it to astonish, disturb, seduce, convince."[2] His art accomplishes this end for us.

MB

1. *Quoted by Lawrence Gowing in* Lucian Freud *(London: Thames and Hudson, 1982), pp. 190–91.*
2. *Artist's text in* The Artist's Eye: Lucian Freud, *exhibition catalogue (London: The National Gallery, 1987), p. 12.*

107

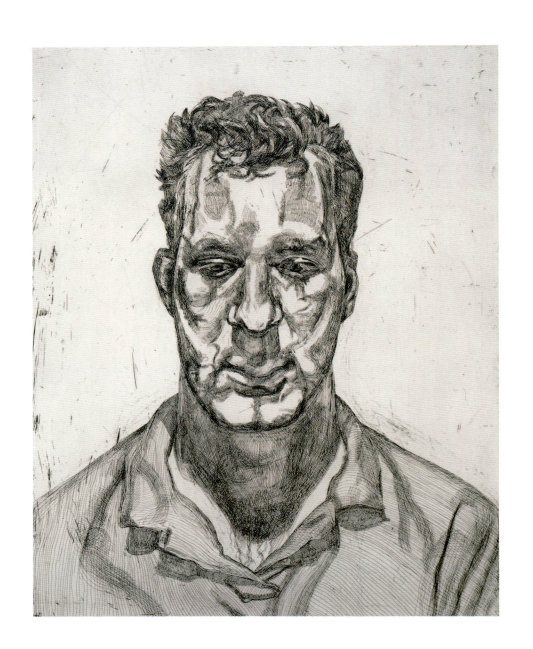

Lucian Freud
Kai. (1992)

(British, born
Germany 1922)

Etching, 22/40

sheet:
31¼ × 25"
(79.4 × 63.5
cm)

Published by
James Kirkman
and Matthew
Marks. 1992

1992.16

In 1982, on the occasion of the publication of a deluxe edition of a monograph of Lucian Freud's work by Lawrence Gowing, the artist returned to printmaking after a thirty-four-year hiatus. In 1936, Freud had made two linocuts; in 1944, a lithograph; and in the late 1940s he had produced four etchings, three of which he published independently in small editions, and the fourth never editioned. Freud's resumption of printmaking in 1982 proved fruitful: fourteen etchings were made in the first year, of which nine were editioned and another twenty-four etchings have been published in the past eleven years.

Freud's earliest achievements as an artist were his drawings: his skill as a draftsman and the hard, linear quality of his early paintings first attracted critical attention in London, where the art historian and critic Herbert Read described him as the "Ingres of Existentialism." It is not surprising that Freud turned to etching as a printmaker, since the essence of etching is line. Yet Freud's prints are not drawings in editions, but works in their own right. In contrast to his etchings, Freud's recent works on paper usually are realized in soft drawing materials, such as pastel (see page 266), watercolor (see page 266), or charcoal and pencil. The artist works on the prepared plate in front of a model, and frequently his paintings and etchings show the same subjects rendered in different ways. Without recourse to paint, Freud relies on composition and line to convey the force of his vision in his prints. The apparent simplicity of line—drawn, bitten, and printed in black on white paper—seems appropriate for the meticulous truth, emotional precision, and psychological realism characterizing Freud's art.

As in his paintings, the primary focus of Freud's printmaking is the human figure. The nine images from 1982 are all heads, generally presented straight on and without accompanying props or surrounding details. Most of the figures and heads in the subsequent prints are located in space by the use of shadows or simple horizon lines which suggest floors or furniture. The starkness of the settings forces the viewer to engage directly with the subject, making the encounter all the more moving and intimate. Frequently the sitter's eyes are closed or the gaze is averted, thus denying a direct confrontation and emphasizing the tension between restraint and intimacy in Freud's portraits. Drama and a sense of incident are provided by the artist's manipulation of the composition, which often removes the very top of a sitter's head or leaves bodies incomplete at an awkward or unexpected point.

In *Kai,* a 1992 etching of the artist's stepson, Freud skillfully uses chiaroscuro to give the head a sculptural presence that belies the delicate web of interlocking lines and crosshatching which describes the form. The most monumental of Freud's portrait heads in etching, *Kai* is one of thirty-three etchings by the artist in the PaineWebber Art Collection, which includes an example of every print by Freud editioned since 1982.

MB

MAD GARDEN
1982
Gilbert + George

Gilbert & George
Mad Garden. 1982

(Gilbert, Italian, born 1943; George, British, born 1942)

Photo-piece: Fifteen black-and-white photographs, mounted and framed

71¼ × 99½" overall (181 × 252.7 cm)

1985.29

In 1968 British artists Gilbert and George began their remarkable life work together as "living sculptures," and the following year commenced to present themselves to the public as works of art. These staged events linked their work with Dada and Surrealism and placed them at the center of the development of performance art. In the following decade the artists also produced paintings, drawings, books, postal pieces, videotapes, postcard sculptures, and photo-pieces. With their public performances all but discontinued in 1977, for the last decade the artists have been focused on object-making activities, principally postcard sculptures and photo-pieces. They nonetheless consider everything they do to be an extension of their life as living sculpture, dedicating themselves to eliminating and resolving the distinctions between art and life. Their works can be as paradoxical as their invention of themselves as sculpture, which by definition is a unique and constant project.

Gilbert and George express the integration of two individuals into a single artistic identity by creating images that are emblems of their shared thoughts, feelings, and observations about the world; thus their work has a strong pedagogical force. In the postcard sculptures they collage mass-produced cultural images. In *Sad,* 1980 (page 267), the vintage postcards acknowledge the value of the past without sentimentality, while also bringing these visions into a present form. The photo-pieces, on the other hand, are made from images the artists generate—usually photographs they have taken, but occasionally their drawings. Unlike performing, the use of photographs and drawings allows Gilbert and George to appear in a vast range of circumstances and contexts limited only by their imagination. The format also permits presentation of an enormous catalogue of subjects, from sex, death, and religion to nature, politics, and madness. Photography also eliminates a potential problem arising from two artists working as a pair: there is no need to consider in their work where one hand stops and another begins. Having established the format of the grid in the photo-pieces of 1974, Gilbert and George have subsequently developed their work through manipulating and expanding the use of images, never using the same photograph or drawing twice.

Mad Garden and *Winter Heads* (page 267) are from the series Modern Faith, in which sexuality and religion are the dominant themes. Madness, a consistent subject in Gilbert and George's art, recalls the eighteenth-century Romantic notion of the artist as a natural, expressive genius, whose basis for art was the self—an idea central to Gilbert and George's work. In *Mad Garden,* Romanticism is given a contemporary incarnation. The stark black-and-white image constitutes a visual elegy enacted by the artists, who strike melancholic poses. George peers down from above while Gilbert stands in the lower right in profile, presenting a vase. Nature appears in the form of plants and flowers with "weeping" blossoms, which expand the poetic vocabulary to include life and death, sexuality and beauty. All are articles in Gilbert and George's program for modern faith.

MB

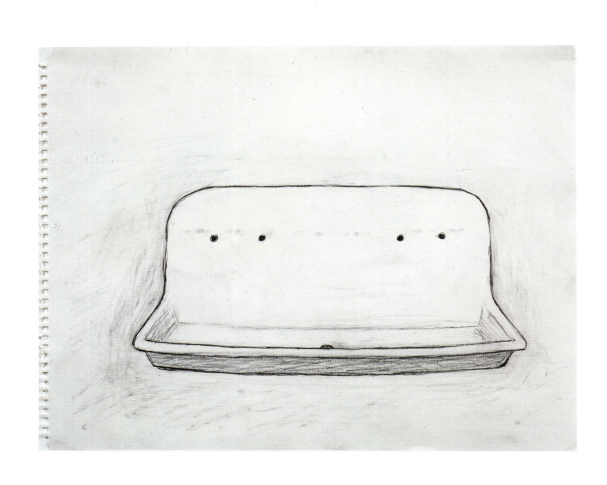

Robert Gober
Untitled #5. 1984

(American,
born 1954)

Graphite on
paper

11 × 14"
(27.9 × 35.6
cm)

1991.35

Robert Gober was first recognized by the art world in 1986, when his sculptures of sinks, which had preoccupied him for two years, were exhibited at the Paula Cooper Gallery in New York. Mounted on a wall, they initially appeared to be everyday white porcelain sinks; only a closer look revealed they had no faucets, no plumbing, and were handmade. Eloquently crafted of plaster, wood, wire lath, steel, latex, and enamel paint, these mute objects deceived the viewer into identifying them as commercially produced and utilitarian.

Gober continued to make sinks of various sizes and shapes, some exaggerated with high backs, others increasingly metamorphosed into bizarre and anthropomorphic forms. Almost surreal is their human presence— holes where the faucets should be register as eyes, rounded contours suggest the naked body, and the drain recalls the body's orifices. Gober was influenced in this pursuit by a recurring dream: "There was a room in my old house that I didn't know existed, full of sinks with running water, and sunlight was pouring into it." His first sinks, however, had no water. "It was a dysfunctional sink without plumbing or fixtures. An image of cleansing without that possibility. It was the early 1980s, the beginning of the [AIDS] epidemic."[1]

Gober later made sculptures of full-size chairs, beds, cribs, and urinals, and wall-paper created for installations. His subjects are nearly all taken from domestic settings and childhood experiences. Unlike many contemporary artists, as well as such historical figures as Marcel Duchamp (critics inevitably compare Gober's sinks to Duchamp's ready-made *Fountain*, a commercially manufactured urinal displayed as a work of art in the 1917 Society of Independent Artists' exhibition in New York), Gober fabricates his pieces rather than using found objects. Thus, his work is emotionally loaded and intricately linked to personal responses from childhood.

Prior to creating the sink sculptures, Gober planned various configurations on paper. As evidenced by the contrasting marks in *Untitled #5*, a study for the sculpture *Double Sink*,[2] he repeatedly erases and reworks lines, shading and filling space to form an illusion of depth. The pentimenti reveal the artist's thought processes and reinforce the anthropomorphic quality of the sink itself. Much like the method of constructing his sculpture, this simplistic technique has a childlike sensibility that reinforces a direct experience.

Seeming to prefer working three-dimensionally, Gober's relatively few works on paper appear to have developed largely out of one of his earliest mature works, *Slides of a Changing Painting*.[3] In 1982 Gober began painting images on a small board, reworking or overpainting parts or scraping them clean altogether, making slides of each stage in the process. The final piece was an edited selection of the slides, which were projected consecutively, creating what the artist has described as a "memoir of a painting."[4] The idea of reworking an image, obliterating it, yet leaving traces under the next image, is exemplified in *Untitled #5*.

JW

1. Quoted by Dodie Kazanjian in "Artist at Odds," Vogue (February 1993), p. 229.
2. Collection Gerald Elliot, Chicago.
3. Collection Walker Art Center, Minneapolis.
4. Quoted in Richard Flood, "Robert Gober: Special Editions, an Interview," The Print Collector's Newsletter, March/April 1990, pp. 6–9.

Philip Guston
Untitled. 1953

(American, born
Canada,
1913–1980)

Ink on paper

18 × 24"
(45.7 × 61 cm)

1987.25

Philip Guston is well-known as a painter of extraordinary abstractions and powerful figurative works (page 116). The importance of his works on paper is also recognized. Drawing was critical for Guston both in the development of his painting and as an independent art. Intense periods of drawing sustained the artist and eased the stylistic transitions that characterize his work. Twice, from 1952 to 1954 and from 1966 to 1968, Guston's concentration on this process indicated the direction his art would take. In 1973 the artist said, "It is the bareness of drawing that I like. The art of drawing is what locates, suggests, discovers. At times it seems enough to draw, without the distraction of color and mass. Yet, it is an age-old ambition to make painting and drawing one."[1]

Untitled, 1953, belongs to a group of drawings that preceded the lyrical abstract paintings that established Guston as a member of the New York School of painting. An exhibition in early 1953 at the Egan Gallery in New York met with critical success and engendered the term "Abstract Impressionism" to describe the beautiful, reverberating, light-filled canvases that Guston exhibited. The structure of his abstract work from the early 1950s was achieved through the use of vertical and horizontal brushstrokes, which recall the Cubistic works of Piet Mondrian. Clusters of brushstrokes coalesce into forms emerging from the delicate tones of the surrounding space, and line is employed to articulate both form and space.

Like all Guston's drawings from this period, *Untitled,* 1953, is black and white, underscoring the essential and immediate nature of the medium. Guston exploited both the expressive and the defining qualities of drawing. In *Untitled,* 1953, the artist used a variety of vertical, horizontal, and diagonal lines to "locate," in his term, the image. Some of the lines are meshed so closely together that they become solid forms, anticipating the rich colors that will later appear in the paintings. The drawn marks, rather than being dispersed over the paper, are concentrated on the left side, foreshadowing the off-center composition of such paintings as *Beggar's Joy,* 1954–55.[2] The mass on the left is balanced by a few vertical strokes on the right, which seem to recede in space. Their fluid elegance recalls Far Eastern brush painting, which Guston admired, especially that of the Chinese Sung period. In *Untitled,* 1953, (as in many of Guston's works from the early 1950s), figure and ground carry equal weight, interacting to describe landscapes that seem to exist in terrain more mental than physical.

The PaineWebber Art Collection includes *Midnight,* another ink drawing from 1953 by Guston (page 267), as well as a later, figurative charcoal on paper entitled *Artist in His Studio* (page 268).

MB

1. Quoted by Magdalena Dabrowski in The Drawings of Philip Guston, *exhibition catalogue (New York: The Museum of Modern Art, 1988), p. 9.*
2. Collection of Boris and Sophie Leavitt, on loan to the National Gallery of Art, Washington, D.C.

115

Philip Guston
In the Studio. 1975

(American, born
Canada,
1913–1980)

Oil on canvas

82 × 79"
(208.3 × 200.7
cm)

1989.41

Philip Guston, who came of age as an artist during the ascendancy of Abstract Expressionism, produced a remarkably varied body of work. The mural paintings of the 1930s and the classical figurative works of the 1940s were followed by the abstractions of the 1950s and 1960s, and then succeeded by the astonishing figurative work of the artist's last decade. Yet despite these stylistic breaks, Guston's oeuvre is characterized by a vigorous coherence generated from the artist's restless exploration, regeneration, and ability to balance and accommodate alternatives. Commenting on the overwhelming multiplicity of meanings in his figurative paintings, the artist wrote in 1976, "I comfort myself, at times, with the thought that *perhaps* one's whole work—I mean all the images and structures I have made—is all one image anyway."[1]

In the Studio demonstrates Guston's fluency in combining the formal means of picture making with unique figurative imagery that is at once personal and universal. The authority of the artist's line, composition, manipulation of space, and use of color support the somewhat absurd but emotionally powerful cartoonlike narrative that is the subject of the painting. In the work, a large head, the artist's alter ego, stares intensely at a small painting propped on an easel in a crowded studio interior.

Evidence of the figure's concentration (and an instance of comic relief) is provided by the two cigarettes that the artist smokes simultaneously, one in his mouth, the other in his hand. The white horizontal bars of the cigarettes formally establish the foreground and middle ground of the painting's shallow space. The viewer's eye travels from the cigarette in the artist's mouth to the painted red foot and finally to the green shade pulled down over the window at the back of the room, which heightens the compressed space of the picture. As Dore Ashton noted, Guston engages here in what he called "the mystery of when you deal with forms in front of forms, as in a deck of playing cards."[2] In a remarkable feat of prestidigitation, Guston transforms the contents of his studio—easel, canvas, window, and artist—into the elements of painting.

Like several other paintings of 1975, *In the Studio* is divided by a horizontal line above which sits the crowded studio composition. Below the line is a band of pink and the sketched form of an open trapdoor. The openness of the lower half balances the composition, and, as in the predella of a Renaissance altarpiece (or a thought bubble in reverse), the inferior zone provides a key to what takes place above. (As a student in Los Angeles, Guston developed an interest in Italian Renaissance art, which he was to sustain throughout his life.) The presence of the hatch intensifies the image of the artist's ongoing struggle with the balancing act of painting, and of his effort to keep from falling psychologically through the floor into an open abyss.

MB

1. Quoted in "Artist's
Statements," in
Philip Guston, by
Robert Storr (New
York: Abbeville
Press, 1983), p. 109.
2. Dore Ashton,
A Critical Study of
Philip Guston
(Berkeley: University
of California Press,
1990), p. 182.

117

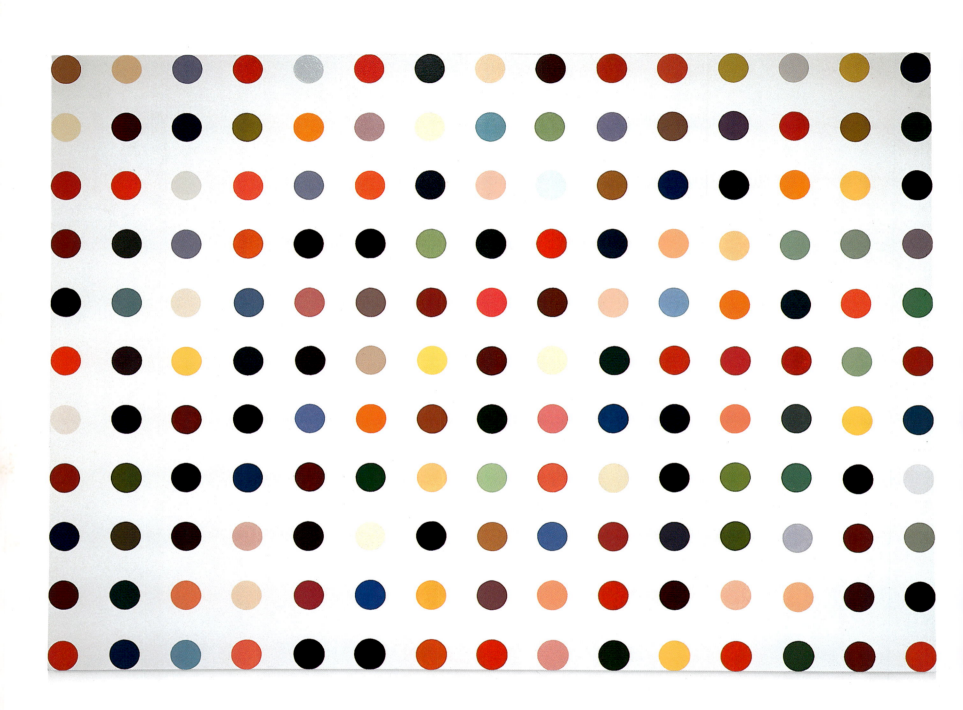

Damien Hirst
Albumin, Human, Glycated. (1992)

(British, born
1965)

Oil-based
household gloss
and acrylic on
canvas

84 × 116"
(213.4 × 294.6
cm)

1992.18

Damien Hirst is one of a group of young British artists who studied at Goldsmith's College, London, and came to critical attention at the end of the 1980s with a series of exhibitions organized in London warehouses. Hirst's work includes paintings, installations, cabinets, boxes, and cases. Issues fundamental to human existence are raised, often in a way that might cause viewers mental discomfort and physical unease. Questions about relationships between life/death, life/art, art/nature, body/mind are presented without answers, thus forcing the viewer into the discussion. The installations and presentations of objects often look scientific or informative, but their meanings are metaphorical and associative. "I try to say and deny many things to imply meaning," he has said, "so that when you work out a reading you implicate yourself."[1] Frequently the titles of his works approach the metaphysical although the works' appearances are clinical, as in *Isolated Elements Swimming in the Same Direction for the Purpose of Understanding*, 1991,[2] in which dozens of various species of fish preserved in formaldehyde float in clear specimen boxes placed in a cabinet. His work reveals a fascination with both social and formal relationships.

Hirst's pharmaceutical paintings are a continuous background to his work in three dimensions and they too are constructed through decisions of display and placement. Executed in household paint, they follow an established format: rows of spots are painted on a white background (usually canvas, but sometimes a wall), with the space between the spots equivalent to the diameter of the spots. The size of the ground and the spots varies within the series. There is no predetermined formula for the order of colors, and the same color is never repeated within a canvas. The titles are selected sequentially from an alphabetical list of pharmaceutical compounds.

Albumin, Human, Glycated is one of the largest paintings in the series, which Hirst began in 1989. The 143 spots of color in *Albumin, Human, Glycated* suggest endless choice, abundance, and variety and resemble manufactured goods such as pills or candies. Although Hirst has spoken of "emotional" decisions in the ordering of colors, the placement appears random; the viewer's eye tries to impose order but fails to find the key to the composition. No particular tone or value dominates, so the effect is of overall balance rather than hierarchy. The spots are isolated from one another yet related to each other through color as the viewer's eye scans the surface of the painting, breaking down the boundaries established by form. While the pharmaceutical paintings invite comparison with Ellsworth Kelly's early pure abstractions or Gerhard Richter's color chart paintings of the 1960s and 1970s, in which paint is reduced to its basic formal components, they differ in intention. Hirst sees them in the context of his own work as underlying structures, observed as if under a microscope. They are "not straight paintings," he says. Rather, each is "more like a sculpture of a painting."[3]

MB

1. *Interview with Damien Hirst by Sophie Calle in* Damien Hirst, *exhibition catalogue (London: Jay Jopling and the Institute of Contemporary Arts, 1991), p. 10.*
2. *Collection of Daniel Moynihan, London.*
3. *Damien Hirst, p. 11.*

119

David Hockney
House behind Château Marmont. 1976

(British, born
1937)

Graphite and
colored crayons
on paper

13¾ × 16¾"
(34.9 × 42.6
cm)

1988.4

David Hockney first established his reputation as a British Pop art painter in the early 1960s and now is widely acclaimed as an innovative printmaker, set designer, and photographer as well. In all these activities, Hockney has been a constant observer of the material world, concerned with the description of the people and things constituting the physical reality of his surroundings. Hockney frequently uses drawings as a diary (the sheets are often precisely dated and include locations); they form an immediate and direct record of his observations. Both drawings and photographs have been used by the artist as studies for his paintings. In 1982, fascinated by theories of visual perception, Hockney began a series of collaged photographs that attempted to record a scene as the eye sees it, with the perception of multiple fractured images and elapsed time, as opposed to the frozen, one-point perspective view of traditional art. *Luncheon at the British Embassy,* 1983, in PaineWebber's collection, is one of these "camera works." Hockney's paintings and prints from the mid-1980s also have this sense of moving focus that connects the artist's later work to Cubism.

Hockney began using colored crayons in 1962, employing them to make works that have the presence of small paintings. In 1964 the artist moved from England to Los Angeles, where he still resides most of the year. *House behind Château Marmont,* drawn by the artist on the grounds of a Hollywood landmark, was executed during a transitional

period in Hockney's career. Between 1974 and 1978 Hockney made many drawings and photographs but relatively few paintings. At this time he also designed the sets for two operas (*The Rake's Progress* and *The Magic Flute*) and published one of his most important portfolios of prints (*The Blue Guitar,* 1977). The artist had become dissatisfied with his painting during this period and the experience of drawing became even more important to him. In an interview early in 1979, he said: "The drawings rarely get labored because they're done with some speed. . . . Now, what I've always longed to be able to do is to paint like I can draw. . . . But in California I'm beginning to find the way."[1]

House behind Château Marmont recalls the drawings Hockney made of Los Angeles when he first arrived there in 1964. The depiction of the scene is accomplished through both description and suggestion: the center of the composition is entirely resolved, but the edges are left blank. The continuation of the foliage on the left side of the house is merely sketched in, while the blue of the sky is indicated by a swatch of color adjacent to the red tile roof. The form of the house is described through the effects of light and shadow on the walls of the building, no two surfaces of which seem to be the same color. The lack of detail and the use of the white of the paper to set off the color and composition together suggest that what is drawn has been captured in the blink of an eye.

MB

1. Quoted by Marco Livingstone in David Hockney *(London: Thames and Hudson, 1987), p. 207.*

121

Howard Hodgkin
In Bed in Venice. 1984–88

(British, born 1932)

Oil on wood in artist's frame

38⅝ × 48⅞" (98.1 × 124.2 cm)

1988.44

Howard Hodgkin's paintings, generally small in size, often represent interiors, gardens, and people. These subjects align Hodgkin with the great French modern painters of interior and domestic scenes, including Pierre Bonnard, Edouard Vuillard, and Henri Matisse. Of these, it is Matisse to whom Hodgkin seems closest, both in his bold use of color and in his determination to translate his immediate sensations in front of a given subject into art. Another often cited source for Hodgkin's art is his interest in Indian miniatures, which he collects. Although the miniatures usually are richly detailed, their flattened space, brilliant colors, and sense of inhabiting a favored realm are also found in Hodgkin's work. Hodgkin presents the interior as a privileged zone, where private thoughts and actions occur, isolated from the outside world.

Since 1970 Hodgkin has painted on wood, preferring its solid, resistant surface for recording his remembered, and therefore ephemeral, subjects. Usually the support incorporates a frame that is over-painted as part of the composition. The space in the paintings is flat, crowded, and slightly theatrical. (Sometimes Hodgkin accentuates the theatricality by adding a painted curtain to frame the composition.) Hodgkin uses broad, vivid brushstrokes, so that the scene is abstracted. The apparent quickness of the brushstrokes is refuted by the lengthy passage of time it takes for a painting to be completed. The pictures have the appearance of having been collaged together or assembled, blurring the image, avoiding accurate depiction, and heightening the feeling that a recollected rather than a live subject is being presented. The viewer must decipher the brushstrokes before the composition can be understood.

In Bed in Venice is one of a group of paintings of subjects set in Venice, most of which were begun in 1984, the year the artist represented Britain at the forty-first Venice Biennale. In the painting, a figure is lying on a bed in front of a window through which light streams. The space in the painting, although more easily read than in most of Hodgkin's compositions, is layered, almost like a collapsed stage set or a child's pop-up book that has been folded. The painted frame and the edge of the composition are covered in a thinly brushed layer of red, which softens the edges, helps to focus attention on the room, and intensifies a sense of voyeurism by directing the viewer's gaze into a framed, protected world. The voluptuous texture and the rich color of *In Bed in Venice* evoke Old Master paintings. Indeed, in its composition and sensuousness, the work recalls the series of luxurious paintings of the reclining Venus painted in the mid-sixteenth century by Titian, the most celebrated of Venetian artists.

MB

123

Bryan Hunt
Sister Ship. (1976)

(American, born 1947)

Lacquer on silk paper over spruce and balsa

5½ × 42 × 5½" (14 × 106.7 × 14 cm)

1986.35

In the mid-1970s, at the end of a ten-year period in which American and European artists had sought to redefine radically the notion of sculpture, Bryan Hunt began making a series of gravity-defying objects called "airships." The first airship appeared as part of a wood and silk construction that depicted a zeppelin moored to the spire of the Empire State Building, a coupling of two modern technological innovations. For his next works, Hunt detached the dirigible from the skyscraper, streamlined it, and relocated it directly on the wall, thus opposing the conventional notion of sculpture as solid and floor-related, and adapting the Minimalist, reductive attitude toward form. Light, abstract, horizontal, and overhead, the airship symbolized another direction for the reinterpretation of sculpture.

Although Hunt had worked in the mid-1960s as an engineer's aide at the Kennedy Space Center at Cape Canaveral in Florida, it was not the aerodynamic aspect of the airship that interested him so much as its classical form. Like such artists as Robert Moskowitz (page 168), Elizabeth Murray (page 174), and Susan Rothenberg (pages 196–203, 277)—painters who were establishing their artistic identity in the mid-1970s—Hunt found a way to isolate a representational image and employ it for his own formal and expressive purposes. *Sister Ship* has the simple, refined, elliptical shape characteristic of Hunt's early airships. Cantilevered from the wall, it hovers,

a buoyant and slightly mysterious object projecting into the surrounding space. The point of intersection with the wall, the shadows cast by the form, and the viewer's shifting perspective of the object all contribute to the articulation of the space in which the airship is installed. The sense of equilibrium in the piece is underscored by Hunt's carefully calibrated use of color: the form's shorter, denser black end visually balances the elegant longer white section that is attached to the wall. Scale, the relationship of the sculpture to the viewer and its surroundings, is dramatized by locating the work over the viewer's head, out of reach. In its state of suspension, the airship suggests a meditative, calm, and liberating presence.

While making the airships, Hunt also has employed another, more traditional method of sculpture: cast bronze. The two techniques stand in opposition to each other. The airships are hand-crafted, delicate, and cerebral, while the bronzes are formed by an established fine-arts process and are durable and physical. Hunt uses each approach to suit his particular ends. In *Cloak of Lorenzo* (page 269), for example, the cast-bronze form of the sculpture suggests both body and garment, thereby simultaneously articulating structure and void and, in contrast to the airships, linking his work to an older, descriptive tradition in art.

MB

125

Bill Jensen
Chord. 1982–83

(American, born 1945)

Oil on linen

24 1/8 × 28 1/4" (61.3 × 71.7 cm)

1986.33

Although Bill Jensen's art is clearly within the tradition of twentieth-century American abstraction, the size and the imagery of his paintings link him more closely with the transcendental works of the first generation of American modernists (including Arthur Dove, Marsden Hartley, and Georgia O'Keeffe) than with the larger, more explosive work of the New York School. Jensen also is influenced by the experimental obsessions of Albert Pinkham Ryder (1847–1917), whom he reveres as an artist willing to risk the physical stability of his art in order to explore the symbolic language of untried painting methods. Jensen first saw Ryder's work at the Brooklyn Museum in 1971, after Jensen moved to New York from Minneapolis earlier that year. In Ryder's dense, painterly landscapes, natural forms—land, sea, and sky—are vehicles for expressing profound emotions. Jensen, an accomplished printmaker and draftsman (page 269), as well as painter, uses process and form in his art as signifiers of the numinous.

Common to all his art is Jensen's ability to exploit the surface for its expressive potential. Jensen works the surfaces of his paintings by employing a variety of techniques including the use of thick impasto, scraping, and incising. The spiral, a natural form evocative of the abstract concepts of infinity and expanding energy held in reserve, is one of

Jensen's most commonly used motifs. An early oil painting in PaineWebber's collection, *December 1976* (page 269), shows a tightly coiled bright blue geometric form resonating against a white field. Close examination reveals that the blue paint has been carefully built up, layer upon layer, while the white ground has been scraped away to the point of revealing the rough surface of the linen support in areas.

Jensen's art is generated both by instinct and intellect. The size of his paintings and his emphasis on their construction invite the viewer to look closely and to enter into a meditation that requires deep concentration. The vibrant physical presence of the work and the artist's use of simple, organic forms result in an art that is highly individual and personal, yet draws on common, universal experience.

In *Chord* the spiral form suggests both a mystical landscape and a musical instrument, a horn through which sound emanates. The combined intensity of the swirling brushstrokes and the rich colors gives an overtone of ecstasy to the work. The title underscores the visual and symbolic richness of the painting. Like a group of notes sounded together, the formal properties of *Chord*—its gesture, color, and surface—unite to describe not only the instrument, but the effect of the resonant sound it produces.

MB

Jasper Johns
0–9. 1960–63

(American,
born 1930)

Portfolio of ten
lithographs,
8/10

sheet: 20½ ×
15¾" each
(approx.)
(52.1 × 40 cm)

Published by
U.L.A.E.

1988.34 a-j

At the urging of Tatyana Grosman, proprietor of Universal Limited Art Editions, Jasper Johns began making prints rather reluctantly in 1960. Since then, like many other contemporary artists, Johns has adopted printmaking as another means, along with painting and drawing, to make art. However, no other contemporary artist has been so expansive in the use and understanding of the various printmaking techniques. "I like to repeat an image in another medium to observe the play between the two: the image and the medium," Johns said in 1978. "In a sense, one does the same thing two ways and can observe differences and samenesses—the stress the image takes in different media."[1] Almost exclusively, Johns has employed printmaking not to make new images, but to refine and develop those he has already presented in paintings and drawings.

The components of printmaking—its necessary reversal of the image, procedural breaking down of an image into parts, and the additive, layering process—suit the exploration of the problems of language and perception that is intrinsic to Johns's art. In *0–9*, his first print portfolio, Johns exploited lithography to make an extended visual pun on the nature and process of printmaking by using repetition as an agent of transformation.

In 1960, having been given a lithographic stone by Mrs. Grosman as an inducement to begin work, Johns drew a zero on it and then set it aside, returning to it only after he had finished several other prints (among them *Coat Hanger, False Start I, False Start II,* and *Painting with Two Balls,* all in PaineWebber's collection). Yet zero was an appropriate and auspicious start. Because of its complete symmetry, the image is the same when reversed; and as the starting point in our numerical system, it is the beginning of a closed set of figures that expresses infinity and contains potentially endless possibilities of combinations. Johns had begun to use numerals as a subject in his art in 1955. In 1958 he began to paint the digits 0 through 9 in two rows, and in 1960 he completed three sets of drawings entitled *Ten Numbers,* in which each numeral from 0 to 9 is executed on a separate sheet of paper.

Johns resumed working on the stone in the summer of 1963 and produced *0–9* that year. The portfolio consists of ten images printed from the same stone, with each consecutive image bearing traces of the previous images. Each print consists of a single number in the sequence 0 through 9, located beneath the complete number sequence, in two rows, a frieze with 0 through 4 above and 5 through 9 below. To reinforce the idea of the variability of the repeated image, the edition—which numbers thirty—is printed in three colors: ten in black, ten in gray, and ten in full color, and each portfolio has one overprinted numeral that corresponds to its number in the edition.

Printed in gray, *0–9* is one of thirty-four prints by Johns in PaineWebber's collection.

MB

1. Quoted in Riva Castleman, Jasper Johns: A Print Retrospective, *exhibition catalogue (New York: The Museum of Modern Art, 1986), p. 36.*

129

Jasper Johns
Untitled. 1981

(American, born
1930)

Paintstick on
tracing paper

21 1/2 × 32 1/8"
(54.6 × 81.6
cm)

1985.41

The paintings in Jasper Johns's astonishing first solo exhibition in 1958 were of easily recognizable objects: flags, targets, and numbers. In choosing these subjects, Johns purposely avoided the subjective and personal in his art, freeing himself to focus on painting alone. His decision to paint commonplace items also indicated the central concerns of the artist's oeuvre: the relationship of one thing to another, the uncertain nature of meaning, and the relationship of the work of art to the viewer, whose perceptual faculties Johns always is challenging. Like other Pop artists—such as Roy Lichtenstein, Claes Oldenburg, Robert Rauschenberg, Edward Ruscha, and Andy Warhol—Johns turned to images from popular culture as a means of distancing his work from the tradition of abstraction dominant in American art of the 1950s. Nevertheless, Johns has remained committed to painting and its related disciplines, drawing and printmaking. For four decades he has continued to reexamine and redefine our notion of what art is, producing an extraordinary body of work as varied in its images as in its use of mediums.

Beginning in 1972, Johns became engaged for roughly a decade in making works in which the dominant motif is the crosshatch, an interlocking abstract form. The artist has attributed the source of this motif to a fleeting glimpse of a pattern painted on a passing car that he saw while on a trip to the Hamptons in Long Island. From this haphazard remembered encounter, Johns forged a new nonfigurative style grounded in the crosshatch, a basic unit

of graphic description. Although the works from this period are the artist's most abstract, they are nonetheless rich in associations, with the occasional symbols and clues that do appear seeming all the more meaningful for their presence. These works often are divided into sections, with each part related by a complex, predetermined system. Frequently, different mediums are used within one work, heightening the sense of the pattern repeating itself, but with differences.

Untitled dates from 1981, the year Johns painted two of three versions of *Between the Clock and the Bed.*[1] These final paintings in the crosshatch series are named after a late self-portrait by Edvard Munch, in which the Norwegian artist stands between two symbols of approaching death: a clock and a bed covered with a rough interlocking diagonal pattern similar to the crosshatch. Like many of the crosshatch paintings, *Untitled,* 1981, is divided into three parts. Here each section is dedicated to a primary color (red, yellow, blue) and its complement (green, purple, orange). The dominant yellow middle recalls the brilliant yellow of Munch's studio, which occupies the center background of his self-portrait. The tripartite division into primary colors and the framing device along the bottom edge of the drawing also recall *Weeping Women,* 1975,[2] a key work from the crosshatch series. In *Untitled,* 1981, the two color systems, marked in loose, urgent strokes, play against each other. The result is a vibrant, highly keyed exercise, resonant with invention as Johns tests the expressive properties of the abstract motif.

MB

1. Collection of The Museum of Modern Art. New York; Collection of the artist.
2. Collection of David Geffen.

131

Donald Judd
Untitled. 1967

(American,
1928–1994)

Lacquer on gal-
vanized iron,
1/3

5 × 40 × 8½"
(12.7 × 101.6 ×
21.6 cm)

1983.30

The Museum
of Modern
Art, New York.
Fractional
gift of
PaineWebber
Group, Inc.

Writing in an article entitled "Specific Objects" in 1964, Donald Judd proclaimed, "Half or more of the best work in the last few years has been neither painting nor sculpture."[1] He was referring to works of art made in New York by himself, Carl Andre, Sol LeWitt, and Robert Morris, among others. In these artists' works, composition, the armature of traditional art, was replaced by the concept of order: metaphor and allusion were succeeded by an emphasis on the nature of materials, and space was not illusionistic but real and three-dimensional. Art was intended to be holistic: "The shape, image, color, and surface are single and not partial and scattered. . . . The thing as a whole, its quality as a whole is what is interesting,"[2] wrote Judd in his essay that later became the manifesto of Minimalism. While a system could provide a way of making a piece, it would be the viewer's perception of the piece as a whole (rather than of the system) that was important. The form of the work was not meant to be symbolic or personally expressive, but rather the coherent expression of an inner logic.

In an attempt to formulate a radical new art that reacted both against recent European art and against American Abstract Expressionism, Judd and his fellow artists sought to make work that was impersonal, nongestural, unsentimental, and, above all, rational. Industrial processes and materials were preferred to conventional artistic means, and creating a series of works that were systematically linked to each other became a way of reinforcing and giving meaning to individual works. In a sense, these artists' ambition was utopian; they were seeking an art that could attain a state of absoluteness.

From painting and reliefs, Judd proceeded to making freestanding objects in the early 1960s. In 1964 he began a series known as Progressions, in which the components of sculpture are organized according to mathematical formulations. *Untitled,* 1967, is one of a subseries of six that have the same form but are fabricated in different materials. The form of the piece, made up of six elements and five intervals, is determined by an arithmetical progression through which a rhythm of positive and negative spaces is established. Reading from left to right, the first element, which measures five inches, is twice the length of the first interval. The size of each subsequent element decreases by one-half inch as the size of each interval increases by the same amount. Element and interval reach identical lengths in the middle of the work, with the progression continuing until the last element is reduced to the size of the first interval. The piece is fabricated from galvanized iron, an industrial material, and coated in a motorcycle paint, Harley-Davidson Hi-Fi Red. The materials give the work a clean, mechanical look, and the color lends the appropriate glamour to the simulation of art made on a production line.

MB

1. Donald Judd, "Specific Objects," reprinted in Donald Judd: Complete Writings (Eindhoven, The Netherlands: Van Abbemuseum, 1987), p. 115.
2. Ibid., p. 122.

133

Alex Katz
Good Morning I. 1974

(American,
born 1927)

Oil on canvas

96 × 72"
(243.8 × 182.9
cm)

1986.14

Working figuratively, Alex Katz has reconciled two apparently opposite modes of depiction: abstraction and realism. He accomplishes this in his paintings by emphasizing formal compositional elements over specific detail and by avoiding particular description in favor of large, flat areas of color linked by light. "A lot of great representational art is not involved with being realistic at all," he has said. "Matisse is my hero for realistic painting. People think realism is in detail, but realism has to do with an allover light and having every surface appear distinctive."[1]

This approach is evident in *Good Morning I,* one of a series executed by the artist in 1974 of four paintings (*Good Morning I* and *II* and *Good Afternoon I* and *II*) that show one or two people in a canoe on Coleman Pond, a lake adjacent to Katz's summer home in Maine. Katz has remarked that the series is concerned with "Water, Light, [and] Time of Day."[2] Seen together, the paintings form a cycle marked by the sense of natural rhythms and elapsed time.

The Good Morning paintings show two young men in a canoe surrounded by deep blue water. While there is no sky depicted in *Good Morning I,* the effects of light are everywhere, bouncing off the white of the boys'

T-shirts and the birchbark of the canoe and creating the apparent reflection of the canoe on the water surface. The pairing of the canoe with its reflection and the absence of a horizon line heighten the tension between the flatness of the painting and the depth and movement of the athletic scene it depicts.

Matisse, Picasso, and Léger are influences acknowledged by the artist, but Robert Rosenblum has written about Katz's paintings (particularly those of canoes) as being part of an American pictorial tradition of expressive figures set in watery landscapes that includes the work of George Caleb Bingham and William Sidney Mount, as well as Thomas Eakins.[3] Katz's paintings are related in scale to the work of the American Abstract Expressionist and color field painters, who came to prominence in the 1950s and 1960s. However, Katz also is influenced by two monuments of American visual culture, the billboard and the movie screen. People portrayed in Katz's paintings often seem as innocent and optimistic as those once depicted in advertising and film. In 1977 this association was reinforced when Katz produced *Times Square Billboard,* an epic work some 247 feet long consisting of twenty-three glamorous portraits of women painted on billboards above New York City's most frantic intersection.

MB

1. Quoted by Richard Marshall in "Alex Katz: Sources of Style," in Alex Katz, exhibition catalog (New York: Whitney Museum of American Art and Rizzoli International Publications, 1986), p. 15.
2. Artist's questionnaire, PaineWebber Art Collection.
3. Robert Rosenblum, "Alex Katz's American Accent," in Alex Katz, p. 28.

135

Anselm Kiefer
Wege der Weltweisheit: Die Hermannsschlacht [Ways of Worldly Wisdom: Arminius's Battle]. 1978

(German, born 1945)

Oil on woodcut on paper mounted on canvas

77¼ × 94¼" (196.2 × 239.4 cm)

1984.46

History, myth, transformation, and change are themes interwoven throughout Anselm Kiefer's art. In 1984 he said, "Art is the only possibility of making a connection between disparate things and thus creating a meaning . . . . I see history as synchronous, whether it's the Sumerians with their Epic of Gilgamesh or German mythology."[1] Like such other postwar German painters as Georg Baselitz (pages 56–59, 258), Markus Lüpertz (pages 271–72), and A. R. Penck (page 275), Kiefer at first used art to examine his own identity, as well as his national heritage. Although Kiefer's work is didactic, the meaning of his allegories often is imprecise, suggesting that the artist acknowledges both the need for definitive answers and the difficulty in providing them. This conscious ambiguity reflects his appreciation of the mutability of meaning. For Kiefer, art's role in society is as an illuminating, regenerative, and redemptive force, but it is also vulnerable to misuse.

In *Occupations,* a series of photographs made in 1969, Kiefer focused on Nazi history, an artistic strategy that was both disturbing and controversial, but, to Kiefer's mind, impossible to avoid. Consistent with his view of art and history as synchronous, his subsequent themes have included the Old Testament, Egyptian legends, the Kabbalah, the French Revolution, and Babylon. The importance of texts in Kiefer's art is underscored by the production of his own monumental books and the inclusion of handwritten inscriptions in his paintings and drawings. In dealing with the past, the artist assumes the dual roles of historian and epic poet. He conflates historical and mythological themes and communicates them through powerful iconographic and visual images. His metaphorical use of materials adds to the process of reification. The influence of Joseph Beuys, with whom Kiefer studied, is evident in Kiefer's use of art as a means to better understand society, in his examination of myths, and in his use of unusual materials. Like many of Beuys's pupils, Kiefer has found an independent way to make art by extending the boundaries beyond traditional methods.

It was his belief in art as a means of cultural and historical transformation that motivated Kiefer to examine Nazi Germany's use of mythic and romantic imagery to justify its repression of cultural life. Growing up in West Germany after the Second World War, Kiefer was sensitive to the double suppression of the past, first by the Third Reich and then by postwar German society. Kiefer argued that art, having been employed in the perversion of history by ideology, should now afford a means to redeem the past by providing a way to comprehend it in the present.

The Ways of Worldly Wisdom: Arminius's Battle, a large collage of woodcuts over which Kiefer painted, is his own treatment of a tale used throughout German history as an allegory of independence. The story, set in Germany's Teutoburg Forest, recounts the first German victory (in A.D. 9) over the invading Romans. The hero of the battle was Arminius (Hermann), who may be one of the sources for the legend of Siegfried. First told by Tacitus, over time the story became

137

Anselm Kiefer
Dem unbekannten Maler [To the Unknown Painter]. 1982

(German, born 1945)

Watercolor and graphite on paper, three sheets

25 × 52¼" overall (63.5 × 132.7 cm)

1988.3

(continued from previous page)

a part of German culture, particularly in the nineteenth and twentieth centuries, when it was the subject of poems, plays, philosophical essays, moralist tracts, Nazi propaganda, and even the inspiration for military strategies. In Kiefer's visually compelling interpretation, the only direct reference to the tale is in the work's title, which appears handwritten in the upper left corner of the work. The artist instead focuses on the protagonists who manipulated the legend—the German writers, philosophers, and generals—assembling woodblock portraits of them and other German cultural heroes enmeshed in a painted network that resembles both the grain of wood and a web. A log fire blazes in the center of the composition.

Kiefer's choice of woodblock is significant and evocative. Black-and-white wood engravings are an established German art form, employed since the Middle Ages in the dissemination of religious iconography as well as in political propaganda. The use of wood also acts as a reminder of the location of the action of the story, a forest, which is the setting for many German legends. Wood is susceptible to fire, which in Kiefer's art is both a destructive and a purifying element. Thus the fire in the center of the work signifies both obliteration and salvation. This ambiguity makes precise decoding of the work impossible, but it does not dilute the force of the image, which comfortably accommodates conflicting interpretations.

Contrary meanings in *To the Unknown Painter,* a watercolor, also reinforce each other and enrich the work. A mythic palette supported on a thin pole sits in the center of a neoclassical courtyard—the architectural style recalling Albert Speer's neoclassical buildings for the Third Reich. The volatile, ominous sky is painted in swirling shades of blue, black, and gray and is intersected by a bolt of lightning that strikes above the palette. Although small by comparison with the surrounding structure, the palette dominates the composition by virtue of its placement, the perspectival drawing that is visible beneath the watercolor, and the tripartite division of the work. The palette stands as a symbol both of the creative and the destructive power of art. Kiefer's watercolor commemorates the actual and potential artists annihilated by the Nazis, but it is also a reminder of the pernicious use of art by the Third Reich.

In *A.D.* (page 270), a lead painting dedicated to the great German painter and printmaker Albrecht Dürer, Kiefer again used material symbolically. Here, the rich surface of chemically treated lead invokes alchemy, a process of transformation. Kiefer began using lead as a support for his works in the mid-1980s, and his exploitation of its malleable and expressive properties resulted in a move toward greater abstraction in his work.

MB

1. Quoted by Armin Zweite in Anselm Kiefer: The High Priestess *(London: Thames and Hudson, 1989), p. 98.*

R. B. Kitaj
Notre Dame de Paris. 1984–86

(American,
born 1932)

Oil on canvas

60 × 60"
(152.4 × 152.4
cm)

1986.16

An American artist living in London, R. B. Kitaj draws on his comprehensive knowledge of history and literary and visual culture in his art. A broad range of themes, from poetry to literature, sports, Hollywood, European history, and more recently, Jewish culture and the Holocaust, has been treated in Kitaj's work. It was his interest in popular culture that led to his being associated with Pop art in the 1960s. For Kitaj, art is part of a larger experience of ideas, and the viewer is invited to plunge into the stream of associations that he traps on paper and canvas. "Books are for me what trees are for a landscape painter," he has said. "They inspire."[1] Kitaj's paintings are not strict narratives, but they continue the philosophical arguments and observations advanced in his writings and manifestos. In counterpoint to his dynamic paintings, Kitaj also makes charcoal drawings, which are among the most accomplished figurative works of our time. Often these are portraits of friends, such as the late poet Robert Duncan (page 270) and David Hockney, with whom he attended the Royal College of Art in 1960–61.

According to Kitaj, *Notre Dame de Paris,* executed while the artist was living in Paris, is a meditation on notions of sin and free will: "I've invented for this painting a kind of 'Path of Life,' littered and confused, from and upon which men stray toward 'sin' . . . as if there might be a better or 'right' path. I have no idea if there be such a path but I rather enjoy listening to advocates of either way. . . ."[2] The references in the painting, collaged together to illustrate a fable enacted by fantastic characters with human bodies and bird heads, are primarily artistic. Specific homage is paid to Henri Matisse in the title and style that recall his 1914 paintings of the same subject and in the bright green triangular swath of color on the right side, which is borrowed from the French artist's 1916 painting *Piano Lesson.*[3] The construction of the space in the painting into separate architectural rooms is reminiscent of the narrative devices of Italian quattrocento painting and derives from a panel by Fra Angelico in the Louvre, *The Dream of Pope Innocent III.* The figure lying face down on the red bed is a reprise of one of Kitaj's own works, a 1979 drawing entitled *Marynka on Her Stomach.* Like the other, male figures in the painting, the woman has a bird's head, a device employed in "the famous Bird's Head Haggadah, the medieval Passover prayer book illuminated so as not to contravene the second Commandment against idolatry."[4] In other words, these hybrid figures symbolize an ingenious artistic solution devised to avoid sin without compromising the illuminator's own intentions.

MB

1. Interview with R. B. Kitaj by Krzysztof Z. Cieskowski, "Problems in Kitaj, Mostly Iconographic" in Art Libraries Journal, *1989. 14/2. p. 37.*
2. From a statement about the painting provided by the artist. PaineWebber Art Collection files.
3. Collection of The Museum of Modern Art, New York.
4. Artist's statement, PaineWebber Art Collection files.

141

Franz Kline
Study for **Black and White #1.** (c. 1952)

(American,
1910–1962)

Gouache and
ink on paper
mounted on
board

11 1/8 × 9"
(28.3 × 22.9
cm)

1989.21

Although Abstract Expressionism was more a shared attitude than a single style, one of the common characteristics of the Abstract Expressionists is the importance they gave to drawing. Many of the artists—in particular Arshile Gorky, Philip Guston (page 114), Franz Kline, Willem de Kooning (page 86), Lee Krasner, and Jackson Pollock—incorporated drawing into their painting technique. Gesture also is essential to the nature of Abstract Expressionism, and of all these artists it is Kline whose work is the most purely gestural. Kline did not move toward abstraction in his art until he was in his late thirties at the end of the 1940s. This was sparked in part by his friendship with de Kooning. Evidently the effect of seeing some of his drawings enlarged on a Bell-Opticon projector in de Kooning's studio in 1948 or 1949 helped Kline to realize the possibility of abstraction for his art.

Kline's full-blown style, which emerged in the early 1950s, is characterized by bold black brushstrokes on white grounds in compositions that synthesize Cubism by using drawing to define the complex spatial relationships of pictorial planes. There is a close correspondence between Kline's drawings and his paintings. While his drawings usually

1. Private collection.

were not made as studies per se, often they were the basis for his abstract paintings of the 1950s. Unable to afford expensive materials, Kline made drawings in black ink on the pages of telephone books. The artist kept these drawings in piles in his studio and would select from these stacks a composition for use in making a painting. He would mount the chosen drawing on cardboard and either tack it up or hold it next to a canvas to consult while painting. Then he would follow the composition of the drawing closely, without using a projector and rarely relying on a grid system for transferring, confident in the ability of his arm to translate with fuller gestures the forms freely described by his hand.

The white gouache background of this study for *Black and White #1* suggests that Kline possibly intended, when it was made, to use it as the basis of a painting, or, more likely, that he added the ground after pasting the drawing on cardboard, then referring to it when painting *Black and White #1* in 1952.[1] Although the oil painting measures fifty by thirty-nine inches, some four-and-a-half times larger than the drawing, there is an astonishing relationship between the sense of scale in the two works. The drawing anticipates the strength and presence of the larger work, while it records the immediate energy and fervent concentration of the initial creative act.

MB

143

Jannis Kounellis
Untitled. (1980)

(Greek, born
1936)

Glass, ink on
paper, and two
painted plaster
heads on steel
shelves

46 × 29½ × 8"
overall
(116.8 ×
74.9 × 20.3
cm)

1987.4

Arte Povera is the term invented in 1967 by the critic Germano Celant to link a group of artists working in Italy who were committed to making works that eroded the barriers between art and its environment. These artists responded to the past while affirming the present. Their approach eliminated representation, instead emphasizing physical presence by employing commonplace materials, which often could be heard, smelled, tasted, or felt, as well as seen. Born in Greece in 1936, Jannis Kounellis moved to Italy in 1956 and was identified with the Arte Povera group from its inception.

In 1967, after a two-year break from making art, Kounellis focused his activities on sculpture and performance. The artist has incorporated a variety of materials—bedframes, burlap, stones, coal, smoke, fire, hair, eggs, spices, grains, wool, plaster fragments of classical sculpture, even animals and musicians—into his work, assembling these diverse components into sculptures and installations. By bringing them together to form an artistic whole, Kounellis underscores the importance of the artist as a "transformer" in the artistic process. The references to culture and history are both poetic and confrontational; the artist himself has referred to his art as the "iconography of iconoclasm."[1] His art seems simultaneously to break with the past in its use of materials while using the past to constitute a new present. This is perhaps an intrinsic response to the pervasive presence of history in Mediterranean culture.

Untitled, 1980, a work made up entirely of fragments placed on steel shelves, is composed of broken plaster casts, splintered glass, and drawings that have been ripped from a larger sheet. The use of shelves as a place where objects from the past are collected can be considered a metaphor for history. Two of the components in *Untitled,* 1980, refer to earlier works by Kounellis, thereby recalling his own artistic past as well as broader cultural history.

The paper elements were torn from a large drawing the artist had exhibited at Sonnabend Gallery in New York that year. These skull-like paper heads recall the figure in Edvard Munch's famous painting *Der Schrei* (*The Cry,* 1893)[2] and serve as a *memento mori.* Kounellis has used plaster casts in his art since 1973. That year, the artist did a two-week performance in Rome, during which he held a mask of Apollo to his face while sitting at a table that supported fragments of classical sculpture and a stuffed blackbird perched atop one of the torso fragments. Beside him, a flautist repeatedly played a thirty-second segment from Mozart at two-minute intervals. Apollo, the sun god of the Greeks and the Romans, traditionally is associated with music, intellect, and culture, and the yellow-painted heads in *Untitled,* 1980, invoke his image and are an optimistic balance to the melancholic presence of the paper heads. The glass shards, unrelated to any earlier work, reinforce the sense of fragmentation and temporality in the piece.

MB

1. Quoted by Thomas McEvilley in "Mute Prophecies: The Art of Jannis Kounellis" in Jannis Kounellis, *exhibition catalogue (Chicago: The Museum of Contemporary Art, 1986), p. 118.*
2. Collection of Nasjonalgalleriet, Oslo.

Guillermo Kuitca
Children's Corner. 1990

1. Lynn Zelevansky in Projects: Guillermo Kuitca, exhibition brochure (New York: The Museum of Modern Art, 1991). n.p.

(Argentine, born 1961)

Acrylic on canvas

58 × 116"
(147.3 × 294.6 cm)

1991.7

The formation of identity, a theme addressed by many contemporary artists in Latin America, is largely a response to their recent history, as well as an investigation into the past. Working in Buenos Aires, Guillermo Kuitca makes paintings of diagrams and systems: floor plans, stage sets, road maps, and, recently, family trees. His work shares the painterly gestures of German, Italian, and American Neo-Expressionism of the mid-1980s, combined with the regional realism of South American art. Narratives of longing and dislocation pervade Kuitca's images, as do moods of sorrow or disillusionment.

Beginning in 1982 Kuitca made paintings of domestic props: beds, tables, chairs, and small figures. Isolated or situated in large spaces, the objects appear incomplete, their narrative quality open-ended. The prominent image of a bed, crudely rendered and tightly made, remains a constant in Kuitca's work. "Despite common associations with birth, passion, and death, these clean and neatly kept beds seem more like the resting places of childhood. They represent security, but also banishment from the mysteries of the adult world, for whom it is not yet bedtime. For Kuitca, the bed is ironically a site of emotional turmoil, alienation, and constriction."[1]

During the early 1980s, Kuitca directed several experimental theater productions, and the expansiveness of the stage set began to assert itself in the composition of his paintings. In Children's Corner, tiny beds and chairs inhabit a vast theatrical space, where walls are distinguished by a decorative floral pattern suggestive of wallpaper that might be found in the home. Each bed is accompanied by a chair: one at the head, another at the side, a third overturned. A fourth chair stands alone. These object relationships evoke the sentiments of abandonment and desire in family interactions, perhaps, as if seen in a child's dream.

In 1987 Kuitca made his first paintings of maps. Although taken from every corner of the world, his choice of topography appears to be random. Whether covering areas of a country or a city, roads and highways read as veins and arteries. Working initially with maps of places unfamiliar to him, Kuitca concentrated on the abstract qualities of geography—and used them as compositions. Thus, in many instances, he complicated the narrative and made it impossible to identify the locale.

By 1989, using the bed motif in a very literal approach, he began painting maps on actual mattresses. A very personal and private space, the bed is now infused with a very public image. Nordrhein (page 271), also in PaineWebber's collection, is a recent example of this genre. Kuitca draws and paints on the vinyl slipcase of the foam mattress as if it were canvas, but allows for accidental effect—the coarse, smudged surface reveals the force of his hand. Buttons, hand-sewn by the artist at specific points that mark various German cities where he met with curators or exhibited work, chart his summer travels through the region to which the title refers.

JW

147

Christopher LeBrun
Prow. 1983

(British, born
1951)

Oil on canvas

102 × 102"
(259.1 × 259.1
cm)

1983.25

The Museum
of Modern
Art, New York.
Fractional
gift of
PaineWebber
Group, Inc.

Christopher LeBrun did not set out to paint horses; the image initially was generated by the artist's response to a stroke of white paint he had put down on canvas. This mark appeared to resemble a blaze, the white patch in the center of a horse's forehead, and became the focal point of the composition. LeBrun's figurative paintings tend to move away from representation and towards abstraction, neatly balancing the two impulses. The artist has taken up the tradition of painting in an era dominated by photographic and recycled images. Although his paintings were first recognized as part of the international revival of figurative painting that occurred in the beginning of the 1980s, LeBrun avoids the irony intrinsic to postmodernism and seeks to restore classical painting to the present in a way that is free from nostalgia or anachronism. Both romantic and modern, LeBrun's art inherits the full tradition of Western painting, from Poussin to Pollock.

Prow is one of a number of paintings centered on the image of a horse that LeBrun made in the early 1980s. From the Uffington White Horse, a first-century chalk pattern cut into turf in Oxfordshire, to the eighteenth-century equine portraits by George Stubbs, horses are commonplace in British art. LeBrun's use of the image seems closer to nineteenth-century French painting, however, particularly the Romantic tradition of Delacroix and Géricault and the later mythological subjects of the Symbolist Odilon Redon. Horses are a dynamic motif in Romantic painting, and Delacroix in particular often showed them as wild, untamed spirits charged with a supernatural energy. LeBrun has painted a variety of traditional subjects—landscapes, horses, trees, heraldic figures, and wings—and he doubtless would agree with *both* Delacroix's statements that "painting does not always need a subject" and "the subjects of fable are always new."[1]

LeBrun invests his figurative work with the sublime, painterly qualities of modern abstract art. His paintings are characterized by a rich surface texture, ranging from densely marked to lightly inflected. They are constructed by the artist in layers, in which the surface and the images are built up and reworked over time in the studio. As is evident in *Prow*, the center of the composition often is dominated by a recognizable form, while the surrounding area is structured by overlapping brushstrokes, which have a range of antecedents from the exquisite gestures of Gustave Moreau to the lyrical abstractions of Philip Guston (pages 114, 267). In *Prow*, the loose, liberated brushstrokes are as critical to the meaning of the painting as those that describe the white horse rising triumphantly at the center of the composition. The soaring image recalls Pegasus, a mythological winged horse symbolic of the creative spirit and of poetic inspiration. It serves here as a heroic embodiment of a renewed belief in painting.

In *Bay* (page 271), a later painting by the artist in PaineWebber's collection, LeBrun employed a network of painted lines and tonal relationships to structure a completely abstract work.

MB

1. The Journal of Eugène Delacroix, *translated from the French by Walter Pach* (New York: Crown Publishers, 1948), p. 543.

Roy Lichtenstein
Mirror #10. 1970

(American, born 1923)

Oil and Magna on canvas

24" dia. (61 cm)

1986.37

Roy Lichtenstein is most often identified with the comic-strip paintings that he began making in 1961. In using comic books, advertising, and cartoons as the basis for his art, Lichtenstein shared with fellow Pop artists Claes Oldenburg and Andy Warhol the determination to reshape art in the image of contemporary life. Lichtenstein sought to stylize his images of the contemporary world through the vocabulary of technology, particularly that of the printing process. Using Benday dots as a stylistic device, restricting his palette to the four colors employed in commercial printing (red, yellow, blue, and black), and graphically manipulating scale, Lichtenstein developed the means to parody a range of subjects drawn from both popular culture and high art. His interest in the definition of symbolic language in commercial and fine art (such as Benday dots and brushstrokes), and in the presentation of images and styles as archetypes has been central to his art, which continues the traditions of painting yet is imbued with irony and humor.

Mirror #10 is one of a series of about fifty Mirror paintings completed by the artist between 1970 and 1972. In light of Lichtenstein's Pop paintings from the previous decade—usually based on preexisting images and generic artistic subjects or styles—the subject matter of this series is unexpected. However, the mirror seems to be a perfect vehicle for the artist's multilayered investigation of abstraction and representation. A stock prop in the history of art, mirrors have been put to a variety of compositional and iconographic uses: from Velázquez's *Venus and Cupid* [1] to the twentieth-century interiors of Matisse and Picasso, mirrors have been employed to engage the viewer, establish psychological states, and expand the interior space in paintings. Lichtenstein's more prosaic mirror compositions are based on motifs drawn from advertisements and sales catalogues as well as from his own photographs. His mirrors reflect light, shadows, and indistinct objects. The paintings in the series were executed in three formats: circles, ovals, and rectangles (Lichtenstein created shaped canvases for the two rounded forms). The reliance on formal properties alone places the Mirror series among the most abstract works in Lichtenstein's oeuvre. Yet in their shapes and simulated "reflective" surfaces, the paintings are very like the models themselves, much as Jasper Johns's flag paintings resemble flags.

The Mirror paintings seem to be analogies for abstract art and witty comments on abstract styles, especially parodying the Minimalist insistence on nonillusionistic art, so prevalent at the time. The versatility and flexibility of the mirror device gave Lichtenstein the opportunity to manipulate freely the formal elements in the paintings. The composition of *Mirror #10* consists of light and dark forms, which play against each other. They are contained by a circular border, describing the beveled edge of a mirror and the refraction of light that occurs there. The imitative glassy surface of the painting causes the viewer first to react with a double-take, only to be stymied by the void that is frozen on the canvas. The artist's skillful use of the deadpan mirror image results in a painting that shows nothing but nevertheless is loaded with contradictory meanings.

MB

1. Collection of the National Gallery, London.

Roy Lichtenstein
Final Study for **Landscape with Figures and Sun. 1980**

(American, born 1923)

Graphite and colored pencils on paper

16 × 20" (40.6 × 50.8 cm)

1991.4

During the 1970s the examination of symbolic language was the main focus of Roy Lichtenstein's art, but his attention shifted from his famous images derived from comic strips and popular culture to those of high art, which he analyzed through a process of stylization. This analysis furthered the investigations that he had begun in the previous decade with the adaptation of commercial reproduction processes into the format of painting. In making "copies" of well-known artists' works and quoting hallmarks of twentieth-century art, Lichtenstein produced a body of work that is at once completely original while simultaneously questioning the established concept of originality.

In 1973 Lichtenstein produced *Bull I–VI*, a witty series of prints in which the initially recognizable form of a bull is transformed into a geometric abstraction, recalling the paintings of the Dutch modern masters Theo van Doesburg and Piet Mondrian. Beginning with the Studio Pictures of 1973, artists such as Matisse, Picasso, de Kooning, and Léger, as well as styles such as Surrealism, Cubism, Purism, and German Expressionism were specifically quoted, analyzed, and reinvented in Lichtenstein's work.

As usual, the artist achieved the stylistic analysis of his chosen subject through drawing. Since 1963 Lichtenstein has projected his drawings onto canvases to achieve the compositions for his paintings. The artist's sketches, drawn to the scale of the proposed painting, are put in an overhead projector, and the composition is then transferred to canvas by pencil. The artist has deftly summarized the relationship of one medium to the other, stating, "It's all thought up in the drawings and all accomplished in the paintings."[1]

As the title suggests, this is the study for a painting that is six times its size. There is also another small drawing (4 × 4^{15}⁄16 inches), in which the compositional elements of the two larger works were established. Thus the final study is an intermediate state between the initial conceptualization and the finished work, acting as a rehearsal for Lichtenstein's invented composition. This final study for *Landscape with Figures and Sun* is one of a series of works based on modern German art that Lichtenstein completed in 1980. Its source is not the work of a particular artist, but it recalls the art of Die Brücke and Der Blaue Reiter, the two dominant movements in German art at the start of this century. In keeping with the angularity characteristic of Die Brücke, Lichtenstein's German Expressionist compositions are primarily created from lines rather than dots; hence figure and ground seem locked together like the pieces of a jigsaw puzzle. The flatness of the composition and the diagonal stripes recall German Expressionist woodcuts as well as paintings. Broken down into their formal components, Lichtenstein's synthetic German Expressionist works no longer convey the meaning of their models; they are not idealized landscapes but stylistic ones, inviting a new interpretation.

1. Quoted by Bernice Rose in The Drawings of Roy Lichtenstein, *exhibition catalogue* (New York: The Museum of Modern Art, 1987), p. 28.

153

MB

Roy Lichtenstein
Post Visual. 1993

(American, born 1923)

Oil and Magna on canvas

96 × 80"
(243.8 × 203.2 cm)

1993.38

In his most recent work, Roy Lichtenstein has returned to a subject that has been on the periphery of his work since his early 1970s paintings of still-life scenes from his studio, that of the interior. Collectively known as Interiors, this new body of work, begun in 1989, is concerned with the room itself. The depicted bedrooms and living rooms are likewise hosts to a quirky mixture of generic modernistic furniture, patterned walls and floors, and assorted works of art. They appear to parody contemporary art, decor, and "good taste," as well as Lichtenstein's own thirty-year career.

Just as Lichtenstein's early works appropriated such printed material as comic books, his most recent imagery draws inspiration from the illustrated advertisements in the Yellow Pages. The graphic quality of these ads complements Lichtenstein's pristine trademark style—black outlines, Benday dots and stripes—which he first defined in the Pop paintings. In *Post Visual,* the black outline defines the room itself and the objects within it; repeating black parallel lines delineate the floors and the sofas, as well as the reductivist painting on the wall. Departing from his earlier palette, Lichtenstein introduces into the work pale sherbet tones of peach and light yellow, which contrast with the other, more typically commercial colors.

In *Post Visual,* the scale of the room is depicted slightly larger-than-life, seemingly inviting the viewer to walk into the interior and sit down. One critic described this sensation as similar to watching "the actors entering Toontown in 'Who Framed Roger Rabbit.'"[1] The monumental scale consistent throughout the Interiors series dynamically presents the contradiction of pictorial space and the two-dimensionality of the canvas itself. The black, diagonal lines of the floor create illusionistic space in the paintings, and the corner of the adjoining walls draws the viewer into the room.

Although Lichtenstein delves into new territory in this series, he also has integrated concepts from his earlier work. In much the same way as he reinvented specific artists' works in his paintings of the early 1980s, here Lichtenstein brings together a number of styles, which he largely accomplishes by boldly representing his own as well as other artists' works on the walls. For example, in *Post Visual* a painting of a hanger is included, most likely a reference to the Jasper Johns print of the same image. However, in deciphering each image, the viewer also confronts the rendered generic scene outside, suggesting the presence of a window and further complicating the spatial illusion by reinforcing the contrasting allusions both to painted and real space.

The abstract composition prominently featured and titled in *Post Visual* recalls Lichtenstein's 1964 work *Non-objective Painting I,*[2] an appropriation of a painting by Piet Mondrian. The image also seems to be a witty commentary on the fluorescent 1980s geometric abstraction ("neo-geo") paintings of young artists such as Peter Halley. The words *Post Visual* perhaps reveal Lichtenstein's personal response to this postmodern form of art making.

JW

1. Roberta Smith, "'Inviting' (if Fanciful) Rooms from the View of Roy Lichtenstein," The New York Times, February 7, 1992, Section C, p. 26.
2. The Eli and Edythe L. Broad Collection.

155

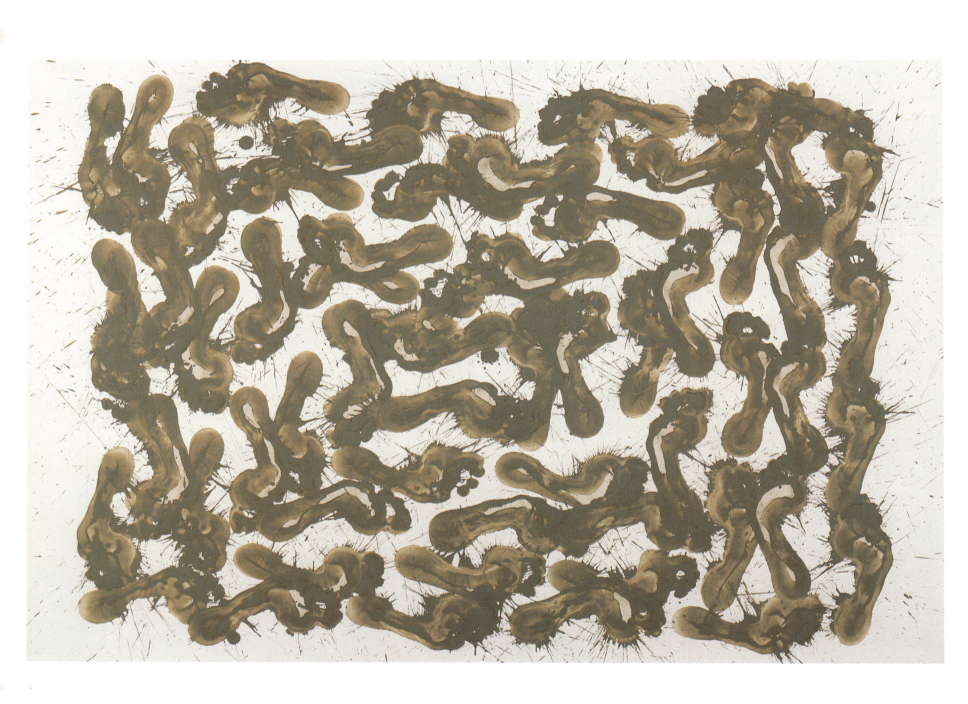

Richard Long
Untitled. 1987

(British, born
1945)

River Avon
mud on paper

44 × 64"
(111.8 × 162.6
cm)

1987.17

By his own description, Richard Long makes art that is "simple and practical."[1] It takes the form of extended walks, through which the artist uses his footsteps to take the measure of the world. Long has walked all over the globe, in such places as Japan's Mt. Fuji region, the Arctic circle, the Atlas Mountains of North Africa, and the West Country of England. The artist records his walks in a variety of ways: by marking a map; through text describing places, signs, and sounds; by photographing a site; or by a sculpture or marks made during his journey, which he sometimes documents in photographs.

By locating his work in nature Long acts as an intermediary between mankind and the environment and radically extends the landscape tradition in art. Through use of the most basic forms, usually a circle and a line, and materials such as wood, stone, mud, snow, chalk, and water, the artist articulates his direct engagement with the natural world; his works are left in the landscape, unmarked and unprotected. Long also makes indoor and outdoor installations for gallery or private spaces, in which he uses simple forms and natural materials. Often the stone used for such installations is locally quarried and selected by the artist. In these pieces, which are permanent and can be dismantled and reinstalled, Long communicates the authentic and direct experience of the natural world with the same power as his works in

the landscape. His use of ordinary objects, real space, text, and photography relates Long's work to Minimal and Conceptual art and to Arte Povera, movements that came to prominence in the 1960s when he was beginning to work as an artist.

The tension between permanence and impermanence is a constant in Long's work, which ranges from ephemeral to durable. These states are emphasized particularly in the pieces in which the artist uses mud (usually for wall or floor pieces, but occasionally—as in *Untitled,* 1987—in works on paper). Metaphorically, mud is a primordial substance, evocative of creation. Geologically, mud is the mixture of finely pulverized particles of rock with water. Thus it represents the combination of two of Long's principal sculptural materials; water erodes stone and stone gives water its substance in the formation of river mud. The mud in *Untitled,* 1987, is from the River Avon (Long was born and lives in Bristol, England, located near the river's mouth). By using his muddy footprints as gesture in this unusual drawing, Long evokes his journeys and reminds us that through such experiences we literally touch the ground and make physical contact with the earth. The parameters of the walk, rather than being established by geographical limits, are set by the margins of the paper. The dense activity of the artist's footprints and the expressive bursts of mud surrounding each mark communicate the fervor of the artist's performance.

MB

1. Remarks made in
exhibition brochure for
a one-person exhibition,
Richard Long, *at the
Dallas Museum of Art,
March 31–May 20,
1984.*

157

Robert Longo
Untitled. 1981

(American, born
1953)

Charcoal and
graphite on
paper

96 × 60"
(243.8 × 152.4
cm)

1981.14

Tense and isolated, this larger-than-life figure is one of some sixty monumental black-and-white drawings collectively known as the Men in the Cities series. Created between 1979 and 1982, the group of chic young men and women drawn in contorted poses and floating on empty backgrounds constitutes Robert Longo's first body of mature work.

The stance of the figure—caught in motion—reveals the consistent and strong cinematic feeling in Longo's work. Men in the Cities, the artist has said, grew out of a relief he made after seeing a film still from Rainer Werner Fassbinder's *The American Soldier* that captured the moment when two gangsters are shot. However, the isolated and dramatic gestures, if not body language, that appear inextricably linked to Longo's protagonists also appear to be the result of the artist's interest in the rhythms of contemporary music, including those of such bands as Talking Heads and The Contortions. These bands might also be credited with inspiring dance styles characterized by sharp, jerking movements.

All the drawings in this series are based on photographs that Longo took of his friends, mostly other artists, on the roof of his South Street loft in New York. Although the subjects are known to the artist, he intended them to represent the young men and women of contemporary urban America—their frenetic lives and the general malaise and pressures of life in the city. To force the twisted

postures that he wanted, Longo threw tennis balls and other objects at his models and then quickly snapped pictures as they writhed and jerked away from the flying articles. Using an overhead projector, Longo magnified the photographs and traced the images onto large sheets of paper with graphite. Later, his assistants would complete much of the detail, obscuring the artist's original markings. As Longo has described, "It is the artist's job to catch his time. When you look at a Hopper you think of a specific time. I am obviously choosing a 20th-century uniform in my work, but it is the gestures rather than the fashion that link the work to the time. People run around the baseball diamond a lot differently now than they did in the 1920s."

In the PaineWebber Art Collection drawing, the male figure seems to be caught in a state of movement between dancing and dying. The upward thrust of his head, the angle of his feet, and the tension of his fingers suggest that he might be falling backward, be hanging, or even be impaled. With nowhere to go, he appears trapped in the claustrophobic composition. The action itself takes place in the imagination of the viewer, who must provide the narrative and become implicated in the completion of the work.

JW

159

Allan McCollum
Five Surrogate Paintings. 1980–81

(American,
born 1944)

Acrylic on
wood and
museum board
in five parts,
various sizes

Clockwise from
top:
10 × 11½";
7 × 10";
7½ × 7⅞";
9¼ × 10¼";
10⅞ × 14¼"
(25.4 × 29.2
cm; 17.8 ×
25.4 cm;
19.1 × 20 cm;
23.5 × 26 cm;
27.6 × 36.2
cm)

1982.3a–e

Allan McCollum is concerned with the originality and preciousness of art. At a distance his objects resemble framed paintings arranged in a cluster and hung in a haphazard manner on the wall. Upon closer examination, however, there is something odd about these objects: no art is apparent within the frame, only simple black rectangles—they are pictures of nothing. In dislocating the object's content, denying the individuality of art by replacing it with a universal sign for a painting, he undermines the tendency to equate commercial and aesthetic value.

As McCollum explains, his work "grew out of an interest in the idea of defining painting, the notion of reducing painting to a simple set of essential terms, and then expressing yourself within those terms. . . . It seemed to me that every conceivable description of painting that one might offer to define its essence or its terms could always be found to also define some other similar object which was not a painting—except for one: a painting always has the identity of a painting, a painting is what it is because it is a convention."[1]

McCollum's first impulse was "to make only one painting and exhibit it over and over again, to create a sort of archival object—like the government's Bureau of Standards maintains the standard 'inch' in platinum. But this solution eliminated the possibility of exchange transactions—and how could a thing represent an art object if it couldn't be bought and sold? I ultimately decided to use a single but repeatable image, one which I could vary minimally in size and proportion, but which remained essentially the same: a frame, a mat and a black center."[2]

After several attempts, in 1978 McCollum arrived at the generic form seen in the PaineWebber piece, which he would continue to use through the 1980s. Initially the entire surface of these works was painted in a single color, but, shortly thereafter, as seen in PaineWebber's work, he decided to paint the frame and center in different colors. In the final version he painted the frames black or brown, the surrounding mattes white, and the center image black. *Five Surrogate Paintings* is among the first works McCollum made using wood, paper, and acrylic. By 1982 he was casting pieces in plaster from rubber molds entitled *Plaster Surrogates*. McCollum chose plaster as a medium not only because of its association with mass-produced replicas, but also because it provided a quick and easy way to meet the demand for his work, particularly in large-scale installations.

JW

1. Quoted by David Robbins, "An Interview with Allan McCollum," Arts Magazine, vol. 60, no. 2. (October 1985), p. 41.
2. Ibid.

161

Brice Marden
Study II. 1981

(American, born
1938)

Oil and
graphite on
paper

18½ × 39½"
(47 × 100.3 cm)

1990.10

Brice Marden has established his reputation as a formidable painter of rigorous, deliberate abstractions that communicate his observations and investigations both of the physical and the immaterial worlds. "The rectangle, the plane, the structure, the picture are but sounding boards for a spirit," he proclaimed in his writings of 1971–72.[1] In his earliest works, executed from the mid-1960s until the mid-1970s, the artist restricted himself to the simplest means of expression, while retaining a remarkable sensuousness in his art. His work of that period, which insists on the primacy of the picture plane, takes the form of panels of flat color, which frequently are broadly divided into rectangular elements and enlivened by expressive marks on the surface and at the bottom edge. The surfaces of both of his drawings (page 272) and paintings are built up in layers of graphite or oil enriched with wax. The use of wax paradoxically dissolves the plane by making it more light-receptive and asserts its material presence by making it more physical. Many of the titles of Marden's early works refer either to landscape or to individuals, thereby evoking the visual perceptions, memories, and emotions of the artist for specific people and places. For example, the resonant beauty of *Grove Group,*[2] a cycle of paintings from 1972–76, was shaped by Marden's reaction to the landscape of Greece—the sky, sea, earth, and olive trees—as well as his response to the spiritual sense of the place as an ancient, sacred grove of the Muses.

In 1977 the artist was commissioned by the Basel Cathedral Stained Glass Trust to make a proposal for stained glass windows. Although the plan was never realized, Marden spent nearly a decade working on the project, and it was to have a profound effect on his art. He began to think of painting in terms of transparent planes expressive of light and spatial depth. Also in 1977 the artist visited Pompeii, where he was influenced by the wall paintings and decorations of Roman and Greek architecture.

Study II draws on these experiences. The columns of color structuring the work recall the post-and-lintel construction and the balance and harmony found in classical architecture. Exterior and interior space are suggested by the juxtaposition of dark and light colors and the use of scale. The rich, translucent color in *Study II* is metaphorical as well as formal: while working on the Basel windows, Marden became interested in alchemy and began using the four colors expressive of the basic natural elements—yellow for air, red for fire, green for earth, and blue for water. These colors, and brown, were used by the Greeks to decorate their temples, and they are also found in the wall decorations of Pompeii. The rough edge of the paper and the artist's use of the entire sheet emphasize the drawing's physicality, as if it were a section of a fresco removed from an ancient wall.

MB

1. *Quoted in* Brice Marden: Paintings, Drawings and Prints, *exhibition catalogue (London: Whitechapel Art Gallery, 1981), p. 54.*
2. *Collection of Mimi and Peter Haas, San Francisco.*

163

THE CITY '66   a. martin

Agnes Martin
The Field. 1966

(American, born
Canada 1912)

Ink and
graphite on
paper

9 × 9"
(22.9 × 22.9
cm)

1990.9

In twentieth-century art, from the abstractions of Mondrian and Malevich to the process art of the Minimalists, the grid—a classical form—has been associated with the concepts of order and the ideal. Agnes Martin's grids (and her related compositions of horizontal and vertical bands) structure the expression of an interior world of order and feeling and provide a meditative focus for the viewer. Unlike the work of her younger contemporaries, the Minimalists, Martin's art does not represent the demonstration of a process or the investigation of a system. Her work is neither depictive nor derivative from nature, although the titles sometimes suggest associations with the real world. Martin intends her abstractions to act as instruments to provoke transcendental revelations that may be attained through looking. By using grids to plot the immaterial, Martin communicates her belief in the existence of perfection.

In *The Field*, a work on paper from 1966, the format of the composition is a grid. The work comprises not only the lines that form the grid pattern, but the effect of the relationship of the horizontal to the vertical, expressed in the intersections of the lines—at which small dark squares are created—and in the open rectangular spaces between the lines. In counterpoint to the structural formality of the grid, Martin emphasizes variations in the density of the pale ink line, as well as irregu-

larities that arise from the function of the human hand, the surface of the paper, and the properties of the drawing materials. Through repetition and by establishing an internal scale, the form of the grid expands the space of the drawing. In *The Field* Martin creates an open, luminous landscape for the mind to roam. Because of its austerity, every incident and particular condition of the drawing's construction is brought up for consideration by the viewer.

The structure of *The Field* is established by a surrounding pencil line that determines the border of the composition and by pencil dots marking the vertical and horizontal coordinates. The ink lines are drawn freehand, with the verticals sometimes not quite reaching their destination at the bottom. The drawing has an atmospheric, floating quality and the effect is one of delicate strength, the impact of which increases over time and with contemplation. In her writings and lectures the artist possesses the quiet voice of a visionary. She urges her audience not to be complacent or distracted, rather to see actively, to respond, and to recall. In a 1976 lecture at Yale in which she emphasized the anagogical force of art, the artist observed: "We are in the midst of reality responding with joy. It is an absolutely satisfying experience but extremely elusive. . . . Joy is perception."[1]

MB

1. Handwritten text of artist's lecture reproduced in Agnes Martin, Paintings and Drawings, 1957–1975, *exhibition catalogue (London: Arts Council of Great Britain, 1977), pp. 19, 27.*

165

Yasumasa Morimura
Angels Descending Staircase. 1991

(Japanese, born
1953)

Color photo-
graph var-
nished and
mounted on
board in two
panels
in artist's
frame, A.P.

102½ × 89"
overall
(260.4 × 226.1
cm)

1992.1

Since 1985 Yasumasa Morimura has created photographic reproductions derived from paintings considered to be icons of Western art. His appropriation and transformation of such revered and analyzed paintings as Vincent van Gogh's *Self-Portrait with Pipe and Bandaged Ear*[1] and Edouard Manet's *Olympia*[2] is both elusive and compelling. Morimura's work is also based on his understanding of the symbiotic process through which one culture infiltrates and influences another in the age of the printed reproduction. "If I had used a canvas to explore my themes," Morimura explained, "it would have shown a partiality to a Western language. But photographs are neither Japanese nor Western; they represent my sense of existing between two worlds."[3]

In these early works, such as *Daughter of Art History: Princess B* (page 273), his version of Velázquez's portrait of the young Spanish Infanta Margarita in *Las Meninas*,[4] Morimura fabricated three-dimensional tableaux that replicated the background of each painting. Dressing himself in the appropriate costume and makeup as the subject, he would literally "insert" himself into the picture. To further blur the lines between painting and photographing, the artist sealed each image with a thick, translucent varnish before framing it in an elaborate gilt frame, comparable to the way the original Old Master painting might currently be presented.

Morimura is often compared to Cindy Sherman (pages 220, 279–80) in that he undergoes a similar transformation into the subject. However, where Sherman's work is a dialogue with styles from 1950s movies or Renaissance portraits, Morimura reenacts specific works.

In 1991, in preparation for an exhibition of his work at the Tate Gallery in Liverpool, Morimura appropriated six famous nineteenth-century paintings by the British Pre-Raphaelite artists found in the collection of the Tate Gallery collection in London. It is, perhaps, no coincidence that these works date from the time when Victorian painting was popular in Japan and likewise Japanese art was fashionable in England. Among the works transformed was Edward Burne-Jones's *The Golden Stairs*,[5] which Morimura flopped, the image thus creating a mirror image with a kaleidoscopic dimension. Entitled *Angels Descending Staircase*, it is a likely reference to Marcel Duchamp's landmark modernist painting *Nude Descending a Staircase*.[6] For these new works, Morimura used a high-resolution computer to superimpose multiples of his photographed images onto a transparency of the original painting. In this work, Morimura has captured the complexity of the composition by replicating the numerous and precise gestures of each figure, which are heightened by the exquisite drapery of the gown. His skill as a photographer along with his attention to detail in the conception of costumes, makeup, and props creates confusion in the viewer's mind between the original and the restaged version. So as not to baffle the viewer altogether, Morimura introduces his own kitsch details, such as the subjects' pink toenails.

JW

1. *Collection Courtauld Institute, London.*
2. *Collection Musée d'Orsay, Paris.*
3. *Quoted in Carol Lufty, "Morimura: Photographer of Colliding Cultures," International Herald Tribune (March 2, 1990), p. 7.*
4. *Collection Museo del Prado, Madrid.*
5. *Collection Tate Gallery, London.*
6. *Collection Philadelphia Museum of Art.*

Robert Moskowitz
Eddystone. 1984

(American, born 1935)

Pastel on paper

108 × 48"
(274.3 × 121.9 cm)

1986.12

Robert Moskowitz's images seem at once familiar and strange: familiar, because they are taken from the artist's immediate environment and nature as well as from the history of art; strange, because they are rendered in highly stark terms, giving them an eerie cast. This use of archetypal imagery, stripped of contextual detail, also marks the work of several other painters of Moskowitz's generation, such as Susan Rothenberg and Elizabeth Murray, dubbed "New Image" painters in a 1978 Whitney Museum of American Art exhibition. The work of these artists, though evolved from a Minimalist aesthetic, was part of a general return to figuration in painting beginning in the late 1970s.

Eddystone represents a lighthouse off the coast of England. Moskowitz first explored the subject in a 1979 painting;[1] one of a group of vertical canvases of epic and phallic proportions based on well-known Manhattan architectural themes, including the World Trade Center towers, the Empire State Building, and the Flatiron Building. Simplistically rendered and reduced to flat shapes, these stark images are set against monochromatic grounds.

Moskowitz has returned to the subject of the lighthouse several times both in his paintings and pastels (two other large-scale works on paper of the lighthouse exist). The latter are not in any way studies, and in fact are often produced afterwards. "I had the idea of making a drawing, full scale, of every painting I've done within the last ten years. I don't know what that means, but I just like it. I like to draw, I like the physicality of drawing. The marks in the ground basically come out of making the drawing, whereas in the painting that's not true."[2] In *Eddystone,* as in other works on paper, the opacity and weight of the structure is transmuted by pigment, which Moskowitz applies with force, allowing smudges, erasures, and fingermarks to remain as evidence of his hand.

The crisp cylindrical silhouette of the lighthouse is rendered schematically flat. Monumental in scale, the tower looms over the viewer. The tall black vertical expanse set against a dark blue ground suggests a night with little or no moonlight and makes for difficult reading. Usually, Moskowitz's images first read literally, as flat compositional elements; they then assume the shapes of familiar, nameable things, only to lapse back into a secondary order of abstraction as the demarcators—the defining instruments—of a fathomless conceptual/symbolic space.[3] In *Eddystone,* the effect of two closely related areas of color in direct proximity—black object against dark blue field—is a delayed perceptual shift that undermines our conception of a lighthouse: this beacon of safety for ships at sea is here lost in the dark.

1. Collection The Museum of Modern Art, New York.
2. Quoted by Katy Kline, in Robert Moskowitz: Recent Paintings and Pastels, *exhibition catalogue (Cambridge: Hayden Gallery, Massachusetts Institute of Technology, 1985), n.p.*
3. Prudence Carlson in "Building, Statue, Cliff," Art in America, *vol. 71, no. 5 (May 1983), p. 145.*

169

JW

Robert Motherwell
Untitled. 1958

(American,
1915–1992)

Oil and
graphite on
cardboard

10½ × 13½"
(26.7 × 34.3
cm)

1985.19

Robert Motherwell was the youngest of the Abstract Expressionists, the predominant group of artists in the United States during the 1950s. Born in 1915, the artist studied philosophy at Harvard and painting and French literature in Paris before coming to New York in 1940 to study art history with Meyer Schapiro at Columbia University. The artists of the New York School, as the Abstract Expressionists came to be called, were not unified by a single style, but by their approach to making non-objective art. Their work was characterized by a break with traditional styles and techniques; by a re-examination of the notion of completion in a work of art; and by an emphasis on individuality, self-determination, and spontaneous freedom of expression.

For Motherwell, modern art was a philosophical and poetic endeavor rather than a literal, imagistic one, and it is characteristic that he paraphrased the French poet Stéphane Mallarmé in his definition of his work: "The expression of the mysterious meaning of aspects of existence, through human language brought back to its essential rhythm: in this way, it endows our sojourn with authenticity and constitutes the only spiritual task."[1] Consistent with the idea of painting as a metaphorical form of writing was Motherwell's interest in the simple forms of Far Eastern brush painting.

Motherwell's paintings, usually either very large or very small, have a finely tuned, unerring sense of scale. He tended to work in series over long periods of time, producing groups of works (such as the Elegies, Plato's Cave, Iberia, and Opens) that were linked by formal themes. The Elegies to the Spanish Republic, perhaps his best-known series, was begun at the end of 1948 and continued throughout his career. Motherwell had a great affection for Spain, and this body of work refers not only to the disastrous defeat of the republicans in the Spanish Civil War, but also to the rich culture and landscape of the country.

1958 was a productive year for Motherwell. He commenced work on the Iberia series and finished a suite of works on paper, the Madrid drawings. Both groups were derived from a visit to Spain that he had made in the spring and summer with the painter Helen Frankenthaler, whom he married that year. In all, he completed over eighty paintings in 1958. He also created a series of small oil sketches on cardboard based on the theme of two figures. *Untitled,* 1958, a small but powerful work, seems to be related to this group of lively and intense paintings. The exuberant brushstrokes and furious pencil scribbles communicate a sense of passionate and physical urgency, and the earthy colors are those of the Elegies—and of Spain itself—black, white, and ocher, with a few traces of red.

MB

1. Quoted in a letter from Robert Motherwell to Frank O'Hara in Robert Motherwell with Selections from the Artist's Writing, *exhibition catalogue (New York: The Museum of Modern Art, 1965), p. 70.*

171

Matt Mullican
Untitled. 1986–87

(American,
born 1951)

Oilstick and
acrylic on
canvas in four
panels

96 × 192"
overall
(243.8 × 487.7
cm)

1988.5

In all his works, New York artist Matt Mullican utilizes a personal glossary of signs, symbols, and abstract forms. Although these symbols seem familiar and mostly recognizable, their precise meanings remain elusive. Working in a wide variety of media, including banners, posters, oilstick rubbings, fabric, etched stone, and leaded glass, Mullican uses this personalized glossary of signs to express his vision of an ordered model of the world, an ideal city.

Mullican's pictograms create a visual vocabulary that brings to mind international signage, from road directions to warning labels. Some are invented by the artist, while others are the universally understood images that we automatically process every day. As Mullican has explained, "Symbols are parts of the landscape. Every airport, every railroad station has these things, and I am interested in the manner in which people express themselves unconsciously, as a culture."[1]

Mullican attended the California Institute of the Arts in Valencia, a school well known for its emphasis on art as idea. There he studied with Conceptual artist John Baldessari (page 52), whose work also comments on information in the world at large. Most of his work at this time was based on performances he did, including allowing himself to be hypnotized. In about 1980 Mullican began to develop his hermetic system of signs, which continues to be the center of his work. This symbology is further accentuated and broken down into levels by color-coding,

which he describes in the following terms: subjectivity (red); language (black and white); the arts or "The World Framed" (yellow); daily living or "The World Unframed" (blue); the elements (green).

PaineWebber's wall-size mural is composed of four canvases that were originally part of *Untitled 1986/7,* an installation of fifty-two panels exhibited at the Brooklyn Museum in 1988.[2] Using a process closer to printmaking than painting, Mullican made rubbings on the canvas over templates he had fashioned out of paper and Masonite to create rough, almost spectral images.

For the central image in this work, Mullican used a cutaway view of the Paris Opera, which was built by Charles Garnier in 1875. The stage is relatively small, dwarfed by the adjoining wings and dressing rooms, the areas in which the performances are prepared and their illusion sustained. We are, by implication, in the space of the audience, which was arranged according to rigid social hierarchies. This view of the Opera, real and implied, illuminates the reciprocally supportive relationship between a stratified society and its culture.[3]

The grand structure, drawn in yellow to represent the arts, is set against a series of disks on which Mullican rendered black-and-white pennants and emblems. These images are less abstracted than is usual for Mullican; we can read, among other signifiers, a palette, a musical note, a telephone, and an airplane. Ultimately, Mullican's cacophony of symbols and signs attempts to make order out of our chaotic world.

JW

173

1. Quoted by Sue Graze in Concentrations 15: Matt Mullican, *exhibition brochure (Dallas: Dallas Museum of Art, 1987), n.p.*
2. This installation was slightly different from the installation of canvases shown at the Dallas Museum of Art in 1987.
3. Nancy Princenthal in Matt Mullican: Untitled 1986/7, *exhibition brochure (New York: Michael Klein, 1988), p. 4.*

Elizabeth Murray
Southern California. 1976

(American,
born 1940)

Oil on canvas

79⅛ × 75½"
(201 × 191.8
cm)

1985.3

Southern California was painted by Elizabeth Murray while she was a visiting instructor at the California Institute of the Arts in Valencia. It belongs to a group of abstract paintings made by the artist in the late 1970s, which preceded the fragmentation of image and canvas that has become the stylistic hallmark of her work. In the 1970s Murray was reexamining her work (which had been figurative and narrative) and pushing it to accommodate both European and American art influences, including the contemporary work she saw in New York, where she had moved in 1967. Since then, Murray has made some of the most visually sophisticated and inventive paintings in contemporary art. In these, she reconciles painterly and narrative concerns, formal and emotional content, and popular culture and high art.

In *Southern California,* Murray employed the biomorphic shapes reminiscent of the abstract forms of Miró, Arp, and Kandinsky, which became the basic vocabulary of her new formal language. The artist invests these forms with the exuberance of cartoons, inflates them, and allows them to float freely in the composition. The purple, blue, and green shapes hover above the red circle, like elements that can be removed and reapplied as in the children's game of Mr. Potato Head. There is no need to read the imagery in Murray's paintings; they are so tightly composed

and finely balanced that they are gratifying merely as formal inventions. But part of the pleasure and challenge of looking at her works, many of which approach visual overload, is to decipher the content as well as the form.

Southern California, about which the artist says, "the place had a lot to do with the color and space of the painting,"[1] appears to be an abstracted landscape. The composition is anchored by the small white dot in the lower right, which deepens the sense of space in the painting and suggests a shift in internal scale. The white dot and blue and green commalike forms are used as punctuation points in the composition. The pentimenti of a spiral embedded in the surface of the red form intensifies the sensation of motion provided by the hovering forms. The loud, vibrant colors play off each other and add to a sense of joy, and the thick, brushed surface communicates the artist's delight in her medium.

As soon as the viewer has taken in the formal composition, other interpretations emerge. A face comes into focus, with the purple shape as lips (or mustache), the blue as nose and the green as an arched eyebrow; or the red form suggests a gigantic contemporary version of one of Cézanne's apples, which in Murray's characterization "sometimes feel like they weigh hundreds of pounds and other times they're as ethereal as feathers."[2]

MB

1. Artist's questionnaire, PaineWebber Art Collection.
2. Quoted in an interview with the artist by Sue Graze and Kathy Halbreich in Elizabeth Murray: Paintings and Drawings, *exhibition catalogue (New York: Harry N. Abrams, Inc., 1987), p. 123.*

175

Bruce Nauman
Read/Reap. 1983

(American, born 1941)

Colored chalks, masking tape, acrylic wash, and paper collage on paper mounted on canvas

71 × 70 3/8" (180.3 × 178.8 cm)

1985.4

Bruce Nauman works in drawing, sculpture, printmaking, photography, and with videos, neon signs, structures, and installations. His artistic flexibility and mental gymnastics have made him one of the most important and influential artists working today. The broad range of materials he uses includes concrete, fiberglass, steel, iron, plaster, wax, and rubber. Yet despite its variety and invention, his work is unified by the consistency of the artist's ideas and the concentrated scope of his investigations, which consider, to cite the title of a neon piece Nauman made in 1983, *Human Nature/Life Death.*

Nauman's two principal mediums are the body and language. His use of the body includes casts, performance (usually recorded on video), and installations in which the viewer is often invited to complete the work by entering into constructed spaces. The active participation of the spectator is almost always solicited in Nauman's work. We are asked to watch, to listen, to read, and, to cite the title of another Nauman work, to *Pay Attention.* The artist's use of wordplay in his works ranges from double entendres, anagrams, puns, and paradoxes to clichés and commands. Frequently, antonyms are employed, such as "live and die" or "good and bad." These pairings incorporate the idea of opposition, establishing a sense of tension as the viewer considers both propositions.

Nauman's use of body parts and of double meanings recalls the art of Marcel Duchamp and of Jasper Johns, and his inquiry into the levels of meaning of language has an affinity with the word paintings of Edward Ruscha

(pages 206–7, 277–78). In Nauman's first neon sign, *Window or Wall Sign* of 1966–67, the phrase "The true artist helps the world by revealing mystic truths" is written in blue neon and contained within a red neon spiral. The form of the piece recalls the disks inscribed with puns that Duchamp and Man Ray used in their 1926 film *Anemic Cinema,* while the use of neon, a commercial and industrial medium, is related to Pop art's appropriations of advertising and commercial processes. Because it is a linear form that facilitates writing or drawing in space, Nauman's utilization of neon is practical; but the medium also transcends practicality by altering the space surrounding the work with light. The intermittent flashing of neon signs (originally intended to attract attention) underscores the either/or propositions in Nauman's work and allows him to isolate and combine words, symbols, and sequences, thereby manipulating and shading their meanings.

Nauman makes drawings both as diagrams for projects and as fully realized, independent works of art. *Read/Reap,* a large, exceptionally rich collage, relates to a neon piece fabricated in 1986. A slip of the tongue or of the pen changes "read" to "reap," thereby modifying the meaning and provoking a sequence of associations. "To reap" (an active, physical process) has associations of judgment and consequence and allegorically represents death in the form of the Grim Reaper, while "to read" (a passive, mental occupation) gives meaning to written symbols or words, a good description of an important function of Nauman's art.

MB

177

Claes Oldenburg
A Sock and Fifteen Cents (Studies for Store Objects). (1961), dated 1962

(American, born
Sweden 1929)

Watercolor,
crayon, and
paper collage
mounted on
paper

24 × 18¾"
(60.9 × 47.6
cm)

1986.46

"I am for Kool art, 7-Up art, Pepsi art, Sun-shine art, 39 cents art, 15 cents art," declared Claes Oldenburg in his notebook in May 1961.[1] These words found concrete expression in December of that year in *The Store,* an environmental work made by Oldenburg in his storefront studio at 107 East Second Street on the Lower East Side of Manhattan. Since arriving in New York in 1956, Oldenburg had become one of a group of young artists that included Jim Dine, Red Grooms, Allan Kaprow, and Lucas Samaras. Reacting against the formal means of Abstract Expressionism, these artists were using performance, happenings, and environments to express their ideas. Their art tended to be figurative and to employ such Dada and Surrealist devices as assemblage and collage. For Oldenburg, it was important to integrate art with life—particularly American urban life—and to study the unfolding contradictions. He wanted to find a way to make a new, realistic art which would restore emotional content, subvert bourgeois values, and involve the spectator. His approach was to combine paintings, sculpture, architecture, and theater in a series of installations made between 1960 and 1964 centered on the street, the store, and the home.

The version of *The Store* that Oldenburg installed in December 1961 consisted of plaster reliefs and three-dimensional objects depicting clothing, food, and advertisements, thereby transforming the commodities of a materialistic culture into art. *A Sock and*

Fifteen Cents (Studies for Store Objects) is a collage assembled in 1961 from torn paper fragments and a magazine advertisement and mounted on a sheet of paper in 1962. Oldenburg has written that in the store drawings "the paper becomes the store window,"[2] and that seems to be the case here, with the small, delicately painted studies for objects representing their counterparts in art. The torn edges of the paper convey the roughness of the finished objects, and the bright pink, blue, yellow orange, and black evoke the atmosphere of exuberant vulgarity in the installation.

Oldenburg has continued to make objects and to work in performance. Drawing, which allows his imagination to operate freely, has remained an essential component of his art. "Drawing is my basic method. I think of drawing as a form of writing. My concrete images are drawings realized—'monumentalizations.'"[3] In 1965 Oldenburg began a series of drawings for monuments in which he placed fantastic, often allegorical, symbols in mostly urban settings; among these is the *Proposed Colossal Monument to Replace the Nelson Column in Trafalgar Square—Gearshift in Motion,* 1966 (page 275). In September 1985 Oldenburg, Coosje van Bruggen, and Frank Gehry presented a performance in Venice entitled *Il Corso del Coltello (The Course of the Knife).* A watercolor in the PaineWebber Art Collection (page 275) is related to this event.

179

1. Claes Oldenburg and Emmett Williams, Store Days: Documents from "The Store" *(1961) and* "Ray Gun Theater" *(1962) (New York: Something Else Press, 1967), p. 41.*
2. Quoted by Barbara Rose in Claes Oldenburg, *exhibition catalogue (New York: The Museum of Modern Art, 1970), p. 195.*
3. Claes Oldenburg, "Items toward an Introduction," in Claes Oldenburg, *exhibition catalogue (London: Tate Gallery, 1970), p. 7.*

MB

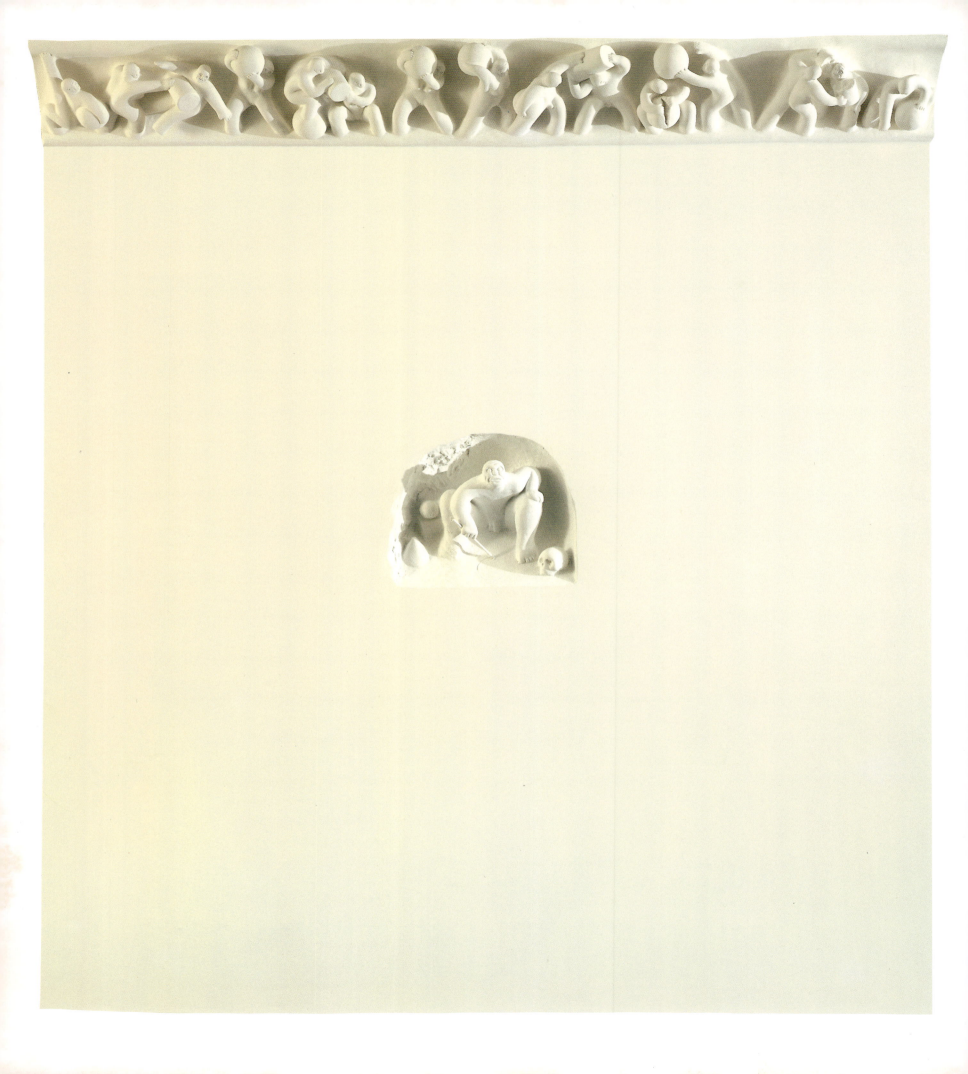

Tom Otterness

Frieze Installation of **The Battle of the Sexes** and **Hermit Philosopher.** 1983–85

(American, born 1952)

Cast plaster and painted cast Polyadam

98¼ × 84⅝ × 8½" overall (249.6 × 215 × 21.6 cm)

1985.25

In May 1985 PaineWebber commissioned Tom Otterness to create an installation on the occasion of the opening of a new worldwide corporate headquarters. Located at the intersection of two corridors on the fifteenth floor, the eight-by-seven-foot wall features a narrative frieze forming a border at the top and an inset sculptural relief in the center. Separate but related, the two pieces form one installation.

Otterness's small figures, a hybrid of the Pillsbury Doughboy and the Michelin tire man, Bibendum, are plump forms with cylindrical limbs and round heads that evoke smiley-face buttons. Simple and playful (Otterness ascribes gender to identical columnar bodies), these forms are imbued with humor and their actions display the snappy rhythm of comic strips. At first glance their movements appear to be innocuous; A more careful examination of the frieze nestled against the ceiling reveals that in this procession male and female figures are engaged in battle.

A founding member in 1977 of the artists' activist group Colab, Otterness has always been interested in public sculpture. Between the years 1978 and 1982 he made a series of cast Hydrocal figurines which he then sold for $4.99 each. The artist saw them as small monuments: "The figurines have bases and a mock monumentality. They were

in some sense public sculpture, and public also because they were affordable."[1] Sold by the foot, these friezes were intended for both private residences and public buildings.

In 1983, for his first solo exhibition at the Brooke Alexander Gallery in New York, Otterness adorned the walls and doorways of the gallery with a white plaster frieze depicting scenes of love and war between the sexes. In appropriating this antique format for his own animated ideology, he was admittedly influenced by diverse sources—Indian temple reliefs, Greek altars, and Christian churches—all public monuments designed to extol military victories or propagate a faith. As one critic observed, "instinctively he understood and strategically he capitalized on the merger of private concerns with social agendas—how a battle between the sexes translated into architectural ornament that is legibly antique and visibly humorous."[2]

Carved out of a Polyadam plaque, the central sculptural relief, *Hermit Philosopher,* sits in a rough concave niche, below the frenzy of the frieze. A small enigmatic figure, this character crouches in his cave and draws in the sand with a compass; a cone and a skull rest on the ground at either side of his feet. Alone and contemplative, the figure glares out at the viewer as if he has been disturbed.

JW

1. Quoted by Hayden Herrera, Tom Otterness, *exhibition catalogue (Los Angeles and New York: James Corcoran Gallery and Brooke Alexander Gallery,* 1990), n.p.
2. Judith Russi Kirshner in "Tom Otterness' Frieze," Artfotum, vol. 22, no. 2 (October 1983), p. 57.

Mimmo Paladino
Tre Comete [Three Comets]. 1983

(Italian,
born 1948)

Oil on canvas
with painted
wood and ani-
mal skull in
artist's frame

81 × 120½ × 8"
(205.7 × 306.1
× 20.3 cm)

1983.32

Mimmo Paladino is one of several Italian artists associated with the Transavantgarde, a group that came to prominence in the early 1980s and was identified with the revival of the past and the return to traditional art forms. Paladino constructs an iconography and depicts rituals based on a variety of cultural and art historical sources, including prehistoric, Etruscan, Egyptian, Early Christian, Romanesque, and Medieval art. In addition, the artist refers to the formal aspects of the art of these various civilizations: he evokes cave paintings and wall paintings through the use of stucco, encaustic, and mosaic; and employs such conventional formats of religious art as the tondo and the triptych. Christian, primitive, and pagan artifacts are freely mixed in the ceremonies the artist devises. The mythopoeic power of art is invoked in Paladino's work. "It is the artist's job to navigate mystery," he has said. "He is a magician, shaman, juggler of this great mystery, art."[1] Thus art is given sacred status and the artist is a romantic figure.

In *Tre Comete* the artist seems to take on the role of archaeologist, unearthing objects and rituals. In the painting, which is saturated in deep red, a color suggestive of sacrament and sacrifice, there are three layers of meaning and construction. The first is the painted animal skull and the large daubed timber, resembling a fragment from a destroyed structure that the artist has attached across the top of the painting. In the center of the work there is a richly painted ceremony centered around a banquet, appearing to suggest martyrdom and cannibalism. A headless ghostly torso dominates this group. This scene, painted in white and ocher with a surface that resembles stucco, is distinguished from the more flatly painted third level. Here the vague marks of cave paintings, a tribal mask and shields, and an ecclesiastical building are depicted.

Paladino combines pagan and Christian rites in this work. We are not definitely in the realm of the living nor of the dead, but in some other spiritual world that the artist has imagined. The title reinforces the mystical and somewhat sinister overtones of the painting. Throughout history comets traditionally have been considered harbingers of strange or calamitous events, and the title refers to three occurrences. In numerology, three is a powerful number and in Christianity it is aligned with the spiritual force of the Trinity. Paladino recognizes the enduring force of myth and, by drawing on the past and collective memory, invents powerful visions for contemporary life.

MB

1. *Quoted in* Process and Product: The Making of Eight Contemporary Masterworks, *exhibition catalogue (Annandale-on-Hudson, New York: Edith C. Blum Art Institute, Bard College, 1987),* p. 109.

183

Blinky Palermo
Untitled. 1968

(German,
1943–1977)

Oil, black
chalk, and
graphite
on canvas

17¾ × 37½"
(45.1 × 95.3
cm)

1987.23

The Museum
of Modern
Art, New York.
Fractional
gift of
PaineWebber
Group, Inc.

Born in 1943 in Leipzig, Germany, Peter Heisterkamp in 1964 adopted the pseudonym Blinky Palermo after the famous 1930s gangster and fight promoter. From 1962 to 1967 Palermo studied closely with Joseph Beuys (pages 64, 259). The artist's education with Beuys can be seen in his use of materials to stress the connection between art and life. For Palermo, art was not intended as an ornament, but as a way to structure a space and to suggest new ways of seeing to the viewer. "Painting for me," he said in 1968, "is the translation of visual and material reality into aesthetic norms: art as interpretation, as seeing afresh, as the extension of consciousness."[1] His body of work includes objects, paintings, drawings, cloth pictures (made of stretched yard goods), wall paintings, and paintings on metal. All his art shares an enigmatic quality—it is at once straightforward and allusive. While reducing his means of expression, in Barnett Newman's phrase, to "the grammar of art," Palermo increased the expressive potential of his work, making art which is not only easily grasped but is also rich in meaning and contemplative.

By 1968 Palermo had established his mature artistic language. That year he had three exhibitions in Germany: one of cloth paintings, one of paintings and objects, and one of wall paintings. In the wall paintings, the wall itself became the ground for the paintings and the area of artistic activity was transferred from an object on a wall to the space of the room itself. Palermo's interest in the relationship of paintings and objects and in the connection of art to its surrounding space is similar to Donald Judd's (page 132) concern with the rejection of illusionism. Palermo's art, however, reveals a spiritual aspect, while the American artist's work is more empirical.

Throughout his brief career, Palermo used the triangle in paintings, room installations, and multiples. In addition to being an easily recognizable geometric form, the triangle is a universal religious symbol, found in pagan mythology as well as in Christianity. Palermo employed the triangle as a standard image that he placed in different locations, thereby focusing on the potential for form to change its significance according to its context.

In *Untitled*, 1968, the triangle sits on a white field, an object securely located within a defined space. The rich black surface of the triangle has been enhanced with chalk, intensifying the contrast with the flatness of the meticulously painted ground and giving the form additional resonance. Viewed hanging on a wall, the painting is both an object and a painting of an object. When the painting is examined closely, a vertical pencil line is seen above the peak of the triangle. The perception of this line alters the spatial reading of the painting by articulating an interior space into which the viewer is drawn. This establishes a complex situation in which the viewer is simultaneously aware of the real space of the room and the depicted space of the painting.

MB

1. Quoted by Marianne Stockebrand in Watercolors by Joseph Beuys, Blinky Palermo, Sigmar Polke, Gerhard Richter, exhibition catalogue (London: Goethe Institute, 1987), p. 8.

185

Sigmar Polke
Untitled. 1985

(German,
born 1941)

Dispensing ink
and wash on
cardboard

38¾ × 29¼"
(98.4 × 74.3
cm)

1987.19

Working in mysterious ways and with un-orthodox materials, Sigmar Polke is one of the most prolific artists of the last three decades and one of the most elusive. Although he has had only intermittent exposure in the United States, his influence on American artists of the 1980s such as David Salle (page 212) and Julian Schnabel (page 214) is significant.

As a student in the early 1960s at the Düsseldorf Art Academy, Polke, along with Gerhard Richter, was aware of the American Pop artists and concurrently turned to commercial illustration for the iconography of his paintings. Distinctly different from that of his American counterparts, however, Polke's work appropriated the pictorial style of advertising, reproducing consumer items in an idealized form. In contrast to the bright, flashy images of advertisements and the related work of American Pop artists, Polke's images are flat and banal. However, making use of Benday dot reproduction as does Roy Lichtenstein (pages 150–55), he painted such immediately identifiable images as newspaper ads. Where Lichtenstein used even repetition, Polke contrastingly preferred imperfection, emphasizing instead the off-register, awkward quality of mechanical reproduction.

Polke's work took various forms through the 1970s as he began utilizing printed fabric as a ground or backdrop for his paintings. His subject matter shifted to art itself, by way of satirizing modern, abstract paintings, often creating works on printed fabric with patterns that possibly might mock a particular artist's design. Polke also experimented with superimposed images and figural motifs over the fabric, alluding to several layers of consciousness simultaneously (and revealing an affinity for Francis Picabia's multiple, overlaid images).

In the early 1980s, Polke embarked upon a series of works that he currently pursues—works that have been termed alchemical. Utilizing chemicals on canvas that effect changes in color and appearance relative to changes in temperature and humidity, the paintings themselves become his laboratory. As the curator John Caldwell noted, "Characteristically, Polke's experiments did not proceed in a single direction or toward a simple goal . . . not so much paintings in the traditional sense, whether figurative or abstract, but rather objects that existed independently of what they represented or communicated and on which certain processes had left their traces."[1]

In *Untitled,* 1985, the mechanical and the handmade interact. Representative of Polke's brash style of mixing painting with drawing in both deliberate and accidental ways, this work displays the random quality characteristic of much of the artist's work. Here, Polke repeatedly tips the sheet of paper in the process of painting. Demonstrating fluidity of motion, through the process of painting, Polke attempts to capture the moment of pouring paint, whether it spatters, creates a weblike pattern, or forms a pool of paint. Thus the resulting composition implies natural processes rather than conventional forms of expression. The colors Polke employs also appear to be arbitrary, not chosen for any particular aesthetic or contextual reason. *Untitled,* 1985, is an arbitrary rather than consciously composed work in its pure reliance on the effect of the medium. Unresolvable in conventional terms, this work is about the process of painting.

JW

1. Quoted in John Caldwell, Sigmar Polke (San Francisco: San Francisco Museum of Modern Art, pp. 13–14).

187

Robert Rauschenberg
Untitled. 1958

(American,
born 1925)

Solvent transfer,
watercolor,
gouache,
colored pencils,
and graphite on
paper

22¾ × 29"
(57.8 × 73.7
cm)

1989.55

Included in Robert Rauschenberg's controversial first solo exhibition at the Leo Castelli Gallery in New York in 1958 were a number of "combine paintings," works that incorporate various objects from the everyday world into the traditional structure of paintings. In the combine paintings, each element is situated to retain its identity and uniqueness, while also becoming a part of the whole. "There is no more subject in a combine than there is in a page from a newspaper," the composer John Cage remarked in 1964. "Each thing that is there is a subject. It is a situation involving multiplicity."[1] The randomness, multiple meanings, and sense of accident that Cage perceived in these works are central to Rauschenberg's art.

Also in 1958 Rauschenberg began to make a series of works on paper, called "transfer drawings," that extended his investigation of unconventional materials and his interest in associative meaning by deriving images from printed media, particularly from newspapers and magazines. The process was simple: the selected illustration was placed face down on a sheet of paper, moistened with solvent (usually turpentine or lighter fluid), and then rubbed from the back with an instrument to achieve the transfer of the image onto the sheet. This process satisfied Rauschenberg's desire to make use of images originally produced for other contexts while allowing him to contain the finished work within the plane of the sheet of paper. Through transfer drawing, the artist was able to continue to explore the principle of assemblage that he had incorporated in his work since about 1950 with brilliant and poetic

results. Unlike combine paintings, the transfer process unified the work rather than disrupted it. Given the size of the source materials Rauschenberg employed for these drawings, paper provided not only a receptive surface but also the appropriate scale.

Untitled, 1958, is a virtual sampler of drawing techniques. In addition to transfer methods, the artist used frottage and gouache, as well as watercolor and pencil, which he manipulated in graphic, expressive ways. While inventing an imagistic alternative to Abstract Expressionism, Rauschenberg retained some of its vocabulary in his use of a grid and gestural marking. The artistic elements in *Untitled,* 1958, are balanced by images taken from sports, transportation, commerce, politics, and rural America. Motion is supplied by the coins that tumble down the left side of the page as if they were in a slot or vending machine and by the baseball player who races across the page from the right (in one instance he seems to pursue one of the large coins). The race car, jockeys, and jet intensify the sense of speed. Without providing a narrative, the artist presents the noisy, bustling, real world.

The combine paintings and transfer drawings form a critical bridge between Abstract Expressionism and Pop art. The appropriation of images from mass culture in the transfer drawings was further developed by Rauschenberg in his silk-screen paintings from 1962 to 1964 and signaled a new direction for the coming generation of postmodern artists.

MB

1. *Quoted in* Robert Rauschenberg: Paintings, Drawings and Combines, 1949–64, *exhibition catalogue (London: Whitechapel Art Gallery, 1964), p. 11.*

Gerhard Richter
Helen. 1963

(German,
born 1932)

Oil and
graphite on
canvas

42¾ × 39⅛"
(108.6 × 99.4
cm)

1987.7

Gerhard Richter explores the limits of painting. In the three decades since completing his first "photo paintings," the German artist has undertaken a radical analysis of painting and its complex and often difficult relationship with photography. Richter has produced a body of work marked by stylistic diversity, a characteristic he shares with other contemporary German artists, including Joseph Beuys (pages 64, 259), Blinky Palermo (page 184), and Sigmar Polke (page 186), suggesting the remarkable capacity of these artists to embrace apparent contradictions in their work. Richter's stylistic variations result from his deliberate consideration of the schism between abstraction and representation in contemporary art.

In choosing to use found photographs as the basis for his work from 1962 through 1966, Richter was influenced by Marcel Duchamp, the Fluxus movement in Europe, and American Pop art. In 1962, a reproduction of a Lichtenstein painting in an art magazine strengthened Richter's conviction that art could be generated from a neutral, impersonal source such as a photograph. However, unlike the Pop artists, such as Lichtenstein, Rauschenberg, and Warhol, Richter did not filter the photographic image through another process, such as printing, transfer, or silk screen, but made painted versions of the photographs, thereby calling attention to the differences between the two mediums.

In his earliest photo paintings, such as *Helen,* Richter enlarged and projected images from newspapers and magazines or amateur snapshots onto canvas, a method serving to eliminate basic aesthetic decisions and personal expression. The subjects are usually anonymous people or objects that have been torn from their surroundings and relocated on canvas, thereby imbuing them with a certain poignancy that contradicts their banality. The paintings are monochromatic and have the indistinct focus associated with cheap, disposable mass-media illustrations or photographs taken by novices. This lack of clear focus is carefully and intentionally rendered through the artist's painting technique. In the catalogue for the 1972 German pavilion at the Venice Biennale, Richter stated: "Paintings are different, they are never blurred. . . . Since paintings are not made in order to compare them with reality they cannot be indistinct or inexact or different (different from what?)."[1] Richter believes that paintings constitute their own reality, one that is not subject to the same tests of accuracy or representation that are applied to photographs.

Gerhard Richter
Confus. 1986

(German,
born 1932)

Oil on canvas

$102\frac{1}{2} \times 78\frac{3}{4}$"
$(260.4 \times 200$
cm)

1987.6

(continued from previous page)

Nevertheless, he insists, "art must be truthful—that's its moral aspect."[2] It is revealing that Richter often refers both to his abstract and to his representational paintings as "pictures," a designation emphasizing that both modes operate as forms of depiction in his art. In some paintings, such as the townscapes or studies of clouds from the late 1960s, the border between representation and abstraction is eroded.

Since the mid-1970s Richter has painted pure abstractions and landscapes, as well as still lifes and occasional portraits derived from photographs that he has taken himself. Together these works present a balanced program of painting's possibilities. In 1976 Richter began making resolutely abstract paintings initially based on photographs; soon, however, he abandoned this procedure in favor of directly executing paintings without photographic reference or intervention. In these later abstract works Richter walks a careful line between spontaneity and planned articulation. He seems to value the process of abstract painting as a challenge of invention and controlled expression. "The abstract works are my presence, my reality, my problems, my difficulties and contradictions," he said in 1985. "They are very topical for me."[3] Usually he works in series, in which individual works are autonomous, although linked thematically. These paintings are executed over a period of several months, during which the final version of each work is reached through the overlaying and reworking of color, brushstrokes, lines, and textures. Each step in the process is studied carefully. In a striking reversal of roles, the slick, glamorous surfaces of the paintings and their rich, saturated colors often evoke the glossy intensity of color photographs.

Confus is the first in a series executed in 1986 of four large vertical paintings (the others are *Dunkel*, *Untitled*, and *Rot*), which was exhibited in New York in 1987. Each painting in the series is organized around vertical divisions in the composition. In *Confus*, as the title suggests, the painting is so loaded with contradictory impulses that it approaches a collapse of pictorial unity. The electrifying palette and the vivid, almost brutal surface of the painting are offset by the open composition and the delicacy of a few lines drawn into the top layer of paint. The center of the painting seems to recede into cool blue and green, as if it were a portal, while the right edge bursts into a flamboyant yellow. A crimson veil descends over the surface, adding a majestic note. Richter risks everything in this painting, even the presence of beauty.

MB

1. *Interview with Rolf Schon in* Gerhard Richter: 36th Biennale in Venice, German Pavilion, *exhibition catalogue (Essen, Germany: Museum Folkwang, 1972), p. 24.*
2. *Quoted by Coosje van Bruggen in "Gerhard Richter: Painting as a Moral Act,"* Artforum, *vol. 23, no. 9 (May 1985), p. 82.*
3. *Dorothea Dietrich in "Gerhard Richter: An Interview,"* Print Collector's Newsletter, *vol. 16 (September–October 1985), p. 128.*

192

James Rosenquist
Sketch for **House of Fire. 1981**

(American,
born 1933)

Colored ink and
graphite on
mylar

33⅛ × 63½"
(84.1 × 161.3
cm)

1982.1

1. Interviewed by
Judith Goldman in
James Rosenquist:
The Early Pictures,
1961–64 (New York:
Gagosian Gallery
and Rizzoli Interna-
tional Publications,
Inc., 1992), p. 103.
2. Collection of the
Metropolitan Museum
of Art, New York.

195

Like his fellow Pop artists Jasper Johns, Roy Lichtenstein, Claes Oldenburg, and Andy Warhol, James Rosenquist employs familiar images in his art. The alteration of scale, odd juxtapositions, disjunctive use of color, and fragmented images that characterize Rosenquist's work derive from his experience as a billboard painter in New York in the late 1950s. Not only did this training provide him with the basis of his painting technique, it taught him to focus on the abstract properties of forms, since the paintings on billboards are so large as to be unrecognizable when viewed close up. By collaging together realistic fragments, Rosenquist constructs poetic compositions in which narrative is implied but left unrealized. This indirect meaning is reinforced by the abstraction and fragmentation of objects, which gives his work a mysterious, dreamlike quality. The artist's strategy of manipulating images is balanced by his strength as a colorist and his keen sense of composition.

Rosenquist usually represents objects that are commercial goods. The natural elements that appear in his work are most often in an idealized, packaged form, such as the bag of groceries containing fruits and vegetables in this sketch for *House of Fire*. Interviewed in 1991, Rosenquist said, "I think of myself as an American artist, growing up in America, thinking about America."[1] In his skillful appropriation of advertising forms in his art, Rosenquist has adopted the most prevalent and typical means of communication in the United States not to celebrate, but rather to comment on, contemporary life.

To live in the United States in the late twentieth century is to experience image saturation and the questioning of the belief in a world constantly made better by technological innovation. The sketch for *House of Fire* is related to the painting *House of Fire*,[2] one of a group of tripartite paintings in which the juxtaposition of images conveys a sense of impending disorder and chaos. As in the painting, the commercial products depicted in the study have a sinister quality: the wrench usually felt in confronting objects removed from their daily context has here a violent undertone. The bag of groceries floats upside-down and the lipsticks on the right, stacked like bullets, are aggressively thrust into the composition. In the center a smelting bucket, symbolic of a nearly exhausted process that was once a mainstay of American industry, bursts through the window, sending a shower of sparks into the room. The sense of danger is heightened by the red background, which oozes down the left side.

The study is executed in colored ink on mylar, a plastic material that the artist likens to the surface of a lithographic stone or plate (Rosenquist is an accomplished printmaker as well as painter and draftsman). Since the sheet is nonporous, the inks settle on the surface in pools, thereby breaking down the forms into floating areas of color, and the translucency of the material heightens the effect of a fiery vision.

MB

Susan Rothenberg
Untitled. 1976

(American, born
1943)

Acrylic and
graphite on
paper

10½ × 10½"
(26.7 × 26.7
cm)

1984.38

Untitled, 1976, is related to the celebrated
series of horse paintings shown in Susan
Rothenberg's first solo exhibition at the
Willard Gallery, New York, in April 1976.
The series, which announced Rothenberg as a
serious and ambitious painter, was started
in 1974. The artist arrived almost intuitively
at the form of a horse in a sketch on a small
piece of canvas. "The horse was a vehicle
for me, I think in the same way Johns had to
use his imagery," Rothenberg has said. "I
think it was a surrogate for dealing with a
human being, but at the same time it was
neutral enough."[1] Both Lucas Samaras and
Jasper Johns were important early influences
on Rothenberg for their ability to transform
representations of everyday objects into
resonant works of art. Philip Guston (page
116), who began exhibiting his late figurative
work in 1970, also was a crucial contemporary influence, as much for the emotional
directness and honesty of his work as for his
use of figuration. Rothenberg is one of a number of American artists (others include Jennifer Bartlett, Louisa Chase, Neil Jenney, Lois
Lane, Robert Moskowitz, and Joe Zucker)
working in New York in the 1970s who had
begun painting figuratively, using humans,
animals, and objects as vehicles to express a
range of emotional, formal, and narrative concerns. This interest in balancing content
with form was part of an international shift
toward a new figurative art that occurred
over the next decade and is represented com-
prehensively in PaineWebber's collection.

Rothenberg's first horses are flat, static
emblems depicted in rectangular canvases
that have a lively, painterly surface. As the
series progressed, the horses acquired both a
sense of motion and emotional presence,
while retaining their function as abstracted
images that the artist manipulated for pictorial reasons. The primary formal relationship
in the horse paintings is the balance between
figure and ground, with the composition
typically distributed evenly between the two.
The horse often is divided or intersected by
lines, a device that creates both dramatic and
pictorial tension.

Executed in acrylic, a medium Rothenberg abandoned for oil in 1981, *Untitled*,
1976, is a small painting on paper that
demonstrates her graphic virtuosity and acute
sense of scale. The work shows a muscular
black horse linked to the edges of the sheet
by four lines that serve to anchor the image
to the white ground of the paper. The painted
white outline surrounding the horse acts as
a double image, or shadow, which increases
the vitality of the form, as do the wiry pencil
lines in the composition.

In about 1978 the artist began to
fragment the horse image; the following year
it disappeared from her work altogether to be
replaced by the human figure. In 1989 the
horse reappeared alongside other animal and
landscape images from the American South-
west, where Rothenberg now lives and
works. These motifs can be seen in the vivid
and complex painting *Dogs Killing a Rabbit*
(page 277).

MB

1. *Quoted by Joan
Simon in* Susan
Rothenberg
*(New York: Harry
N. Abrams, Inc.,
1991), p. 29.*

197

Susan Rothenberg
Biker. 1985

(American,
born 1943)

Oil on canvas

74¼ × 69"
(188.6 × 175.3
cm)

1986.6

The Museum
of Modern Art,
New York.
Fractional
gift of
PaineWebber
Group, Inc.

Biker, a pivotal work painted in 1985, is one of several paintings from the mid-1980s in which Susan Rothenberg demonstrates her continued preoccupation with depicting speed and motion. The painting echoes the artist's images of horses from the late 1970s in which the animal, seen from the front, apparently is galloping toward the viewer. The asymmetrical angle of the cyclist in *Biker* recalls the tilt of the horse and its shadow in *For the Light,* 1978–79,[1] in which a horse is located in a solid white field. In *Biker* the artist describes the landscape through which the rider moves. The difference is significant; *Biker* indicates that Rothenberg has come to grips with showing realistic space, as opposed to the flat, more purely modernist space of her earlier work, and has found a way to present human figures rather than emblems. Through a combination of inflected brushstrokes, an almost naturalistic use of color, and a heightened sense of narrative conveyed through a minimum of descriptive details, the artist achieves an important breakthrough.

On the right of the painting a tree balances the composition and establishes the foreground, acting as a static object toward which the biker moves. The cyclist hurtles through a puddle of bright blue water, causing splashes that exaggerate the sense of movement as they bounce off the bike's wheels. In painting the light and the movement of the water, Rothenberg drew on observations from her Long Island home of bodies of water which were the subject of her first oil paintings in 1981–82. Yet despite the legibility of the scene, parts of the image are abstractions, precipitating a tension between literal depiction and the suggestion of sensation. The title figure is identifiable only through fragments—the head, the arm, and the hand, which is raised to shield the biker's eyes. These body parts, frequently employed by Rothenberg in her earlier work, represent the whole, and convey a sense of dynamic motion. The rest of the form dissolves into a red aura of speed as the biker is propelled forward.

Rothenberg has commented that using oil paint, "a medium so luscious that the whole ground of the painting seems that it is moving sometimes,"[2] contributed to achieving the sense of movement in *Biker* and *Bucket of Water,* an earlier work. In *Biker* both speed and motion are conveyed through the quick deftness of the brushstrokes, particularly the bright flashes of white paint, which indicate light bouncing off the moving rider and bike. The sparkling freshness of *Biker* evokes the atmosphere that occurs after rainfall, further adding to the intensity of the depicted moment.

MB

1. Collection of
the Whitney Museum
of American Art,
New York.
2. Interview with the
artist by Michael
Auping in Susan
Rothenberg, *exhibition catalogue (New
York and Buffalo:
Rizzoli International
Publications and the
Albright-Knox Art
Gallery, 1992), p. 69.*

199

Susan Rothenberg
1, 2, 3, 4, 5, 6. 1988

(American,
born 1943)

Oil on wood
in six parts

126¾ × 46⅛"
each
(322 × 117.2
cm)

1988.39

(Detail, left)

Late in 1987 PaineWebber approached Susan Rothenberg to create a work for the series of large meeting and dining rooms located on the top floor of the PaineWebber building in New York. Although the artist had never executed a commission before, she was interested in the idea of making a work for a public space and originally had hoped to execute the paintings during office hours, which would have allowed her some interaction with the employees. The artist suggested a six-part mural for a large dining room, and ingeniously proposed locating the paintings on the structural piers that run through the interior of the building, thereby integrating the commission into the architecture and the interior space of the room. After visiting the site twice, Rothenberg offered three thematic options: spinning dancers, turning bodies, or turning Buddhas. Delighted by the idea of six painted figures moving across a vast space, the company chose the subject of dancers and the commission of six painted panels and accompanying drawings was arranged.

Rothenberg characteristically set herself an ambitious and somewhat risky challenge. Although murals by contemporary artists are rare, the use of dancing figures as a mural subject has many historical precedents, most notably in this century Matisse's extraordinary commission *The Dance,* 1932–33, completed for Dr. Albert C. Barnes. Painted during the summer of 1988 in the artist's Sag Harbor studio, *1, 2, 3, 4, 5, 6* is the culmination of a group of works depicting movement in the form of bodies spinning and turning

that Rothenberg began in 1986. The artist had studied dance as a child in Buffalo, New York, and had worked and performed with choreographer Joan Jonas in New York City in 1969 and 1970, hence her knowledge of the subject was grounded in personal experience. In *1, 2, 3, 4, 5, 6,* each of the six figures performs a different movement, ranging from poised to energetic, from the corner figure crouching sideways in plié to the fifth figure, which, with arms crossed, kicks its foot forward in space. As they seem to move forward and recede in space, the dancers are united by their gestures, which cross the empty spaces created by the windows that intervene between the piers. Set against the sky and skyline of New York, the figures are at once physical and ethereal. They are painted in Rothenberg's distinctive palette of earthy red and vivid blue (which for her is a "spirit" color) and set against black and white backgrounds. The forms dissolve into the painted space surrounding them, thereby heightening the figures' sense of animated motion. The first and last figures are partnered by their shadows or afterimages.

Since 1984 Rothenberg has used drawings to generate images for paintings in addition to creating them as works in their own right. The six drawings related to the commission are studies that were begun before and finished after the paintings (page 277). Rothenberg first sketched in the figures on paper cut in the elongated format of the panels, thereby establishing the compositions. She then returned to work on the drawings in oil paint after the panels were completed.

MB

201

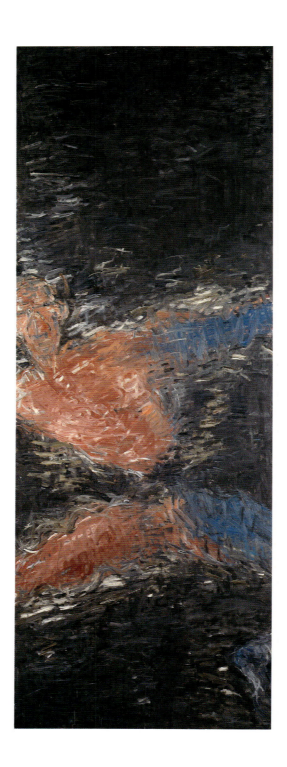

E. Ruscha '65

Edward Ruscha
Museum on Fire. 1968

(American,
born 1937)

Graphite on
paper

8 × 14⅜"
(20.3 × 36.5
cm)

1974.3

In 1956 at age nineteen Edward Ruscha left Oklahoma City for Los Angeles, intending to become a commercial artist. The following year, while a student at Chouinard Art Institute, he saw a reproduction in a magazine of Jasper Johns's painting *Target with Four Faces,* which, he says, inspired him to abandon the Abstract Expressionist style of painting he had been pursuing. By 1961 he was painting single, unrelated words such as "honk," "radio," or "oof" on neutral backgrounds. Rendered in a variety of proportions and graphic styles— tilted, ribboned, dripping—these paintings and drawings of banal words drifted between the boundaries of Pop and Conceptual art.

Intrigued by the fact that words, relative to objects, have no actual size, Ruscha experimented with representing them large, painting the 20th Century-Fox logo the size it might appear on a billboard or a movie screen, and the word *Hollywood* on the legendary sign as if seen close up from within the hills—exaggeratedly large. Around this time he also made a painting of a Standard Oil gasoline station, transforming the ubiquitous California landmark into a monument to consumer culture. Against a dramatic backdrop, the simple service station is ironically elevated to the status of an architectural icon.

In much the same way as he plucked the gasoline station from the urban Los Angeles scene, Ruscha made a monumental painting entitled *The Los Angeles County Museum on Fire,* 1965–68.[1] In the mid-1960s the museum, located on Wilshire Boulevard, was one of the few institutions exhibiting modern art in the western United States. Ruscha depicted it on fire, in a painting and in six studies completed between 1965 and 1968.[2] Working in powdered graphite, Ruscha achieved a pristine, seamless surface. The oblique aerial perspective, similar to that employed in the PaineWebber Art Collection print *Standard Station,* makes the Los Angeles museum appear to float in space, isolated from its environs and curiously, if not mischievously, afire.

The unexpected and surreal addition of these far-reaching flames immediately invites interpretation. But Ruscha's mix of fact with fiction is intentionally provocative and confusing. Showing the museum on fire, Ruscha claimed, is an "attempt to raise thoughts about the nature of an art museum."[3] Others, however, have interpreted the gesture as "a metaphoric rendering of the threat posed by any new kind of art to the preceding artistic generation."[4]

By the late 1960s and early 1970s Ruscha had abandoned representative imagery altogether and was preoccupied with showing words and language in all media: paintings, drawings, prints, and books. A number of these works are in the PaineWebber Art

Edward Ruscha
The End. 1991

(continued from page 205)
Collection (pages 277–78). Despite their deadpan appearance, these works are almost "spoken" into existence. Ruscha achieves visual onomatopoeia by distorting the font or letter spacing, as in *Vanish* (page 277), where the tiny letters spread and disappear into a Technicolor sky. By 1973 he was making drawings and paintings of found phrases—fragments heard on the radio, bits of conversations, things written down—that he painted or drew verbatim, such as *Now Then As I Was About to Say* (page 278) and *Year after Year* (page 278).

By the early 1980s Ruscha stopped painting words almost entirely, generally replacing them with landscapes, spray-painted in soft silhouettes with a fuzzy, slightly out-of-focus quality. These are usually somber and nocturnal works, with enigmatic, silhouetted images—deserted streets, vacant houses, and landscapes. Predominantly rendered in black and white, many of these works are complicated by the presence of simple white "fill-in-the-blank" rectangles that hover above or below the images and suggest a correspondence to the paintings' titles. In *Brother, Sister* (page 278), two bars floating above a pair of four-masted sailing ships listing at parallel angles on a dark sea suggest a sympathetic connection between the two vessels.

Ruscha's most recent work—including *The End*—reintroduces words as subjects.

Somewhere between a single word and a phrase, *The End* also recalls an ever-present cinematic character of Ruscha's art. The two words seemingly flashing before us are reminiscent of the closing credits in a film. The link between Ruscha's art and the cinema has possibly never been as direct. The Gothic typeface suggests a black-and-white movie from a bygone era, perhaps the 1930s or a classic film noir. Motionless, the words appear twice in heavy black lettering: the first time cropped at the top, the second time cropped at the bottom. A thick white line bisects the canvas, appearing like a film frame gone out of sync or nearly broken.

To capture the quality of time and effect, Ruscha re-created the static, aged quality of an old film through carefully rendering dust and debris and long white scratches. The combination of large-scale text and small-scale image further blurs the distinction between painting and the silver screen. Ultimately, we are not allowed to read "The End" in its entirety. This ironic twist, a consistent gesture in Ruscha's work, ensures that the words or message remain empty, so that viewers project their own meaning onto the image.

Ruscha repeated the image of *The End* in a suite of six recent woodcut prints, entitled *Cameo Cuts,* also in the PaineWebber Collection. Featured among the images is similar cinematic imagery, including a test signal used in film sequencing.

JW

(American, born 1937)

Acrylic and graphite on canvas

70 × 112"
(177.8 × 284.5 cm)

1991.24

(Detail, right)

208

1. Collection Hirshhorn Museum and Sculpture Garden, Smithsonian Institution, Washington, D.C.
2. Los Angeles County Museum on Fire *is one of these studies; three other studies are in the collection of the Hirshhorn Museum and Sculpture Garden, Smithsonian Institution, Washington, D.C. According to their records, they were commissioned by Joseph Hirshhorn. The others are in the collection of Jean Pigozzi, Paris, and the collection of the artist.*
3. *Artist's statement in* "object record" *dated April 2, 1980, from the Department of Painting and Sculpture at the Hirshhorn Museum and Sculpture Garden.*
4. *Anne Livet, in introduction to* The Works of Edward Ruscha, *exhibition catalogue (New York: Hudson Hills Press, in association with the San Francisco Museum of Modern Art, 1982), p. 15.*

Robert Ryman
Untitled. 1976

(American,
born 1930)

Pastel and
graphite on
sandblasted
Plexiglas with
black oxide
steel bolts
and fasteners

49½ × 49½"
(125.7 × 125.7
cm)

1976.2

The Museum
of Modern Art,
New York.
Fractional
gift of
PaineWebber
Group, Inc.

In a 1991 lecture at the Guggenheim Museum, Robert Ryman insisted his art is Realist in that he does not picture the external world nor create illusory qualities in his work. His paintings and drawings are expressions of only their physical components: material, surface, edge, and light. For over four decades, Ryman has explored the essentials of painting, while challenging the viewer's perceptual abilities to provoke a greater appreciation and experience of the activity of painting. Ryman started painting in the 1950s in New York, where he had moved in 1952 intending to become a jazz musician. In 1961 he left the Museum of Modern Art after working there for seven years as a guard, and began painting full-time. During this period he established the area of investigation to which he has been dedicated—the application of white pigment on roughly square supports. Choosing white was a means of emphasizing the importance of light. The artist has used an astonishing range of materials for supports—from canvas and various metals to plastic, fiberglass, and Plexiglas—and has exploited the tone and texture of each.

Ryman's approach was sympathetic to the views articulated by the Minimalist and Conceptual artists in the mid-1960s. It is particularly in accord with their objection to pictorial art and the illusionism of painting. But unlike the Minimalists, and despite his practice of working in series, Ryman's exploration of the mechanics of painting is not merely theoretical—rather it constitutes an eloquent discourse on the potential for painting. Supporting his conception of his art as real and therefore part of the real world, Ryman integrates his work into its surroundings without the mediation of a frame.

Untitled, 1976, is one of four works the artist made for an exhibition of 1976 at the Museum of Modern Art, New York, called *Drawing Now.* Drawings are not used by Ryman as preparatory sketches for other works: a drawing is defined by the medium the artist employs (e.g. pencil or pastel) rather than the support he selects. By executing *Untitled* on Plexiglas sandblasted to retain the surface's white pastel covering, Ryman expanded the definition of what a drawing can be. The steel bolts and fasteners establish that the drawing is attached to the wall, as opposed to hanging on the wall's surface and being suspended by invisible hardware. External fasteners first appeared in Ryman's work in 1976 and since have become a significant formal component of his art. In *Untitled* the bolts and plates are also used as important compositional devices. They determine nearly every internal incident that defines the drawing— from the empty borders at the top and bottom to the location of the ruled pencil lines and the shape of the three small squares echoing their form. On the left, a ruled pencil line begins at the top and culminates in Ryman's signature near the bottom; on the right, the translucent Plexiglas is left bare, thereby leaving a rough, unfinished, and open edge to the subtly nuanced and richly textured surface of the drawing.

MB

211

David Salle
My Subjectivity. (1981)

(American,
born 1952)

Oil on canvas
and household
paint on
Masonite in
two panels

86 × 112"
overall
(218.4 × 284.5
cm)

1981.17

David Salle is one of several American artists who came to prominence in the early 1980s with work focusing on the human figure. While such artists as John Ahearn (page 48), Eric Fischl (with whom Salle shared a studio at California Institute of the Arts, pages 96–98, 265), Robert Longo (page 158), Julian Schnabel (page 214), and Cindy Sherman (pages 220, 279–80) adopted the figure for specific narrative or expressive purposes, Salle has employed the human form—most often the female nude—as a requisite component in the construction of an art based on the juxtaposition of dislocated images that carry with them a range of associations. Salle's paintings are ironic, overlaying images borrowed from both high and low culture. The forms are presented without a sense of hierarchy or classical composition, and the finished works are puzzles for which the viewer must try to work out a solution. Often, the possibility of many different, and often conflicting or unrelated, readings in Salle's work serves to negate the idea of meaning itself.

Immediate predecessors for Salle's collaging and fragmenting appropriated images can be found in American Pop art, particularly in the understated eloquence of Jasper Johns (pages 128–30) and the formal language of James Rosenquist (page 195). The artist also cites the influence of American movies, particularly those of Douglas Sirk, in which various images are layered simultaneously on the screen, with each level giving meaning to the others. Stylistically, Salle's use of fragments resembles the dense compositions of Francis Picabia's late work and the crowded, anarchic paintings of the contemporary German painter Sigmar Polke (page 186).

My Subjectivity is a diptych, a standard painting form that Salle began using early in his career to place his disjointed fragments side by side. Two panels, one a deep black construction and the other a painting on canvas, hang mutely next to each other, spliced together like a split-screen projection. The carefully paired images bring to mind a series of conflicting interpretations. Each side represents a set of opposing artistic options: abstraction or figuration, industrial construction or traditional painting, literal or illusionistic space, repetitive series or single image, impersonal or personal expression. The naked young girl shown kneeling uncomfortably on a chair in the right panel projects a feeling of vulnerability, while the left side is a model of impassive detachment. The luminous, electronic green of the painting suggests a television or computer screen, an association that imparts a flickering, ghostly quality to the work. The blank, nihilistic look of the painting, its eerie, empty quality, paradoxically gives it force and presence. The title, *My Subjectivity,* is a teasing suggestion that despite the obliqueness of the visual statement, the artist's personal point of view is being represented.

MB

213

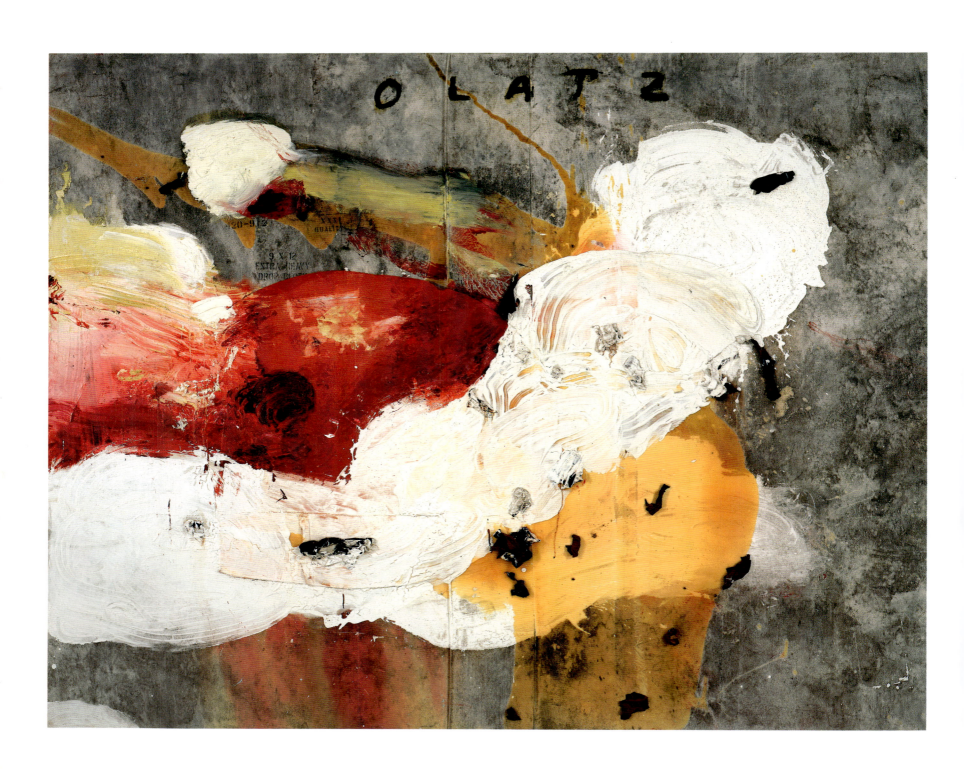

Julian Schnabel
Olatz IV. (1991)

(American,
born 1951)

Oil, gesso,
resin, and
leather
on drop cloth

96 × 120"
(243.8 × 304.8
cm)

1992.11

Not content to develop a single signature style, Julian Schnabel makes paintings, drawings, and sculpture that encompass a variety of styles. His materials are unconventional—he has used broken crockery, animal hide, velvet, tarpaulins, and Kabuki theater backdrops—and he exhausts them for multiple meanings. Even his sources are random and diverse; ultimately, however, each of his works tells a story.

Schnabel's meteoric ascension in the art world began with his first exhibition in 1979, in which he showed huge, colorful paintings covered with an assemblage of broken pottery. Labeled a Neo-Expressionist in the early 1980s, and grouped with such painters as Susan Rothenberg, Georg Baselitz, Anselm Kiefer, and Francesco Clemente, Schnabel eschewed the cool, detached approach to art making that characterized the preceding generation of Pop artists, Minimalists, and Photo-Realists. The raw physical power of his work, its breadth and theatricality, helped free painting from post-Minimalist strictures of the 1970s, opening new paths for the 1980s. "Shifting between the figurative and abstract as his works require, Schnabel fills the canvases with everything that strikes a chord in him. The nature of his obsession is to bring himself into the work. He has a remarkable ability to capture an instant or impulse, to absorb a myriad of visual information, and to respond quickly to issues that interest him. As a painter, he is constantly changing things."[1]

Olatz IV is one of a series of seven paintings completed during the summer of 1991 and is named after a Basque friend of Schnabel's who became a kind of muse for the series. Using an eight-by-ten-foot drop cloth, which Schnabel intentionally distressed to lend a sense of depth and definition, he painted in oil, gesso, and resin (as well as applying leather and appliqués) in both deliberate and accidental movements. He achieved randomness in some areas by flinging paint-saturated rags at the stretched drop cloth.

Despite its heroic scale, there is a soft and lyrical quality to *Olatz IV,* conveyed by the amorphous and viscous white gesso form that was poured onto the surface and shaped by a cloth and by the artist's hands. The contrast between this cloudlike form and the untouched drop cloth is similar to and almost imitative of Cy Twombly's work (pages 242, 246–47). The white form hovers rather magnificently over a passage of brilliant red orange paint and a patch of amber resin, into which are set small pieces of crumpled brown chamois.

Schnabel's paintings are responses to things that exist outside himself—a word, a phrase, an idea, or a material. They trigger feelings and associations. To the artist, the Olatz paintings are "very Mediterranean and very open. They are about different times of day, different locations. They are not landscapes, but places that exist in my mind. I exist in those places."[2] As in most of his work, Schnabel developed a dialogue between accidental and intentional shapes to create an energetic whole.

JW

1. *Gabriella de Ferrari in* Julian Schnabel, *exhibition catalogue (New York: Pace Gallery, 1992), n.p.*
2. *Ibid.*

215

Sean Scully
Us. 1988

(American, born
Ireland 1945)

Oil on canvas
in two panels
with four
inserted panels

96 × 120"
overall
(243.8 × 304.8
cm)

1989.1

For over two decades, Sean Scully has used stripes in his paintings, a direction inspired partly by a visit in 1970 to Morocco, where heavy, striped fabrics are an integral part of the visual background. Scully's paintings from the 1970s are precise, formal statements executed with scarcely a trace of expression. By contrast, his later works are tempered with a sense of doubt about the stability of formal order.

More loosely painted than his earlier work, Scully's paintings since 1981 are characterized by a developed sense of composition and light and a shift in emphasis from the surface qualities of the paintings to their structure. Usually made of joined canvases, the paintings often are composed of some parts that have greater depth, and therefore project more deeply into space, and other parts that actually have panels set into them, like windows in a wall. Both devices allow for a more pronounced manipulation of the picture plane and underscore the reading of the painting as illusory, a fictional object. Scully has spoken of his work in relationship to the paintings of Jasper Johns, but his commitment to a pictorial means of abstraction can be seen in the context of other twentieth-century artists, from Piet Mondrian to Frank Stella and Brice Marden. However, his use of color and his vigorous brushwork often recall the palette of Spanish art, particularly the paintings of Goya and Velázquez.

The emphasis on construction gives Scully's recent work an architectural presence, seemingly developed in the context of the urban environment in which the artist lives. "I see a sort of urban romance in the expedients that people use to keep a place like Manhattan together," he has said, ". . . though, of course, that is the point—it doesn't exactly hold together. It's not contained. There's the grid of the streets and the gridded buildings, and then all of the amazing things people do inside those grids and along those edges."[1]

In *Us* two pairs of identically sized panels are set into two larger canvases that form a diptych. The larger panels are more smoothly painted than the smaller ones, which are executed with edgy brushstrokes forming the vertical and horizontal stripes. The relationship of the smaller stripes to the larger ones and the intersection of the edges of the six canvases give the painting its sense of incidence. The colors are harsh, almost corrosive, with each color painted over a darker, grayer tone. The composition of the painting is locked together by its construction, but the smaller canvases are placed uneasily in their compartments, breaking the coherence of the painting both visually and psychologically. The work speaks of both unity and estrangement. Studying this painting, we are reminded that the correlative of the pronoun *us* is *them*.

1. Quoted in Carter Ratcliff, "Sean Scully and Modernist Painting, The Constitutive Image," Sean Scully: Paintings and Works on Paper, 1982-88, *exhibition catalogue (London: The Whitechapel Art Gallery, 1989), p. 20.*

217

MB

Richard Serra
No Mandatory Patriotism. (1989)

(American,
born 1939)

Paintstick on
two sheets of
paper

93⅛ × 201⅛"
(236.5 × 510.9
cm)

1989.62

In the late 1960s the sculptor Richard Serra wrote a list of verbs on a sheet of paper *(to roll, to fold, to bend, to shorten, to shave, to tear, to chip, to split, to cut, to sever . . .)* as a way of naming activities that could be used to form materials. At that time Serra was not making traditional drawings, but in 1977 he cited this list of verbs as the basis for locating drawing in the defining lines of his early sculptures. Since the actions specified on the list were used conceptually to delineate the form of his sculptures, the activity of drawing was therefore implicit in the making of his work.

Serra's independent drawings fall into three categories: sketches, medium-sized works in charcoal or lithographic crayon on paper, and large Paintstick and oilstick works. With the exception of the sketchbooks, line seldom appears as a single stroke in Serra's drawings, generally having a more sculptural presence. It exists as the contour or edge of a shape or is formed by the relationship of two shapes. In 1971 Serra made the first Paintstick or oilstick drawings on canvas applied to the wall of a room as a plane, thereby altering the perception of the architecture and extending his ongoing experimentation with site and context previously established in his sculptural work. Serra has continued to make large drawings related to interior spaces, sometimes applying drawing materials to the wall directly, other times using a support such as canvas, paper, or forged steel.

No Mandatory Patriotism is one of a series of eight large framed drawings on paper that Serra included in the exhibition *Weights and Measures* at the Leo Castelli Gallery in New York in 1989. Earlier that year, Serra's monumental *Tilted Arc,* a site-specific work that was commissioned by the federal government, had been dismantled by order of the General Accounting Office after years of public protest, debate, and ensuing legal battles. The individual titles of the drawings exhibited in *Weights and Measures* refer to a number of topical issues, including civil rights, censorship, artists' rights, and patriotism.

Like all the drawings in the series, *No Mandatory Patriotism* is a diptych, composed of two deep black planes with rich, dense surfaces layered in strokes of Paintstick. Because the drawing hangs enclosed in a frame on the wall, the two planes of the composition are seen independently, not related to the space of the room. Isolating the drawing from its surrounding or containing space, the frame emphasizes the internal structures of the drawing. The placement of the rectangular plane on the paper, of each panel next to the other, and of the Paintstick to the edge of the paper are calculated precisely, resulting in an acutely balanced work of finesse and strength.

MB

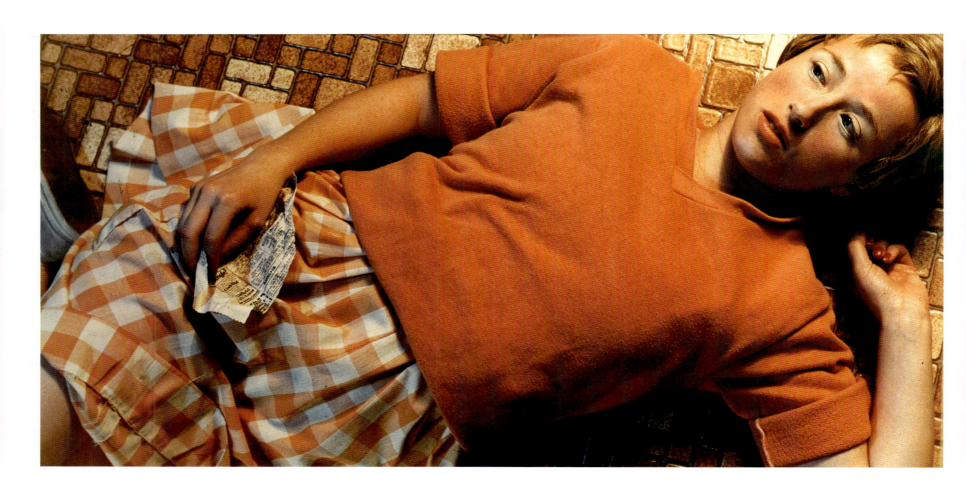

Cindy Sherman
Untitled #96. 1981

(American,
born 1954)

Color photo-
graph, 1/10

24 × 48"
(61 × 122 cm)

1981.15

Cindy Sherman's earliest photographs were black-and-white; dubbed "Film Stills," they were executed between 1977 and 1980. Since 1980 the artist has used color photography to produce a body of work that combines narrative and formal concerns. Until recently, Sherman herself always has been present in her work, thereby fusing the identity of the artist and model and giving her oeuvre, which has dealt with many different subjects, an edgy coherence. Through photography, Sherman examines the way images are constructed and the cultural roles they play. The scope of her investigations has covered the banalities of film, television, and advertising; the horror of fairy tales; the vanity of fashion and portraits; and the fallibility of recorded history. Her pictures emphatically are not self-portraits, but obviously staged photographs in which the artist plays parts. The commercially processed photographs are a way to record the images that the artist herself composes.

The "Film Stills" are small in format and show the artist in a variety of women's roles popularized by movies and television, serving as an index of the stereotypes of women in popular culture. They were shot on location and often, in fact, photographed by other people. In 1980, Sherman moved into her studio to make her photographs, at first using backscreen projections, but then assembling costumes and sets, taking on the roles of director, makeup artist, set designer, cameraman, and propmaster, as well as performer. The following year, having been invited by *Artforum* to publish a portfolio of prints in the magazine, Sherman began a series of horizontal photographs based on the format of conventional magazine centerfolds. *Untitled #96* is from this group. Regarding this image, Sherman said in 1982: "I was thinking of a young girl who may have been cleaning the kitchen for her mother and who ripped something out of the newspaper, something asking 'Are you lonely?' or 'Do you want to be friends?' or 'Do you want to go on a vacation?'"[1] This drama of somewhat trivial, but nevertheless moving, personal desires and expectations is conveyed through the props and through the girl's dreamy, faraway expression. However poignant the narrative, it is the formal presentation of the image that gives the work its strength. This is accomplished by employing pictorial devices borrowed both from film and from more traditional fine art. In addition to telling a good story, Sherman has composed a great picture.

Sherman has continued to use a combination of familiar narrative and sophisticated formal means in her work. In 1983 she was asked by a fashion designer to create a spread for *Interview* magazine. The result was a distinctly unglamorous set of photographs that in the end were not used (see *Untitled #122A*, page 279). Between 1988 and 1990, the artist worked on a series of historical portraits that analyze the stylistic mannerisms of older art while examining the values their subjects embody. These images were derived from sources ranging from the French Revolution to Old Master paintings (see *Untitled #209*, 1989 and *Untitled #228*, 1990, page 280).

MB

1. Quoted by Peter Schjeldahl in "The Oracle of Images" in Cindy Sherman, *exhibition catalogue (New York: Whitney Museum of American Art, 1987), p. 10.*

Lorna Simpson
Untitled. (1992)

(American,
born 1960)

Eighteen color
Polaroids and
eighteen en-
graved plastic
plaques

90 × 162"
overall
(228.6 × 411.5
cm)

1992.13

Since the early 1980s Lorna Simpson's work has addressed issues of identity, race, and gender. Rooted in the tradition of African-American narrative, her photographic images and texts question the way women—primarily black women—are classified and analyzed by white male society; at the same time, they reveal just how ingrained racial and gender stereotypes are in contemporary visual imagery and language.

Simpson's conceptual approach to photography developed after a period of documentary portrait work, when she began to realize that her images were universally understood by predetermined cultural notions. At this point, she began to eliminate all references to the individual, thereby creating faceless portraits. Her purpose was to deny the viewer the opportunity to examine the model's emotional state or expression, a conventional means of reading a photograph, and simultaneously to encourage the viewer to engage in a dialogue with the work. Simpson provided "directions" by pairing images with words and texts. Situated on simple, generic plastic plaques—often used for directional signs or in public places—they ultimately serve as tools to decipher images.

Untitled, 1992, is one of Simpson's largest works to date, comprised of eighteen large-format Polaroids and eighteen plastic plaques. Read vertically, it shows six female figures. As surrogate heads for the six torsos, Simpson mounted plaques over black shoe-boxes bearing the following words: *scars, stories, lies, fears, desires,* and *habits.* Each figure is seen from behind and is clothed in a tailored suit, a garment traditionally worn by a man and adopted by women to disguise and manipulate their sexuality and gender difference. The poses of the figures also seem to suggest different psychological states, which perhaps relate to the sentiments expressed on the plaques. The lower tier features pairs of shoes, four female, one male, and one mixed. The words *she* and *he* appear beneath the shoes, though not always with respect to gender. The result is what Simpson calls "an inquiry into how codes of dress define gender."[1] The juxtapositions also seem to infer that a person has to be genderless to conform to the corporate workplace.

This work confronts body language and the stereotypes accepted and denied in the workplace. In the gestures of the torsos and the coupled words from left to right, a narrative emerges, beginning with the hands clasped behind the back with the word *scars* and ending with the empowered gesture of arms crossed in the front of the body paired with the word *habits.*

Ultimately, the back view of the model's gesture and the absence of a facial expression resist interpretation. Thus, combined with carefully constructed language and props, Simpson uses photography as a medium to transmit her reflections and interpretations of contemporary life. However, she takes her work a step further in redirecting the viewer away from culturally conditioned responses.

JW

1. Beryl J. Wright, Lorna Simpson: For the Sake of the Viewer, *exhibition catalogue* (New York: Universe Publishing and Chicago: Museum of Contemporary Art, 1992), p. 23.

223

Alexis Smith
Seven Wonders. (1988)

(American,
born 1949)

Silk-screen ink,
found paper,
plastic and
metal objects,
and painted
wood frame

47¼ × 41 ×
2½"
(120 × 104.1 ×
6.4 cm)

1992.8

In the tradition of collage, the works of Alexis Smith, a California-based artist who first came to prominence in the 1970s, incorporate image, object, and text. Smith's collages, once described as "part of the narrative or story-art phenomenon, a more talkative, less hermetic branch of Conceptual art,"[1] also have, in their spare use of components, connections to those of Joseph Cornell or Robert Rauschenberg.

Smith is intrigued by the overlooked and forgotten debris of popular culture found in yard sales, thrift shops, and flea markets. The visual narratives that result from using these materials in collage imbue treasures of the past with sentiments from the present. But her combinations of image and text remain cryptic, creating an ironic tension as the viewer tries to solve the visual and literary puzzles. As one writer has observed, "rather than pronouncing any unified notion, these witty, studied elements encourage the oscillation of meanings and instability of fixed connotations."[2]

The texts Smith appropriates—from American classics by John Steinbeck to pulp fiction by Raymond Chandler—furnish a secondary narrative. *Seven Wonders* is one of twenty works in her On the Road series, titled after the 1957 Jack Kerouac novel of the same name. This classic Beat Generation book describes a wild, delirious race to the West and provided Smith with myriad vignettes about the quintessentially American experience of life on the road.

In *Seven Wonders,* a battered roadside advertisement for Camel cigarettes, a 1964 *Life* magazine cover featuring a kimonoed Japanese woman bowling, a ruptured golf ball, a Brownie camera, and a plastic undersea diver (a popular 1950s children's toy) are brought together like travel souvenirs. The rusted and well-worn cigarette sign shares the same cast-off character as the plastic diver, golf ball, and camera. Silk-screened across the sign is a wide-eyed observation from Kerouac, "Everything amazed him, everything he saw," which offers an appropriate response to the oddity of the magazine cover but also mocks and contradicts the pedestrian quality of the objects. Adding further confusion to the interpretation is the original advertising slogan for the cigarettes, "So Mild, So Good."

The title, *Seven Wonders,* conjures up the monuments of ancient art and architecture that were awe-inspiring marvels to the Greeks and Romans. One of the most famous of these monuments, the pyramids of Egypt, is prominently featured in the Camel sign. Despite this direct reference, the grandeur and magnificence of the title jars with the work's assortment of commonplace objects. Perhaps these disposed of and forgotten remnants represent the wonders of Smith's world—one in which the accrued meaning of unrelated, disjunctive images and objects resists complete comprehension.

JW

1. Roberta Smith in "Alexis Smith at the Brooklyn Museum," The New York Times, *January 1, 1988, p. 14.*
2. Andrea Liss in Forty Years of California Assemblage, *exhibition catalogue (Los Angeles: Wight Art Gallery, University of California at Los Angeles, 1989), p. 210.*

225

David Smith
Untitled. (1952)

(American,
1906–1965)

Tempera on
paper

29⅝ × 42½"
(75.3 × 108 cm)

1987.16

Like an inventor who builds a new machine from existing parts, David Smith rethought sculpture in the middle of the twentieth century. Smith reassembled the idea of sculpture by assimilating the great modern European sculpture traditions—Cubism, Surrealism, and Constructivism—into a new, monumental style. The European models provided the process of welding, the idea of collage, the use of found objects, the notion of Cubist space, and the exploitation of chance or accident. To these Smith added the liberation of sculpture from its pedestal, the restoration of color to the surface of sculpture, the use of new materials such as stainless steel, the importance of the relationship of sculpture to landscape, and an ambitious, American sense of scale.

Smith began his artistic career as a painter and continued to paint and draw throughout his life, making some 300 to 400 drawings in ink or paint on paper per year. His conviction that "painting and sculpture aren't very far apart"[1] enabled him to conceive his innovative idea of sculpture, freeing it from the notion of monolithic and volumetric form. The most significant formal element that Smith applied from painting to making sculpture was the importance of the picture plane as a point of departure for his work. For example in *Hudson River Landscape* of 1951[2] he enclosed the composition within a linear frame, or in *Australia*, also of 1951,[3] he formed the sculpture as though it were a drawing in space. The success of later works, particularly the Zigs and Cubis of the 1960s, depends on the planar relationships between the rectangular forms that comprise the sculptures.

Smith saw his "drawings" (as he called his paintings on paper) not simply as studies for sculptures, but as separate, autonomous works, which he valued for directness of expression. "In drawings remain the life force of the artist," he said in a 1955 lecture on the subject. "Especially this is true of the sculptor, who of necessity works in media slow to take realization. And where the original creative impetus must be maintained during labor, drawing is the fast-moving search which keeps physical labor in balance."[4]

Smith's drawings are generally horizontal, rhythmic abstractions that are similar to works on paper by his contemporaries, the Abstract Expressionist painters Willem de Kooning, Arshile Gorky, and Jackson Pollock. In particular, Smith's even distribution of forms over the surface of the paper recalls Pollock's allover format. In *Untitled*, 1952, Smith melded a structure of gray brushstrokes with a network of white paint. The white paint intervenes in the figure/ground relationship of the gray strokes and the paper, locking the surface of the composition together, as if the surrounding space of the linear composition were made solid. The activity of the brushstrokes animates the drawing, and the gray and white paint combine to give a silvery metallic surface, thereby adding to the sense of lightness in the work.

MB

1. *Quoted in* David Smith by David Smith, *edited by Cleve Gray (London: Thames and Hudson, 1968), p. 106.*
2. *Collection of the Whitney Museum of American Art, New York.*
3. *Collection of The Museum of Modern Art, New York.*
4. David Smith by David Smith, *p. 84.*

227

Kiki Smith
Identical Twins. (1990)

(American,
born Germany
1954)

Cast aluminum
with metal
cords in four
parts

10 × 3⅜ ×
2¼"; 10 × 3¾
× 2½";
9 × 4 × 2½";
10⅜ × 4 × 2¼"
(25.4 × 9.2 ×
5.7 cm; 25.4 ×
9.5 × 6.4 cm;
22.9 × 10.2 ×
6.4 cm; 27 ×
10.2 × 5.7 cm)

1990.52

The human body, in all forms and states of being, has dominated Kiki Smith's art making since 1980. Smith's works remind us that it is the body, not the mind, that is "our primary vehicle for experiencing our lives." She finds expressive potential in corporeal aspects and exposes the human condition as simultaneously powerful and vulnerable. With eloquence and candor, she rejects the hierarchic approach to the body, democratically investing fluids, organs, limbs, and joints with equal significance. Her work does not merely talk about the body, it *is* the body in all its variety and complexity.

Smith came of age as an artist during the late 1970s, at the height of Minimalism, Conceptual, and Process art. Through the work of her father, Minimalist sculptor Tony Smith, she gained an understanding of how sculpture conceptually and physically can embrace an awareness of one's bodily experience in the world. Tony Smith also introduced his daughter to the work of his contemporaries, such as Eva Hesse, whose experimentation with materials and explorations of sensuous forms had a profound impact on her nearly two decades later.

In 1980 Smith produced an untitled work of an isolated clay hand, covered by algae and floating in a simple Mason jar of dark green water. It would set the tone for much of the work that would follow. Completed after her father's death, the piece was a simultaneously disturbing and consoling evocation of a life after death. Though most of Smith's more recent works deal with what it means to be alive, this poignant merging of elegy and celebration remains a mainstay of her work.

Distinctly different from many of her contemporaries, Smith relies on a traditional approach to art making, often choosing materials that have a handmade and old-fashioned quality. Preferring to work with diverse mediums and usually with what is at hand, Smith made a number of wax castings in early 1990. *Identical Twins,* included in her first solo exhibition in the Projects Gallery at the Museum of Modern Art in New York, is an aluminum cast made from wax casts of a pair of twins' hands. Despite their industrial medium, these hands are similar to the plaster and wax casts in *Target with Plaster Casts,*[1] the Jasper Johns painting, as well as the wax ex-votos of limbs placed in shrines in Latin countries (an influence Smith acknowledges). The piece was more directly inspired, however, by Smith's preoccupation with the individual human form and the notion that nature never duplicates itself. Intrigued by the indistinguishable characteristics of a set of twins who lived in her neighborhood, Smith invited the pair to her studio and made wax casts of their hands. After casting the wax hands in aluminum, Smith attached cords so that they could be hung, side by side, in a very casual manner. In these seemingly identical pairs of hands, sculptural and genetic duplication are visually and conceptually linked.

1. Private collection.

JW

Frank Stella
The Blanket (IRS #8, 1.875X). 1988

(American,
born 1936)

Mixed medi-
ums on magne-
sium and
aluminum

119¾ × 228¾
× 46"
(304.2 × 581 ×
116.8 cm)

1988.25

(Detail, left)

In 1987 PaineWebber commissioned two artists, Frank Stella and Susan Rothenberg (pages 202–3), to make works for the top floor of the PaineWebber Building in midtown Manhattan. Stella's commitment to the vitality of abstract art, his interest in the relationship of painting to sculpture and architecture, and the baroque grandeur and complexity of his work in the mid-1980s made him a logical choice to execute work for the enormous spaces at the top of the corporate headquarters. For this project, Stella chose the center of the three very large horizontal walls that dominate the reception and dining-room area, a space with views extending from the East River to the Hudson River.

For over three decades, Stella has been engaged in an analysis of the conventions of painting. From the start, it was his practice to work in series, exploring the physical possibilities of shape, color, edge, line, and space. In the mid-1970s, Stella's art appeared to undergo a radical change. The complex spatial relationships always present in the geometry of his paintings found expression in metal reliefs that he flamboyantly painted. "Whether you call what I do painted reliefs or relief paintings," he has said, "It doesn't make much difference. The impulse that goes into them is pictorial, and they live or die on my pictorial abilities, not my abilities as a sculptor. . . . They want to do everything that sculpture doesn't want to do."[1]

Stella has remained primarily concerned with the pictorial space of the picture plane, which is embodied in his later work by the supporting wall. By projecting his work from the wall, the artist imposes an essentially frontal reading of his art on the viewer, but he provides many vantage points so that the paintings can be read in space, as well as within the picture plane. The arrangements of shape, texture, and color explore the plastic and expressive potential of pictorial structure. Stella aims to make art that has the verisimilitude of the art of the sixteenth and seventeenth centuries without employing narrative or figuration, so that his abstract art is imbued with the sense of tension and drama more often found in the grand figurative compositions of artists such as Rubens and Caravaggio. In spite of the sophistication and theoretical basis of his pictorial language, Stella's art has a volubility that is directly communicated. It has a sense of presence that engages the viewer and provokes the kind of exhilaration generated by the ingenuity and beauty of a well-designed suspension bridge or skyscraper. Indeed, Stella's large works belong to the urban landscape of the twentieth century; they celebrate the present.

231

Frank Stella
The Wheelbarrow (B #3, 2X). 1988

1. Quoted by William Rubin in Frank Stella, 1970–1987, exhibition catalogue (New York: The Museum of Modern Art, 1987), p. 20.
2. For a comprehensive discussion of this group of works see Philip Leider, "Shakespearean Fish," Art in America (October 1990), pp. 172–91.
3. Ibid., p. 183.
4. Herman Melville, Moby-Dick (London: Everyman's Library, 1991), p. 305.

(continued from page 231)

Stella's work is constructed; the individual elements are made and the paintings are assembled from these parts. After building the composition, the artist unifies the structure by painting, which he refers to as the "main event." Most often, Stella begins work on a piece by working out the composition in a maquette. Both *The Blanket (IRS #8, 1.875X)* and *The Wheelbarrow (B #3, 2X)* were started in 1986 with paper-covered foam-core reliefs, which were then translated into maquettes and subsequently enlarged. (The painted-metal maquettes are also in the collection, page 280.) The two commissioned pieces belong to a large body of work that makes use of a wave-shaped form and is loosely linked by the theme of *Moby-Dick*, the novel by Herman Melville.[2] Begun in 1986, the group now numbers some 135 pieces. Stella first developed the wave form while working on a portfolio of hand-painted prints entitled *Had Gadya*, which was published in 1984 (some of these prints are in the PaineWebber collection). The other dominant form in the series is a set of shapes derived from a catalogue of cast-iron rain gutters (for example, the large blue shape on the right of *The Wheelbarrow*). Each work is a dynamic concatenation of shape, drawing, color, and movement. In *The Wheelbarrow*, the elements float on a cast-metal dome, decorated with designs which echo Far Eastern latticework.

In *The Blanket* the forms are mounted and stacked on top of each other, moving into space with an elaborate flowing black-and-white scroll at the front, which Philip Leider has shown is related to a 1931 Picasso painting.[3] Both works suggest the rolling of the sea. In *The Blanket (IRS #8, 1.875X)* the movement is furious but graceful; in *The Wheelbarrow (B #3, 2X)* it is more frenzied, with even the ragged edge of the supporting disk echoing the motion.

In the *B* series the B stands for Beluga, another name for the white whale, and the titles of the two works in the commission, *The Blanket* and *The Wheelbarrow*, are taken from chapters in *Moby-Dick*. Though he titled the works with Melville's novel in mind, Stella does not intend them as illustrations but as independent formal statements. The power of the novel is its compelling tale that is narrated through the use of metaphor, an aspect that links it with Stella's ambitions for his art. "The Blanket," chapter 68, falls precisely in the middle of *Moby-Dick* and is a remarkable description of the skin of the white whale, which reads, intriguingly, like an essay on the ambiguity and complexity of visual perception. "The question is," asks Melville, "what and where is the skin of the whale?"[4]

MB

(American, born 1936)

Mixed mediums on cast magnesium and aluminum

108¼ × 109¾ × 43⅜" (275 × 278.8 × 110.2 cm)

1988.23

234

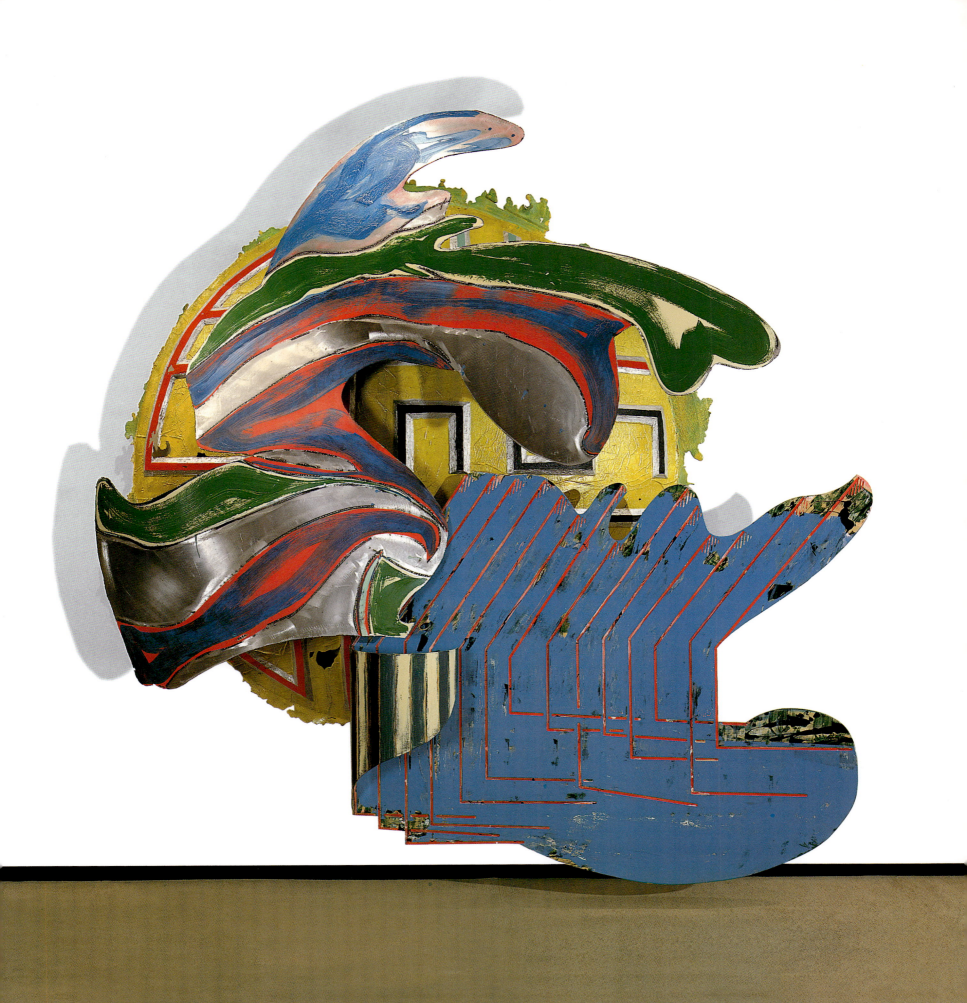

Donald Sultan
Forest Fire, February 27, 1984. (1984)

(American,
born 1951)

Latex, plaster,
and tar on vinyl
tile over wood
in four panels

97 × 97"
(246.4 × 246.4
cm)

1984.16

The seemingly disparate repertory of images portrayed in simple, reductive terms in Donald Sultan's work—from traditional, generic still lifes to gritty, contemporary urban scenes—he derives from the world around him. Factories, street lamps, and smokestacks in his paintings refer to the cluttered cityscape of lower Manhattan; flowers and fruits come from the more immediate environment of the home or the studio; while images of fires and explosions are plucked from newspapers.

Despite this multiplicity of sources, there is a certain logical relationship between Sultan's many subjects. For example, the forms of smokestacks evolved into those of flowers, cigarettes, or even the guns of a battleship. The evolution of choice is due, in part, to Sultan's manipulation and simplification of form to emphasize abstract qualities. By incorporating the date of completion into the title of each work, he keeps a sequential record of his imagery; hence, one can trace the evolution of a particular theme. *Forest Fire, February 27, 1984* is the fifth of nine paintings made over the course of a year and a half.

In contrast to Sultan's choice of simplified forms and straightforward approach toward his subject matter, his working method and materials are complicated. Instead of building up layers with paint, the artist constructs a support that hangs on the wall, jutting out into space, literally projecting the image. Beginning by gluing vinyl tiles—the sort used in offices or homes—to Masonite, Sultan affixes a panel to heavy plywood backing; in turn, the plywood is attached by steel rods to rectangular stretcher bars. The units are constructed in four-foot sections and then combined in groups of two or four. Once the work has been assembled, the tiles are covered with a layer of butyl rubber, a tar-like material used for roofing. After drawing on the tar-covered surface, Sultan then burns the images into the tiles with a blowtorch, gouges and scrapes away the surface, and fills the voids with tar or plaster before painting. Thus, the process appears to be allied more to printmaking than to traditional painting.

The force and seductiveness of destruction is a recurring theme in Sultan's work. While most of his "disaster" pieces focus on man-made catastrophes, *Forest Fire, February 27, 1984* is about the uncontrollable forces of nature. Here Sultan has created great tension between the tranquil silhouette of the totemic cypress trees in the foreground and the gestural flames of color that engulf the charred remains of branches in the distance. In this eerie scene, the viewer's vantage point is ambiguous. As the artist has pointed out, "I want my painting to be almost indecipherable, as if the viewer were inside the painting, in the fire, in a state of confusion. The fact that the image is hard to read is part of the painting."[1]

JW

1. Quoted by Gerritt Henry in "Dark Poetry." Artnews, vol. 86, no. 4 (April 1987). p. 105.

Wayne Thiebaud
Desserts. 1961

(American, born 1920)

Oil on canvas

24⅛ × 30⅛" (61.3 × 76.5 cm)

1984.13

Desserts, one of Wayne Thiebaud's first still-life paintings of common objects, was exhibited in his first solo exhibition in New York in 1962. This exhibition coincided with the emergence of a group of otherwise unrelated artists whose subject matter dealt with mass-produced images and objects. Although Thiebaud's hand-painted style—influenced in part by California figurative painters such as Richard Diebenkorn (pages 90, 264)—contrasted greatly with the mechanical silk-screen and stenciling methods of Roy Lichtenstein and Andy Warhol, his banal imagery was immediately likened to theirs and labeled "Pop."

Thiebaud's still lifes, which collectively represent the quintessential all-American diet of hot dogs, ice cream cones, cakes, and pies, celebrate the ordinary and commonplace. In many instances, the heavy impasto of brushstrokes mimics the luscious consistency of the depicted edibles. Painting from memory, in an improvisational manner, Thiebaud has said that he manipulates the consistency of the paint and the shape of the strokes to render the fluffy white foam of a lemon meringue pie or the rich, sugary frosting on a piece of cake: "I like to see what happens when the relationship between paint and the subject matter comes as close as I can get it—white, gooey, shiny, sticky oil paint [spread] out on top of a painted cake to become frosting. It is

playing with reality—making an illusion which grows out of an exploration of the properties of materials."[1]

A free-lance cartoonist and commercial artist in the 1940s, Thiebaud composes his paintings as if they are magazine layouts, using a white ground and cropping the space around the image to focus attention. In *Desserts* the composition is tightly organized and strongly suggests that everything has been arranged on a pastry shelf. The wedges and slices, enticingly laid out neatly on a receding plane, grow slightly smaller as they move upward, while the broad, blue gray strokes that form a border below the desserts evoke the cool chrome of a counter display. The artist has also carefully varied the size and shape of the pieces so that each has the irregular appearance of a section cut from a whole pie or cake—an illusion further enhanced by the different lengths and shapes of the negative spaces. Although this painting is representational in appearance, Thiebaud has brought all its abstract qualities to the surface.

Beyond perfection, these desserts appear as near caricatures of the objects themselves. Clearly meant to be seen and not eaten, these desserts do not whet our appetites but rather they tease us. By treating them with gentle irony and humor, Thiebaud affirms rather than denies the perpetual riches to be gained from the ordinary experience.

JW

1. *Quoted by Lucy Lippard in* Pop Art *(New York: Praeger, 1966), p. 153.*

239

Rosemarie Trockel
Untitled. 1986

(German, born
1952)

Ink on paper

11 × 8¼"
(28 × 21.1 cm)

1991.33

Highly original and idiosyncratic, Rosemarie
Trockel's art—drawings, paintings, sculptures, fabric pieces, and installations—eludes
categorization. In 1985 Trockel first achieved
recognition for her knitted pieces, fashioned
of machine-woven knit fabric and stretched
and mounted like canvas. The meaning of
her work is not presented in simple, straightforward terms; rather, it is the result of an intri-
cate visual strategy in which the combination
of seemingly unrelated images elicits multiple associations that reverberate on aesthetic,
social, political, and art-historical levels.

Since the early 1980s Trockel has worked
on paper to develop her ideas, many of which
later find their way into three-dimensional
works. On small sheets of paper she uses either
quickly sketched lines or rapid brushstrokes—
capturing the essence of a thought—or carefully rendered images that incorporate traditional techniques. She acknowledges Sigmar
Polke and the late Joseph Beuys (pages 64, 186,
259) as important influences, and strong reso-
nances of their work are apparent throughout
her oeuvre. Ranging from the banal to the
fantastic, Trockel's drawings, figures, and
imagery—borrowed from the sciences, con-
sumerism, the media, and everyday life—are
highly personal and can be viewed as ongoing
entries in a journal. In fact, in their changing
configurations the images form an archive that
the artist returns to over and over again. One
series was inspired by human evolution and
includes images of apes (page 282), skeletons,

skulls, and human heads, rendered alone or
integrated into a more abstract composition.

There is an inescapable obliqueness in
Trockel's work, a wavering between meaning
and nonmeaning. While the actual significance of a sign or juxtaposition of images is
likely to remain unknown, the quality of her
marks and the style of line invite the viewer
to guess and interpret her thoughts. *Untitled,*
1986, a delicate work on paper in PaineWebber's collection, resembles a modified ink-blot
drawing. A stemlike form divides the sheet,
with small appendages branching off to
either side. Surmounting this image is a biomorphic shape at once suggestive of ovaries
or kidneys. A similar shape appears below.
Shooting from the left side of this stalk is
a phallus; to the right is an orifice expelling
waste. Just above floats the familiar logo of
the wool industry which Trockel has appropriated before, most notably and ironically
in knitted pieces. A symbol of purity—100
percent virgin wool—it seems out of place
in this delicate abstraction, although con-
forming to the artist's sense of composition.

JW

241

Cy Twombly
Untitled. 1972

(American,
born 1928)

Rubber stamp,
crayon,
graphite,
and ink on
paper

61½ × 78½"
(156.2 × 199.4
cm)

1991.20

With Jasper Johns and Robert Rauschenberg, Cy Twombly belongs to the generation of contemporary American painters who began working at midcentury, the moment when Abstract Expressionism was emerging as the dominant national voice. In 1951, at the invitation of Rauschenberg, Twombly went to Black Mountain College in North Carolina, where he came into direct contact with the Abstract Expressionist painters Franz Kline and Robert Motherwell. While the influence of both artists is evident in Twombly's paintings from this period (page 282), a more refined, distinct gesture that particularly characterizes his work can also be detected.

By the late 1950s both Johns and Rauschenberg broke with their predecessors' highly personal mode of expression by using subject matter, such as numbers, flags, or found objects, that was considered impersonal. Rather than rejecting the subjective, however, Twombly exploited and celebrated it by merging personal memory and cultural tradition. In 1957, Twombly left the United States for Italy, a country rooted in classical civilization. Here, he entered into a painterly dialogue with Mediterranean culture, in particular its embodiment as Arcadia, an ideal existence of rural, pagan serenity commemorated by Virgil in his *Ecologues*. In looking back to this timeless, pastoral myth, Twombly idealizes the present. Using history, mythology, and poetry as his primary sources, he constructs records of the process of recalling the past. In both paintings and works on paper, line, placed against a white drawing sheet or ground, is the principal means of recording. Line appears as contour drawing,

gesture, and handwriting. In his work, Twombly has exploited the tradition of Surrealist automatic drawing that he inherited from the Abstract Expressionist artists. His use of language and the incorporation of writing into his paintings and drawings invites diaristic intimacy and links his art to a poetic as well as to a pictorial tradition.

The viewer can "read" a painting or drawing by Twombly, but the precise meaning of the work cannot be deciphered. Rather than depicting subjects, he evokes them through marks made on a field. Often, as in the large drawing *Untitled,* 1972, both figure and landscape are suggested through the use of color. In this case, cool blue suggests the haze of the Italian hills, while rosy pink evokes flesh. The accumulation of words, numbers, and forms indicates that this is a mental as well as natural landscape. Numbers are inscribed, suggesting measurement, duration, and repetition (as in "1702 Times" in the upper center). References both to Greek and Roman mythology include the names of the Greek warrior Ajax (center) and Venus (upper left), who also is personified by the outline of a shell. Words and forms are erased and obliterated by crayon and pencil, implying that the melancholic companion of remembrance is forgetting—the word *memory* itself emerges from the lower-left corner. The two rectangles on the left side of the composition are reminiscent of pages of text, but the scrawled phrases they contain are unreadable. These evocative, tantalizing fragments seem to rush past, as if a flood of memories has been released, leaving their traces on the paper.

MB

243

Cy Twombly
Untitled. (1981)

(American,
born 1928)

Various dimen-
sions and medi-
ums in seven
parts, left to
right:

a) pastel on
   paper, 27½ ×
   39½"
   (69.9 ×
   100.3 cm)
b) tempera on
   paper, 27½ ×
   39½"
   (69.9 ×
   100.3 cm)
c) tempera on
   paper, 27½ ×
   39½"
   (69.9 ×
   100.3 cm)
d) Paintstick,
   flat paint,
   crayon, and
   tempera on
   paper, 53½ ×
   59½"
   (135.9 ×
   151.1 cm)
e) Paintstick,
   crayon, and
   tempera
   on paper,
   22¼ × 30"
   (56.5 × 76.2
   cm)
f) Paintstick on
   paper,
   22¼ × 30"
   (56.5 × 76.2
   cm)
g) graphite on
   paper,
   22¼ × 30"
   (56.5 × 76.2
   cm)

1985.32 a–g

(Detail, left)

Drawing and painting are so closely related in Cy Twombly's art that any attempt at simple classification of his work by medium is difficult. His early paintings resemble drawings, with the white surface of the canvas akin to a page that has been scratched and inscribed. Conversely, the later works on paper acquire the characteristics of paintings, particularly in the artist's use of broad areas of color for expressive purposes. Twombly's ability to use mediums interchangeably and expand the potential of each process has resulted in the development of an artistic language that is both eloquent and unique.

During the summer of 1981, while staying in Bassano in Teverino, Italy, Twombly completed a group of drawings and paintings on paper. *Untitled,* 1981, composed of seven sheets each numbered by the artist, is the most complex of the eleven of these works, which were shown in New York at the Sperone Westwater Fischer gallery the following spring. Throughout his career, Twombly has created works on paper in groups, often linked by their titles to specific subjects (for example, *Delian Odes,* 1961; *Virgil,* 1973; and *Natural History,* 1974) or to geographical locations (*Captiva,* 1972–73). While *Untitled,* 1981, lacks the artist's characteristic handwriting and use of words, it unfolds a visual and formal narrative, which begins and ends with two single curved lines. Within these

brackets, one in blue pastel and the other in black pencil, the artist articulates a vivid range of marks, forms, and materials, and reveals a startling display of emotional states, from meditative calm to urgent expression. The mediums used include pencil, pastel, tempera, Paintstick, and flat paint, applied by the artist both with brushes and with his fingers.

The single blue line of the first drawing states the motif for the entire series and provides an armature that links the individual sheets and establishes the rhythm of the work. In the second and third sheets, the pastel line balloons into painted blue spheres. The series culminates in the middle sheet in a drawing that incorporates all the artistic mediums and colors (red, blue, green, black, and white) appearing in the other sheets. The physical energy of the line and the impulse of the brushstrokes and finger marks, which erupt in a torrent of marks and gestures borne on a foam of white paint, give the entire work its dynamic force. References to literature and the use of language in Twombly's earlier work seem to have been replaced here by the raw, surging power of nature. Relative order is restored in the next drawing, in which bands of red and green vibrate, and in the sixth sheet only the red band remains. Tranquility returns at the end, with a single pencil line completing the cycle.

MB

245

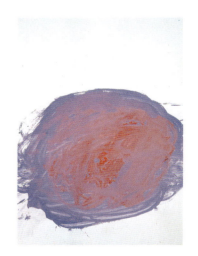

Andy Warhol
Cagney. (1962)

(American,
1928–1987)

Unique silk
screen on paper

30 × 40"
(76.2 × 101.6
cm)

1988.20

In August 1962 Andy Warhol made his first painting using the photo-silk-screen process, a technique that allowed for infinite replication of preexisting images and subsequently became synonymous with his art making. This working method also gave Warhol immediate access to an image bank of the commercial and popular press, and media icons instantly became his subject matter. Among his first endeavors is *Cagney,* a work on paper (there are five additional works of the same image, each unique, printed in 1964).[1]

Based on a publicity still from the 1931 film *The Public Enemy* starring James Cagney, Jean Harlow, and Joan Blondell, the actor is portrayed as a gangster moments before he is gunned down clutching two .38-caliber guns, his back against a wall; the barrel of a machine gun, at almost pointblank range, is aimed directly at him. The strong shadow of Cagney's silhouette creates a strong cinematic presence and the overall composition reveals that the entire film still is silk-screened rather than simply cropping the subject's face as Warhol chose to do in most of his silk-screened images.

Warhol, who most likely screened this work himself, considered *Cagney* to be a unique work on paper and not a print as it was neither editioned nor published. *The Kiss (Bela Lugosi),* 1963, based on a photographic still from another 1931 film, *Dracula,* is another example of such a work. Despite its mechanical form of reproduction, this work retains a handmade look—similar to his earlier paintings of comic-strip characters and newspaper advertisements—because of the irregular inking of the screen and uneven pressure in the printing. The blank streaks that run horizontally through the image indicate the areas where the ink did not come through the screen.

Attracted to movie stars and celebrities since his childhood, Warhol's voyeuristic approach to portraiture in the early 1960s focused primarily on youthful celebrities such as Troy Donahue, Warrren Beatty, and Elvis Presley. Working with publicity stills he collected and acquired, he gradually divested the images of any apparent emotion, often through serial repetition. One of Warhol's first subjects was Marilyn Monroe, who committed suicide shortly before Warhol began experimenting with silk-screening. Working from a publicity still of the actress from the 1953 film *Niagara,* Warhol reproduced her well-known face as both a single image and in repetition up to one hundred times.

Warhol's preoccupation with morbidity and mortality was made more explicit in a series of paintings, known as the Death and Disaster series, that Warhol also began in 1962 and continued through 1966. In these paintings Warhol reproduced gruesome newspaper photos of fiery car crashes, suicides, and, most obviously, the electric chair. Although Cagney, shown here moments before the impending violence, is not considered to be part of this series, it strongly resembles *Suicide* (1964), based on a newspaper image of a patient leaping to his fate from Bellevue Hospital.

Warhol perhaps found his most powerful statement when his fascination with celebrity clashed with death, typified by his paintings of Marilyn Monroe. In a similar vein, *Cagney* can be viewed as a synthesis of the celebrity portrait and disaster series.

JW

1. See Catalogue Raisonné, Feldman, Frayda, and Schellman, Jörg, eds. Andy Warhol Prints (New York: Abbeville Press, 1985).

Robin Winters
Ghent Drawings. 1986

(American,
born 1950)

Graphite on
coffee- and tea-
stained paper
(ninety sheets)
mounted on
paper in ten
parts

11⅝ × 8¼"
each sheet;
(29.5 × 22.2
cm; 34 × 24½"
overall
62.2 × 86.4
cm)

1987.8

In 1986 an unusual exhibition was organized in Ghent, Belgium, entitled *Chambre d'Amis (In Ghent There Is Always a Room for Albrecht Dürer)*. Fifty-one artists were invited to stay in the homes of the residents of Ghent and to make works of art there. The intention was to integrate art into everyday life and, more specifically, to force the interaction of the artist with society at the moment of creation. The artist would be removed from the isolation of the studio, and the mystery of the creative act would be revealed to the public.

Through his writings, performances, objects, and activities with Colab, an artists' cooperative that he cofounded, Robin Winters's art has always had a political edge. He has sought to break down the barriers between culture and society, to involve a broad public in his work, to encourage an awareness of alternative cultures, and to locate his work in a historical context. His paintings, drawings, and performances have been inspired by the subversive spirit of Dada and the expressive directness of Art Brut. Invited to participate in *Chambre d'Amis,* Winters elected to stay in the home of an art historian and to locate his installation in her library, thereby giving himself the opportunity to confront art history. He chose ninety volumes from the bookshelves and selected a photographic reproduction from each. He then drew the image, freehand, on vellum, while making two carbon copies of each drawing. The "originals" were placed in the source books and left for his hostess to discover, thereby extending the performance of

the work over a long period of time. The artist retained one set of copies, and the other set—drawn on paper that had been soaked in coffee and tea and folded and creased to appear aged—was mounted together in ten frames and exhibited at the Museum van Hedendaagse Kunst. The publicly exhibited version is now in PaineWebber's collection.

In this project, Winters raises a number of questions about the traditional criteria for judging works of art. Because all the images are secondhand and copied, the drawings have an awkward, naive quality, which makes establishing a critical hierarchy among them impossible. Notions of appropriation and originality are considered: since the work consists entirely of copies, is it original? (The answer must be yes.) The artist also asks us to examine how objects are placed into the continuum of history and how history itself is constructed. The books chosen covered a broad range of cultural topics and included *Art into Society—Society into Art; Arthur Rimbaud; The Styles of Ornament;* and *Histoire de l'art et lutte des classes* (titles of each source book are typed on the individual drawings). Monographs on famous artists were also selected, thereby posing questions about our belief in the authority of masterpieces. Some of the images Winters selected for reproduction, such as Picasso's Cubist sculpture *Glass of Absinthe* and Piero della Francesca's portrait of Federico da Montefeltro, are so well-known and enduring that even in his schematic versions, they retain their status as icons.

MB

251

Terry Winters
Conjugation. 1986

(American,
born 1949)

Oil on linen

85 × 110"
(215.9 × 279.4
cm)

1990.35

1. From a lecture given October 16, 1990, quoted by Lisa Phillips in Terry Winters, exhibition catalogue (New York: Whitney Museum of American Art and Harry N. Abrams, Inc., 1991), p. 23.

Like Brice Marden and Cy Twombly (pages 162, 242–47), Terry Winters has developed a highly personal vocabulary that is deliberately ambiguous but nevertheless capable of eloquent communication. In his art Winters employs imagery drawn from those systems that structure our understanding of the physical world, including anatomy, astronomy, biology, botany, and zoology, as well as those that give it form, such as architecture and tribal art. Cells, skeletons, crystals, and seeds suggest generation and decay and are metaphors for creativity itself. Modeled on the natural world, Winters's forms are refashioned by the act of painting or drawing, thereby integrating process and image in his work completely.

Conjugation was painted during a period for Winters of intense activity in drawing and printmaking, mediums he uses as deftly as painting. "I have tried to use all three media equally without any kind of hierarchy of importance," he has said.[1] During 1985–86, Winters completed *Folio,* a portfolio of eleven lithographs in PaineWebber's collection. In 1986 he produced *Schema,* a group of seventy-five works on paper (page 283), which were published together as a book. Both projects are a testament to Winters's interest in the development of discrete images in a series. They also demonstrate the importance in Winters's art of drawing, both for its expressive and descriptive properties. The resulting forms often look like phenomena observed through a microscope or telescope, thereby making an analogy with scientific processes and advances. Winters manipulates the relative scale of the images—cells are enlarged and planetary systems are reduced—and relocates them from an illustrational context to an artistic one in order to employ them for his own pictorial ends. At times he handles paint as if it were an organic material, building it up in thick granular formations and using its sensuousness to draw the viewer into an inner world that is both psychologically and emotionally resonant.

Conjugation shows what seems to be two joined cells described in three different states. The first, in the upper left, is a sketchy outline. The second, on the right, fills in the form with modeling in black and gray, and the third shows it in vivid color, luminous in the center and vibrant at the edges. Winters reveals the means of the painting's construction: forms are painted over but still visible, layers of paint are scraped away, surfaces are scumbled, an outline is traced but not filled in, paint is thinned and allowed to run down the canvas, and color has been applied and then reconsidered. The work is an analogy for creation: both the mental and the material processes of painting are described, and the organic forms and rich colors give the painting an erotic charge that is underscored by the title.

MB

253

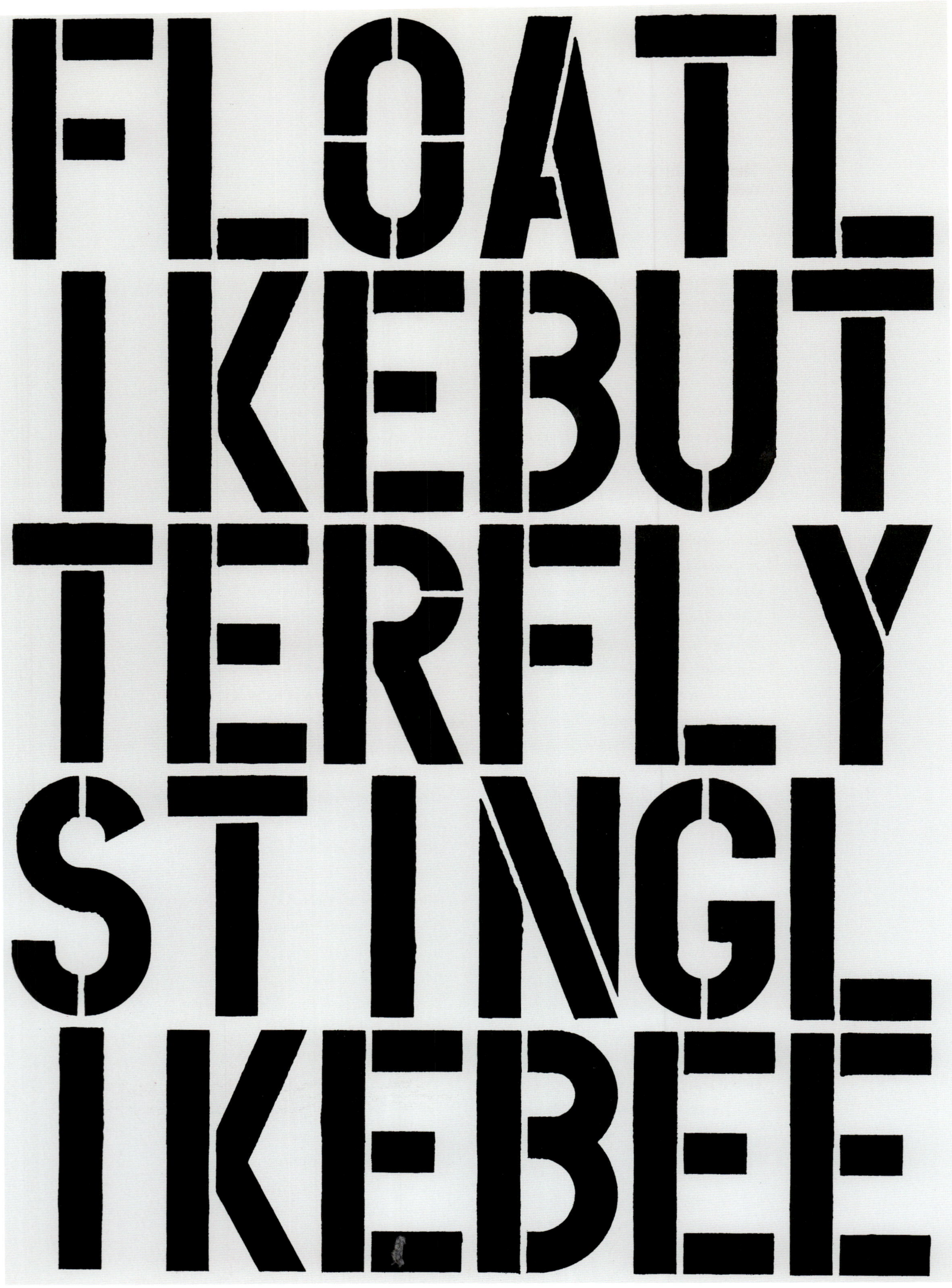

FLOATL
IKEBUT
TERFLY
STINGLI
IKEBEE

Christopher Wool
Untitled. 1988

(American, born
1955)

Alkyd and
Flashe on alu-
minum

84 × 60"
(213.4 × 152.4
cm)

1993.2

For Christopher Wool, the process is the image. He consistently uses mechanical devices, such as rubber stamps, stencils, or decorative rollers, that imitate wallpaper to create a repetitive image or pattern. In this methodical approach, Wool's paintings and works on paper call the nature of painting into question. Rather than uniformity, these works display variety, deliberate proof of his casual approach and of a homemade quality. Wool began his work with allover paint drips or splatters, which resemble Jackson Pollock paintings, and progressed through several patterns (page 284) and motifs such as flowers and leaves before using text as his subject.

Wool's choice of typography is, not surprisingly, that of generic, commercially available stencils. Over a ground of white Flashe on aluminum, Wool applies black alkyd, creating a hard, opaque surface on which the letters seem never completely dry. There is a directness in these works that, regardless of the phrase or word, forces the viewer to reckon not only with the image but with the surface of the work itself.

As Wool had used a rubber roller, widely available in any hardware store, as a pre-existing source for his paintings, he similarly takes his words from movies, books, or advertisements. Using a grid to position the letters into an allover abstract pattern, he shortens the customary space between the lines of text so that the letters form vertical as well as horizontal relationships. In some instances, the line divisions break the word without regard for syllables, making the text difficult to read and thus encouraging the viewer to see the painting first as an abstract cluster of letters. The stark quality of black type on a white aluminum ground, in addition to the tight composition, has the eye-grabbing, graphic quality employed in tabloid headlines. It also creates the sensation of an LED sign releasing letters, one at a time, word by word, announcing the news—good and bad. As in his earlier abstract works, Wool's process is evident with traces left of his gesture and technique: the letters are never perfectly stenciled, and imperfections such as paint drips are allowed to remain.

Despite their familiarity, these works appear at first appear cryptic. *Untitled,* 1988, among his first group of text paintings, demonstrates Wool's appropriation of Muhammad Ali's popular catchphrase "float like a butterfly, sting like a bee," and "transforms it into a pictorial pattern that tampers with the original meaning/logic of the sentence structure."[1] In a similar vein, Wool also borrowed the phrase "sell the house, sell the car, sell the kids," from a scene in Francis Ford Coppola's film *Apocalypse Now.* As one critic wrote, "Notwithstanding appearances to the contrary, Wool's art refuses to deliver a message, making meaning dependent on the spectator's psychological and cultural associations."[2]

JW

1. Joshua Decter in "Christopher Wool," Arts Magazine 63, no. 6 (February 1989) p. 104.
2. Lynne Cooke in Carnegie International 1991 (volume 2), exhibition catalogue (Pittsburgh and New York: The Carnegie Museum of Art and Rizzoli International Publications, 1992), p. 20.

255

Additional works

John Ahearn
(American, born 1951)

Margie. (1980–81)
Acrylic on cast plaster
24 × 16½ × 8"
(61 × 41.9 × 20.3 cm)
1984.12

Stephan Balkenhol
(German, born 1957)

Figurensäule Mann [Column Figure Man]. (1993)
Carved painted wawa wood.
58¼ × 8 × 8¾"
(147.9 × 20.3 × 22.2 cm)
1993.42

The following section is arranged alphabetically by artist and chronologically for the works of each artist. Dates or portions of dates not inscribed on the work by the artist appear in parentheses. For cast sculpture, the cast number and size of the edition are indicated where appropriate. Dimensions are given in inches and centimeters, height preceding width and followed by depth in the case of sculptures and constructions. Sheet sizes are given for works on paper, unless otherwise specified. Dimensions of works in artists' frames include the frame size. The accession number indicates the year in which a work was acquired, for example, 1984.12 is the number assigned to the twelfth work acquired in 1984.

Frank Auerbach
(British, born Germany 1931)

Study for *Primrose Hill, High Summer.* 1959
Colored chalk on paper
8¼ × 11"
(21 × 27.9 cm)
1988.29

Stephan Balkenhol
(German, born 1957)

Figurensäule Frau [Column Figure Woman]. (1993)
Carved painted wawa wood.
58⅜ × 8½ × 7¾"
(148.3 × 21.6 × 19.7 cm)
1993.43

258

Frank Auerbach
(British, born Germany 1931)

J.Y.M. Seated. 1981
Chalk and charcoal on paper
30⅛ × 22⅞"
(76.5 × 58.1 cm)
1986.1

Georg Baselitz
(German, born 1938)

Peitschenfrau [Whip Woman]. 1964
Pen and brush and ink on paper
15⅞ × 16½"
(40.3 × 41.9 cm)
1990.34

Jo Baer
(American, born 1929)

Untitled (Korean). 1962
Oil on canvas
72 × 72"
(182.9 × 182.9 cm)
1992.32

Georg Baselitz
(German, born 1938)

Untitled (Hero). 1966
Brush and ink and graphite on paper
13½ × 8½"
(34.3 × 21.6 cm)
1990.43

Georg Baselitz
(German, born 1938)

Untitled, 12.VI.87. 1987
Colored crayons and
graphite on paper
25⅞ × 19¾"
(65.7 × 50.2 cm)
1988.1

Glen Baxter
(British, born 1944)

The Pleasure Seekers. 1987
Colored crayons and
ink on paper
79 × 59½"
(200.7 × 151.1 cm)
1987.11

Georg Baselitz
(German, born 1938)

Untitled, 2.V.89. 1989
Charcoal and graphite
on paper
30 × 23"
(76.2 × 58.4 cm)
1990.28

Billy Al Bengston
(American, born 1934)

Ventana Dracula. (1972)
Acrylic on canvas
48 × 48"
(121.9 × 121.9 cm)
1973.7

Georg Baselitz
(German, born 1938)

Untitled, 29.I.91. 1991
Gouache, pastel, and
ink on paper
39¼ × 27⅝"
(99.7 × 70.2 cm)
1992.2

Jake Berthot
(American, born 1939)

Nick's Door. 1985–86.
Oil on gessoed hollow
wood door in artist's frame
80 × 36"
(203.2 × 91.4 cm)
1986.18

Georg Baselitz
(German, born 1938)

Untitled, 19.X.91. 1991
Graphite, pastel, and
watercolor on paper
24 × 34"
(61 × 86.4 cm)
1992.12

Joseph Beuys
(German, 1921–1986)

Hirschkuh. (c. 1950)
Collage, gold paint, egg
tempera, watercolor, and
brown paper tape on paper
mounted on glass and metal
12½ × 15½"
(31.8 × 39.4 cm)
1988.35

Domenico Bianchi
(Italian, born 1955)

Untitled. 1984
Watercolor, encaustic,
and oil on burlap
96½ × 84½"
(245.1 × 214.6 cm)
1985.11

Michael Byron
(American, born 1954)

Water. (1983)
Oil on wood
15½ × 30"
(39.4 × 76.2 cm)
1984.45

Richard Bosman
(American, born 1944
India)

Assassin. (1981)
Oil on canvas
85⅛ × 67⅛"
(216.2 × 170.5 cm)
1984.7

Michael Byron
(American, born 1954)

Judas Goat Boy of Love.
1986
Oil on plaster on wood
22⅜ × 19⅜"
(56.8 × 49.2 cm)
1986.49

260

Troy Brauntuch
(American, born 1954)

Untitled. 1981
White pencil on black
paper
44 × 30"
(111.8 × 76.2 cm)
1981.12

Miriam Cahn
(Swiss, born 1949)

Schiff [Boat]. 1982
Charcoal on vellum
34½ × 58" (irreg.)
(87.6 × 147.3 cm)
1986.34

Roger Brown
(American, born 1941)

**Swamp Rose Mallow a
View from Afar.** (1980)
Oil on canvas
72 × 48"
(182.9 × 121.9 cm)
1980.1

Anthony Caro
(British, born 1924)

Odalisque. 1985
Bronze
20 × 33 × 16"
(50.8 × 83.8 × 40.6 cm)
1986.28

Bruno Ceccobelli
(Italian, born 1952)

Virginia. 1985
Oil, tempera, and
sulfur on paper
22¼ × 30¼"
(56.5 × 76.8 cm)
1985.37

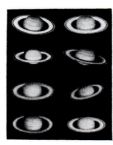

Vija Celmins
(American, born Latvia
1939)

Drawing Saturn. 1982
Graphite on acrylic
ground on paper
14 × 11"
(35.6 × 27.9 cm)
1983.11

Vija Celmins
(American, born Latvia
1939)

Galaxy #1 (Coma Berenices).
1973
Graphite on acrylic
ground on paper
12¼ × 15¼"
(31.1 × 38.7 cm)
1975.2

Louisa Chase
(American, born 1951)

Mist in Mountains. 1982
Oil on canvas
84 × 108"
(213.4 × 274.3 cm)
1982.8

Vija Celmins
(American, born Latvia
1939)

Galaxy #4 (Coma Berenices).
1974
Graphite on acrylic
ground on paper
12¼ × 15¼"
(31.1 × 38.7 cm)
1975.4

Louisa Chase
(American, born 1951)

Saint Joan. 1983–84
Oil on canvas
96 × 84"
(243.8 × 213.4 cm)
1984.14

Vija Celmins
(American, born Latvia
1939)

Galaxy #2 (Coma Berenices).
1974–75
Graphite on acrylic
ground on paper
12¼ × 15¼"
(31.1 × 38.7 cm)
1975.3

Sandro Chia
(Italian, born 1946)

Free Elaboration. (1981)
Oil, colored chalk, pastel,
and charcoal on paper
69⅛ × 58⅜"
(175.6 × 148.3 cm)
1981.13

Francesco Clemente
(Italian, born 1953)

Non Androgino. (1979)
Graphite and gouache on
paper mounted on canvas
27½ × 70⅞"
(69.9 × 180 cm)
1986.11

Greg Colson
(American, born 1956)

El Paso. 1990
Enamel, ink, wood, metal,
found objects, saw, picture
frame, and ink stamp
60 × 54 × 2½" overall
(152.4 × 137.2 × 6.4 cm)
1991.14

Francesco Clemente
(Italian, born 1953)

**Earth (from the series *The
Four Elements*).** (1982)
Pastel on paper
24 × 18"
(61 × 45.8 cm)
1983.4

Bruce Conner
(American, born 1933)

Untitled Drawing. 1972
Pen and ink on paper
11 × 10¾"
(27.9 × 27.3 cm)
1991.36

262

Francesco Clemente
(Italian, born 1953)

Self-Portrait. (1984)
Oil on silver leaf on canvas
70⅞ × 82¾"
(180 × 210.2 cm)
1985.17

Bruce Conner
(American, born 1933)

Sampler. 1991
Pen and ink on paper
22 × 21⅞"
(55.9 × 55.6 cm)
1991.37

Chuck Close
(American, born 1940)

Large Mark Pastel. 1978
Pastel and watercolor on
washed paper mounted
on paper
55¾ × 43¼"
(141.6 × 110 cm)
1991.30

Alan Cote
(American, born 1937)

Approaching. 1983–84
Acrylic on canvas
100¼ × 90"
(250 × 228.6 cm)
1985.14

Gregory Crane
(American, born 1951)

Circular Valley near Big Pink.
(1984)
Oil and tempera on linen
51 × 141"
(129.5 × 358.1 cm)
1985.27

Walter Dahn
(German, born 1954)

Untitled. 1985
Acrylic on paper
11½ × 8¼"
(29.2 × 21 cm)
1987.14

Enzo Cucchi
(Italian, born 1950)

**Leone dei Mari Mediterranea
[Lion of the Mediterranean
Sea].** 1979–80
Oil on canvas mounted
on burlap
83½ × 82"
(212.1 × 208.3 cm)
1981.6

Walter Dahn
(German, born 1954)

Untitled. 1985
Gouache on paper
7⅛ × 7½"
(18.1 × 19.1 cm)
1987.15

Enzo Cucchi
(Italian, born 1950)

Untitled. 1983
Conté crayon on paper
25 × 19⅝"
(63.5 × 50 cm)
1983.11

Walter Dahn
(German, born 1954)

Untitled. 1986
Paper collage and acrylic
on canvas
82½ × 63"
(210 × 160 cm)
1988.42

Enzo Cucchi
(Italian, born 1950)

Untitled. 1986
Charcoal, crayon, and
ink on paper
6¼ × 18⅛"
(15.9 × 46 cm)
1986.38

Walter Dahn
(German, born 1954)

Untitled. 1988
Acrylic on paper
10 × 9½"
(25.4 × 24.1 cm)
1989.31

John Davies
(British, born 1946)

Man with Two Poles. 1975
Pastel, chalk, and ink
on paper
16 × 15½"
(40.6 × 39.4 cm)
1987.31

Jane Dickson
(American, born 1952)

Witness (J.A.). 1991
Oil and Rolotex on canvas
70 × 35"
(177.8 × 88.9 cm)
1992.3

Gianni Dessi
(Italian, born 1955)

Canto Profondo. 1984
Oil and charcoal on
wood and burlap
90½ × 74½"
(229.9 × 189.2 cm)
1986.8

Richard Diebenkorn
(American, 1922–1993)

Two Nudes Standing. 1965
Graphite and brush and
ink on paper
17 × 12½"
(43.2 × 31.8 cm)
1989.2

264

Gianni Dessi
(Italian, born 1955)

Misura. 1985
Oil and gouache on paper
12¾ × 8¾"
(32.4 × 22.2 cm)
1986.9

Richard Diebenkorn
(American, 1922–1993)

Untitled. 1985
Gouache, graphite, and
paper collage on paper
39⅜ × 26⅛"
(100 × 66.4 cm)
1987.26

David Deutsch
(American, born 1943)

Square Pond. (1984–85)
Acrylic, gouache, and
pumice on paper mounted
on canvas
90⅛ × 162¾"
(228.9 × 413.4 cm)
1986.7

Jean Dubuffet
(French, 1901–1985)

Memoration XX. 1978
Black felt-tip pen and
paper collage on paper
20 × 27½"
(50.8 × 69.9 cm)
1979.2

Carroll Dunham
(American, born 1949)

Large Shape with Bands.
1989
Oil and graphite on canvas
91 × 126½"
(231.1 × 321.3 cm)
1990.49

Eric Fischl
(American, born 1948)

Coney Island. 1981
Oil wash on paper
50 × 60"
(127 × 152.4 cm)
1986.45

Barbara Ess
(American, born 1948)

Untitled. 1988
Monochrome color
photograph, 4/4
50 × 71"
(127 × 180.3 cm)
1988.46

Eric Fischl
(American, born 1948)

Untitled. 1984
Watercolor on paper
34⅞ × 46"
(88.6 × 116.9 cm)
1985.36

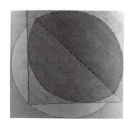

William Fares
(American, born 1942)

Circular Ruins. 1974
Acrylic on canvas
66 × 66"
(167.6 × 167.6 cm)
1974.4

Janet Fish
(American, born 1938)

Chinoiserie. 1984
Oil on canvas
42 × 132"
(106.7 × 335.3 cm)
1985.9

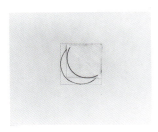

William Fares
(American, born 1942)

Untitled (study for *Circular Ruins*). 1974
Graphite and paper
collage on paper
22½ × 28½"
(57.2 × 72.4 cm)
1974.7

Joel Fisher
(American, born 1947)

Untitled (Drawing No. 12).
(c. 1982)
Graphite and found fiber
on handmade paper
6⅛ × 6" (irreg.)
(15.2 × 15.2 cm)
1989.27

Joel Fisher
(American, born 1947)

Untitled (Drawing No. 1).
(1988–89)
Graphite and found fiber
on handmade paper
6 × 6¼" (irreg.)
(15.2 × 15.9 cm)
1989.26

Lucian Freud
(British, born Germany
1922)

Self-Portrait. (1974)
Watercolor and graphite
on paper
13⅛ × 9½"
(33.3 × 24.1 cm)
1991.22

Joel Fisher
(American, born 1947)

Untitled (Drawing No. 26).
(1988–89)
Graphite and found fiber
on handmade paper
6 × 5¾" (irreg.)
(15.2 × 14.6 cm)
1989.28

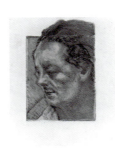

Lucian Freud
(British, born Germany
1922)

Cerith. (1989)
Pastel over etching on
paper
13¾ × 10¼" (irreg.)
(34.9 × 26 cm)
1989.25

266

Günther Förg
(German, born 1952)

Pinakothek, München.
(1983–86)
Black-and-white photo-
graph in artist's frame
110¾ × 51¾"
(281.3 × 131.5 cm)
1988.14

Giuseppe Gallo
(Italian, born 1954)

**Caino e Abele [Cain and
Abel].** (1985)
Oil and wax on canvas
with metal element
95⅝ × 106¼"
(242.9 × 269.9 cm)
1986.22

Günther Förg
(German, born 1952)

Untitled. 1987
Ink and gouache on
paper in ten parts
12½ × 9½" each
(31.8 × 24.1 cm)
1987.33a–j

Jedd Garet
(American, born 1955)

Black Figures #1. 1979
Pastel and acrylic on paper
50 × 38"
(127 × 96.5 cm)
1983.1

Jedd Garet
(American, born 1955)

Picture. 1981
Acrylic on canvas
73 × 57"
(185.4 × 144.8 cm)
1981.11

Frances Cohen Gillespie
(American, born 1939)

Lapis Lazuli. 1983
Oil on canvas
72 × 60"
(182.9 × 152.4 cm)
1984.1

Jedd Garet
(American, born 1955)

Breathing Water. 1982
Acrylic on canvas
73 × 57 × 3"
(185.4 × 144.8 × 7.6 cm)
1983.7

Lawrence Gipe
(American, born 1962)

Study #7 (Fin de Siècle).
1990
Oil on paper
87⅛ × 64"
(236.2 × 177.8 cm)
1990.51

Gilbert & George
(Gilbert, Italian, born
1943; George, British,
born 1942)

Sad. 1980
Postcards mounted on
paper
41¼ × 32¼"
(104.8 × 81.9 cm)
1987.21

Joe Goode
(American, born 1937)

Bed. 1967
Graphite and colored
pencils on paper
20 × 25"
(50.8 × 63.5 cm)
1992.4

Gilbert & George
(Gilbert, Italian, born
1943; George, British,
born 1942)

Winter Heads. 1982
Photo-piece: 20 black-and-
white photographs hand-
colored with ink and dyes,
mounted and framed
95 × 98¾" overall
(241.3 × 250.8 cm)
1983.15

Philip Guston
(American, born Canada,
1913–1980)

Midnight. 1953
Brush and ink on paper
11¾ × 17¾"
(29.9 × 45.1 cm)
1986.31

Philip Guston
(American, born Canada, 1913–1980)

Artist in His Studio. 1969
Charcoal on paper
17¾ × 23⅞"
(45.1 × 60.6 cm)
1986.20

Edward Henderson
(American, born 1951)

Untitled. 1985
Oil, ink, and watercolor on paper
12 × 9"
(30.5 × 22.9 cm)
1985.45

Richard Hamilton
(British, born 1922)

People Again. 1969
Crayon, gouache, and collage on photograph
12¼ × 20"
(31.1 × 50.8 cm)
1991.17

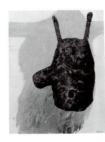

Edward Henderson
(American, born 1951)

Untitled. 1985
Oil, ink, and watercolor on paper
12 × 9"
(30.5 × 22.9 cm)
1985.47

268

Jane Hammond
(American, born 1950)

Untitled (254, 164, 151, 80, 5, 21, 39, 193, 264, 44).
1989
Oil on linen
76 × 60⅛"
(193 × 152.7 cm)
1990.11

Edward Henderson
(American, born 1951)

Untitled. 1985
Oil, ink, and watercolor on paper
12 × 9"
(30.5 × 22.9 cm)
1985.48

Edward Henderson
(American, born 1951)

Untitled. 1984
Oil, ink, and gouache on paper
12 × 9"
(30.5 × 22.9 cm)
1985.46

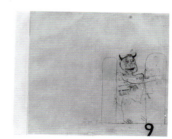

David Hockney
(British, born 1937)

To Queens, New York. 1961
Graphite, colored crayons, rubber stamp, and oil on paper
17⅞ × 21⅞"
(45.4 × 55.6 cm)
1991.25

Roni Horn
(American, born 1955)

Distant Double 2.26x and 2.26y. 1989
Powdered pigment and varnish on paper, in two parts
28¼ × 29¾" each
(71.8 × 75.6 cm)
1989.63a–b

Yvonne Jacquette
(American, born 1934)

Tokyo Billboards II. 1985
Oil on canvas
85⅛ × 100 1/16"
(216.2 × 254.2 cm)
1986.21

Bryan Hunt
(American, born 1947)

Cloak of Lorenzo. 1981
Bronze on cast concrete base, 2/4
sculpture:
53¼ × 35½ × 36½"
(135.3 × 90.2 × 92.7 cm);
base: 37 × 26 × 26"
(94 × 66 × 66 cm)
1981.8

Bill Jensen
(American, born 1945)

December 1976. 1976
Oil on linen
20 × 18"
(50.8 × 45.7 cm)
1984.47

Yvonne Jacquette
(American, born 1934)

Ferry near Battery Park (Dusk). 1981
Oil on canvas
76 × 62"
(193 × 157.5 cm)
1982.4

Bill Jensen
(American, born 1945)

Untitled XVII. 1991
Ink on paper
19¾ × 25⅝"
(50.2 × 65.1 cm)
1992.15

Yvonne Jacquette
(American, born 1934)

Maine Yankee Nuclear Plant V. 1983
Pastel on paper
50⅛ × 42½"
(127.3 × 108 cm)
1983.31

Jasper Johns
(American, born 1930)

Untitled. 1990
Watercolor on paper
38⅝ × 25⅜"
(98.1 × 64.5 cm)
1991.18

Roberto Juarez
(American, born 1952)

Three Birds. (1984)
Acrylic on canvas in
artist's frame
86 × 58"
(218.4 × 147.3 cm)
1985.1

Anselm Kiefer
(German, born 1945)

A.D. (1989)
Chalk and entrails on
treated lead in artist's steel
frame
95⅛ × 51⅞"
(243.1 × 131.8 cm)
1989.32
The Museum of Modern
Art, New York. Fractional
gift of PaineWebber
Group, Inc.

Roberto Juarez
(American, born 1952)

Rattle. 1984
Acrylic, oilstick, and canvas collage on linen
78 × 102"
(198.1 × 259.1 cm)
1985.2

Martin Kippenberger
(German, born 1953)

Untitled. 1989
Acrylic, graphite, ink, and
watercolor on paper
10⅞ × 8¼" (irreg.)
(27.6 × 21 cm)
1989.29

270

R. L. Kaplan
(American, born 1940)

Summit I. 1983
Oil on canvas
48 × 74"
(121.9 × 188 cm)
1984.9

Martin Kippenberger
(German, born 1953)

Untitled. 1989
Acrylic, graphite, ink, and
watercolor on paper
11⅝ × 8¼" (irreg.)
(29.5 × 21 cm)
1989.30

Jon Kessler
(American, born 1957)

Under Venice. 1987
Steel, aluminum, Plexiglas,
fluorescent lights, motors,
photo mural, glass, Mura-
no glass vases, Fresnel lens,
and lacquer paint
84 × 121 × 32"
(213.4 × 307.3 × 81.3 cm)
1988.26

R. B. Kitaj
(American, born 1932)

The Poet Writing. (1982)
Charcoal on green paper
30½ × 27½"
(77.5 × 69.9 cm)
1986.2

Guillermo Kuitca
(Argentine, born 1961)

Nordrhein. 1992
Mixed mediums on
foam mattress
78 × 78 × 3½" (irreg.)
(198 × 198 × 8.9 cm)
1992.31

Roy Lichtenstein
(American, born 1923)

Archaic Head VI. 1988
Patinated bronze, 1/6
57⅞ × 18 × 10"
(147 × 45.7 × 25.4 cm)
1989.38

Christopher LeBrun
(British, born 1951)

Bay. 1988–89
Oil on canvas
61 × 53⅛"
(155 × 134.9 cm)
1989.59

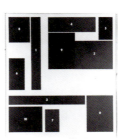

Thomas Locher
(German, born 1956)

1-11. (1987)
Paper collage on paper-
board mounted on paper-
board
55⅛ × 47⅛"
(140 × 119.7 cm)
1987.32

Mark Lere
(American, born 1950)

**You Are the Space That You
Occupy.** 1982
Graphite and watercolor
on vellum
38¼ × 30½"
(97.2 × 77.5 cm)
1986.19

Andrew Lord
(American, born 1950)

**Curves (from the series *Jug
and Dish in the Afternoon*).**
1984
Glazed earthenware in
two parts
jug: 27¼ × 19 × 14¼"
(69.2 × 48.3 × 36.2 cm)
dish: 5 × 24⅛ × 7"
(12.7 × 61.3 × 17.8 cm)
1984.17a-b

Barry Le Va
(American, born 1941)

Centers and Sections. 1975
Ink on paper
42 × 84"
(106.7 × 213.4 cm)
1976.3

Markus Lüpertz
(German, born 1941)

**Untitled (Mann in Anzug
[Man in Suit]).** 1976
Charcoal, gouache crayon,
and graphite on paper
38 × 25¾"
(96.5 × 65.4 cm)
1987.18

Markus Lüpertz
(German, born 1941)

Untitled. (1979–80)
Gouache with charcoal and
graphite on paper
19¾ × 27½"
(50.2 × 69.9 cm)
1986.39

Brice Marden
(American, born 1938)

Untitled. 1971
Graphite and wax on paper
22⅜ × 30½"
(56.8 × 77.5 cm)
1988.13

Mark Luyten
(Belgian, born 1955)

Intermezzo. (1987)
Oil, sand, crayon, and
postcard collage on paper
59 × 39"
(149.9 × 99.1 cm)
1987.22

Brice Marden
(American, born 1938)

Untitled. 1991
Ink on paper
25⅞ × 34⅜"
(65.7 × 87.3 cm)
1993.1

272

John McLaughlin
(American, 1898–1976)

Untitled #20. (1966)
Oil and acrylic on canvas
48 × 60"
(121.9 × 152.4 cm)
1973.8

Louisa Matthiasdottir
(Icelander, born 1917)

Sheep with Pink House.
(1984)
Oil on canvas
38 × 52"
(96.5 × 132.1 cm)
1984.18

Robert Mangold
(American, born 1937)

**Study for Four Color Frame
Painting #4 (B).** 1984
Acrylic and graphite on
paper, four sheets
mounted on canvasboard
40 × 28"
(101.6 × 180.3 cm)
1988.30

Meuser
(German, born 1947)

Untitled. 1986
Graphite, paper collage,
and oil on cardboard
9⅝ × 12½" (irreg.)
(24.5 × 31.8 cm)
1988.38

Meuser
(German, born 1947)

Untitled. 1987
Graphite and oil on card-
board
9⅛ × 12⅝"
(23.2 × 32.1 cm)
1988.36

Yasumasa Morimura
(Japanese, born 1953)

**Daughter of Art History:
Princess B.** 1990
Color photograph var-
nished and mounted on
board in two panels in
artist's frame, 2/5
89¼ × 71⅝"
(226.7 × 181.9 cm)
1991.21

Meuser
(German, born 1947)

Untitled. 1987
Graphite and oil on card-
board
9⅛ × 12⅝"
(23.2 × 32.1 cm)
1988.37

Malcolm Morley
(British, born 1931)

Kite. (1984)
Watercolor on paper
43⅝ × 52"
(110.8 × 132.1 cm)
1988.17

273

Melissa Miller
(American, born 1951)

Territory. 1983
Oil on linen
69 × 116"
(175.3 × 294.7 cm)
1983.21

Jill Moser
(American, born 1956)

Trace. (1986)
Graphite, oilstick, and
conté crayon on mylar
42¼ × 69½"
(107.3 × 176.5 cm)
1987.1

Gerry Morehead
(American, born 1949)

Above Eight Rivers. 1990
Acrylic, tempera, and
gouache on board
40 × 89"
(101.6 × 226.1 cm)
1991.16

James Nares
(American, born England
1953)

Untitled. 1986
Oil on paper
23⅞ × 17⅞"
(60.6 × 45.4 cm)
1987.30a

James Nares
(American, born England
1953)

Untitled. 1986
Oil on paper
23⅞ × 17⅞"
(60.6 × 45.4 cm)
1987.30b

Harry Nickelson
(American, born 1956)

John Tunnard. 1985
Tempera, ink, and gesso
on paper
40 × 45"
(101.6 × 114.3 cm)
1985.42

James Nares
(American, born England
1953)

Untitled. 1986
Oil on paper
23⅞ × 17⅞"
(60.6 × 45.4 cm)
1987.30c

Harry Nickelson
(American, born 1956)

Ignace Paderewski. 1985
Tempera, ink, gesso, and
colored crayons on paper
40 × 45"
(101.6 × 114.3 cm)
1985.43

James Nares
(American, born England
1953)

Untitled. 1986
Oil on paper
23⅞ × 17⅞"
(60.6 × 45.4 cm)
1987.30d

Harry Nickelson
(American, born 1956)

Untitled. 1985
Tempera, ink, gesso, and
colored crayons on paper
53 × 45"
(134.6 × 114.3 cm)
1985.44

James Nares
(American, born England
1953)

Untitled. 1986
Oil on paper
23⅞ × 17⅞"
(60.6 × 45.4 cm)
1987.30e

Harry Nickelson
(American, born 1956)

Quahna Parker. 1986
Tempera, gesso, colored
crayons, and ink on paper
53 × 58"
(134.6 × 147.3 cm)
1986.48

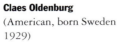

Claes Oldenburg
(American, born Sweden
1929)

**Proposed Colossal Monument
to Replace the Nelson Column
in Trafalgar Square—
Gearshift in Motion.** 1966
Crayon, watercolor, and
paper collage on paper
15¾ × 22¾"
(40 × 57.8 cm)
1987.10

A. R. Penck
(German, born 1939)

Venedig [Venice]. 1980
Gouache on paper
14¼ × 18¾"
(36.2 × 47.6 cm)
1986.41

Claes Oldenburg
(American, born Sweden
1929)

**Proposed Events for *Il Corso
del Coltello*.** 1984
Graphite, crayon, and
watercolor on paper
40 × 30"
(101.6 × 76.2 cm)
1985.13

A. R. Penck
(German, born 1939)

Untitled. 1981
Ink and wash on paper
13 × 16⅛" (irreg.)
(33 × 41 cm)
1986.40

275

Tom Otterness
(American, born 1952)

Creation Myth. 1986
Graphite and watercolor
on paper
18 × 24"
(45.7 × 61 cm)
1987.5

Katherine Porter
(American, born 1941)

To Victor Jara. 1980
Oil on canvas
87¼ × 103¾"
(221.6 × 263.5 cm)
1981.9

Mimmo Paladino
(Italian, born 1948)

Untitled. 1983
Gouache and stucco on
paper
26 × 38¾"
(66 × 98.4 cm)
1984.8

Katherine Porter
(American, born 1941)

Spring. 1984
Oil on canvas mounted
on wood
42 × 77"
(106.7 × 195.6 cm)
1984.42

Katherine Porter
(American, born 1941)

Untitled. 1984
Tempera on rice paper
41 × 76"
(104.1 × 193 cm)
1984.43

Edda Renouf
(American, born Mexico
1943)

New York Sound Drawing #1.
1977
Graphite and colored
chalk on paper
30½ × 28½"
(77.5 × 72.4 cm)
1978.3

Harvey Quaytman
(American, born 1937)

Nuncio. 1986
Pigment, acrylic medium,
and rust on canvas
36 × 36"
(91.4 × 91.4 cm)
1986.44

Edda Renouf
(American, born Mexico
1943)

Visible Sound III. 1978
Acrylic on linen
84½ × 84½"
(214.6 × 214.6 cm)
1978.2

276

Ed Rainey
(American, born 1954)

Successful Farming No. 6.
1985
Colored pencil, acrylic,
charcoal, graphite, and ink
with rubber stamp on
paper
52 × 52"
(132.1 × 132.1 cm)
1985.15

Sam Reveles
(American, born 1958)

Skull Rack (Spanish). 1991
Oil on canvas
66 × 84"
(167.6 × 213.4 cm)
1992.7

Robert Rauschenberg
(American, born 1925)

Sleeping Sweeper. 1988
Acrylic, silk screen, and
enamel on mirrored
anodized aluminum in two
panels
96¾ × 120¾" overall
(245.8 × 306.7 cm)
1989.43

Gerhard Richter
(German, born 1932)

18. Okt. 92. 1992
Watercolor on paper
11¾ × 15¾"
(29.9 × 39.8 cm)
1993.36

Gerhard Richter
(German, born 1932)

22. Okt. 92. 1992
Watercolor on paper
11¾ × 15¾"
(29.9 × 39.8 cm)
1993.37

Edward Ruscha
(American, born 1937)

Accordion Fold with Vaseline Stains. 1972
Gunpowder and petroleum jelly on paper
11½ × 29"
(29.2 × 73.6 cm)
1973.5

Susan Rothenberg
(American, born 1945)

Untitled. 1979
Acrylic, gesso, and graphite on paper
50 × 38" (irreg.)
(127 × 96.5 cm)
1984.39

Edward Ruscha
(American, born 1937)

Fine Wires. 1972
Gunpowder and pastel on paper
11½ × 29"
(29.2 × 73.7 cm)
1972.6

Susan Rothenberg
(American, born 1945)

1, 2, 3, 4, 5, 6. 1988
Graphite, charcoal, and oil on paper in six parts
60 × 20" each
(152.4 × 50.8 cm)
1988.40a–f

Edward Ruscha
(American, born 1937)

Positive. 1972
Gunpowder and pastel on paper
11½ × 29"
(29.2 × 73.7 cm)
1972.7

Susan Rothenberg
(American, born 1945)

Dogs Killing a Rabbit.
1991–92
Oil on canvas
87 × 141"
(221 × 358.1 cm)
1992.14

Edward Ruscha
(American, born 1937)

Vanish. 1972
Oil on linen
20 × 24"
(50.8 × 61 cm)
1973.1

Edward Ruscha
(American, born 1937)

Very. 1973
Pastel on paper
22¾ × 28¾"
(57.8 × 73 cm)
1974.4

Edward Ruscha
(American, born 1937)

Jinx. 1973–74
Oil on canvas
54 × 60"
(137.2 × 152.4 cm)
1974.9

Edward Ruscha
(American, born 1937)

Coiled Paper. 1973
Gunpowder on paper
23 × 29"
(58.4 × 73.7 cm)
1973.6

Edward Ruscha
(American, born 1937)

Brother, Sister. 1987
Acrylic on canvas
72 × 96⅛"
(182.9 × 244.2 cm)
1987.27

278

Edward Ruscha
(American, born 1937)

Year after Year. 1973
Gunpowder on paper
22¼ × 28⅜"
(56.5 × 72.1 cm)
1973.11

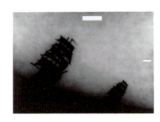

Edward Ruscha
(American, born 1937)

Palette with Hot Colors.
1988
Acrylic on paper
29⅞ × 24"
(75.9 × 61 cm)
1988.43

Edward Ruscha
(American, born 1937)

**Now Then As I Was About
to Say.** (1973)
Shellac on moiré rayon
35¾ × 40"
(90.8 × 101.6 cm)
1973.15

David Salle
(American, born 1952)

Untitled. 1983
Ink wash and oil on paper
18 × 24"
(45.7 × 61 cm)
1983.17

David Salle
(American, born 1952)

Untitled. 1983
Brush and ink and oil
on paper
18 × 24"
(45.7 × 61 cm)
1983.18

Jim Shaw
(American, born 1952)

Study for *Sin of Pride.*
(1988)
Graphite on paper
17 × 14"
(43.2 × 35.6 cm)
1991.2

David Salle
(American, born 1952)

Innocent. (1990)
Acrylic and oil on canvas
with two inserted panels
72 × 90"
(182.9 × 228.6 cm)
1991.5

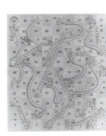

Jim Shaw
(American, born 1952)

**Study for *Snakes and Lad-
ders.*** (1990)
Graphite on paper
17 × 14"
(43.2 × 35.6 cm)
1991.3

Sean Scully
(American, born Ireland
1945)

Untitled. 1989
Watercolor on paper
22 × 30¼"
(55.9 × 76.8 cm)
1990.12

Cindy Sherman
(American, born 1954)

Untitled #122A. 1983
Color photograph, 15/18
comp.: 35¼ × 21¼"
(89.5 × 54.0 cm)
sheet: 40 × 30"
(101.6 × 76.2 cm)
1992.19

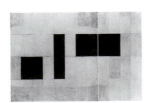

Carole Seborovski
(American, born 1960)

Landscape Diptych. 1986
Graphite and pastel on
paper on two sheets
31 × 44¾" overall
(78.7 × 113.7 cm)
1987.29

Cindy Sherman
(American, born 1954)

Untitled #209. 1989
Color photograph in
artist's frame, 2/6
65 × 49"
(165.1 × 124.5 cm)
1990.5

Cindy Sherman
(American, born 1954)

Untitled #228. 1990
Color photograph in
artist's frame, 6/6
88 × 54"
(223.5 × 137.2 cm)
1991.6

Frank Stella
(American, born 1936)

Untitled. (c. 1971)
Colored crayons on
graph paper
17 × 22"
(43.2 × 55.9 cm)
1989.17

José Maria Sicilia
(Spanish, born 1954)

Red Flower XII. 1986
Acrylic on canvas in
two panels
103 × 118" overall
(261.6 × 299.7 cm)
1987.2

Frank Stella
(American, born 1936)

The Blanket (IRS 8, 1X).
1988
Mixed mediums on
magnesium and aluminum
69½ × 121⅞ × 25"
(176.5 × 312.1 × 63.5 cm)
1988.24

280

Michael Singer
(American, born 1945)

**First Gate Ritual Series
1/30/76.** 1976
Charcoal, chalk, and paper
collage on paper, in artist's
steel frame
45¼ × 84¼"
(114.9 × 214 cm)
1978.11

Frank Stella
(American, born 1936)

The Wheelbarrow (B 3, 1X).
1988
Mixed mediums on
cast aluminum
55¼ × 52¾ × 25"
(140.3 × 134 × 63.5 cm)
1988.22

Ray Smith
(American, born 1959)

**Aves de Rapiña [Birds of
Prey].** 1990
Oil on wood in four panels
96 × 192" overall
(243.8 × 487.7 cm)
1990.25

Donald Sultan
(American, born 1951)

Domino, Feb. 2, 1990. 1990
Tar, latex, and plaster on
tile over wood
12 × 12"
(30.5 × 30.5 cm)
1990.13

Donald Sultan
(American, born 1951)

Dominoes, Aug. 20, 1990.
(1990)
Tar, latex, and plaster on
tile over Masonite in four
parts
98 × 98" overall
(248.9 × 248.9 cm)
1990.42

Wayne Thiebaud
(American, born 1920)

Color Study for *Neighbor-hood Ridge.* 1984
Watercolor, pastel, and
colored pencil over etching
13½ × 10"
(34.3 × 25.4 cm)
1986.15

Volker Tannert
(German, born 1955)

Brot und Spiele [Bread and Circuses]. 1984
Oil on canvas
86½ × 105"
(219.7 × 266.7 cm)
1985.12

James Torlakson
(American, born 1951)

RT Tanker. 1973
Watercolor on paper
11 × 15½"
(27.9 × 39.4 cm)
1973.14

Mark Tansey
(American, born 1949)

Discarding the Frame. 1993
Oil on canvas
84 × 74½"
(213.4 × 189.2 cm)
1993.55

Ernst Trawoeger
(Austrian, born 1955)

Untitled. (1984)
Brush and ink, watercolor,
and collage on paper
23½ × 34"
(59.7 × 86.4 cm)
1985.30

Wayne Thiebaud
(American, born 1920)

Sacramento Riverscape.
1965–66
Pastel on paper
12¼ × 20¼"
(31.1 × 51.4 cm)
1985.21

Ernst Trawoeger
(Austrian, born 1955)

Untitled. 1984
Gouache and brush and
ink on paper
33 × 22"
(83.8 × 55.9 cm)
1985.31

Rosemarie Trockel
(German, born 1952)

Untitled. 1983
Gouache on paper
9⅝ × 7⅜"
(24.5 × 18.7 cm)
1991.31

Cy Twombly
(American, born 1928)

Untitled. 1971–72
Cementite, wax crayon,
and graphite on paper
27½ × 32½"
(69.9 × 82.5 cm)
1988.2

Rosemarie Trockel
(German, born 1952)

Untitled. 1986
Ink and watercolor on
paper
11¼ × 9¼"
(28.6 × 23.5 cm)
1991.32

Meyer Vaisman
(Venezuelan, born 1960)

Jugs. 1989
Process inks and acrylic
on canvas in four panels
96½ × 96½ × 9¾" overall
(245.1 × 245.1 × 24.8 cm)
1990.2

282

William Tucker
(American, born Egypt
1935)

**Untitled (Study for Sculp-
ture).** 1988
Charcoal on paper
60 × 48¼"
(152.4 × 122.6 cm)
1988.45

John Walker
(British, born 1939)

Untitled. 1981
Charcoal and chalk on
paper
32 × 47½"
(81.3 × 120.7 cm)
1984.41

Cy Twombly
(American, born 1928)

Landscape. (1951),
dated 1952
Oil and paper collage
on wood panel
11 × 21"
(27.9 × 53.3 cm)
1989.18

John Walker
(British, born 1939)

Untitled. 1983–84
Oil and canvas collage
on canvas
96 × 120¼"
(243.8 × 305.4 cm)
1985.33

John Walker
(British, born 1939)

Untitled. 1989
Oil on canvas
96 × 84"
(243.8 × 213.4 cm)
1990.3

Christopher Wilmarth
(American, 1943–1987)

Long Given. 1974
Graphite and staples on
layered paper
6 × 12"
(15.2 × 30.5 cm)
1990.33

Andy Warhol
(American, 1928–1987)

Mao. 1973
Graphite on paper
36¼ × 33¾"
(92.1 × 85.7 cm)
1974.10

Robin Winters
(American, born 1950)

Only the Lonely. 1985
Graphite on coffee- and
tea-stained paper (48
sheets) mounted on paper
sheet: 11⅝ × 8¾"
(29.5 × 22.2 cm);
72¼ × 73" overall
(183.5 × 185.4 cm)
1986.17

William Wegman
(American, born 1943)

Art Medal. 1983
Ink and watercolor on
paper
11 × 14"
(27.9 × 35.6 cm)
1990.29

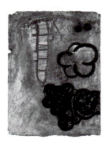

Terry Winters
(American, born 1949)

Schema (74). 1986
Oil and gouache on paper
12 × 8⅝"
(30.5 × 21.9 cm)
1987.9

Margaret Wharton
(American, born 1943)

Family. 1981
Wooden chair, photo-
graph, wood, and concrete
83 × 34 × 30"
(210.8 × 86.4 × 76.2 cm)
1981.7

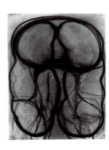

Terry Winters
(American, born 1949)

#8. 1989
Charcoal on paper
30⅛ × 22¼"
(76.5 × 56.5 cm)
1990.24

Paul Wonner
(American, born 1920)

**Still Life on Drawing Table
with Flowers and Clock.**
1979
Acrylic, charcoal, and
pastel on paper
39½ × 27½"
(100.3 × 69.9 cm)
1979.3

Frank Lloyd Wright
(American, 1867–1959)

**Window from the Ward W.
Willis House, Highland Park,
Illinois.** (c. 1901)
Leaded glass
62¾ × 26 × 1½"
(159.4 × 66 × 3.8 cm)
1984.50

Christopher Wool
(American, born 1955)

Untitled. (1988)
Alkyd on rice paper
60 × 35¾"
(152.4 × 90.8 cm)
1988.32

Frank Lloyd Wright
(American, 1867–1959)

**Windows from the Francis
W. Little House, Wayzata,
Minnesota.**
(c. 1913)
Leaded glass in six panels
72¾ × 127½ × 2¼"
(184.8 × 323.9 × 5.7 cm)
1984.48

284

Christopher Wool
(American, born 1955)

Untitled. 1989
Alkyd on acrylic on
aluminum
90 × 60"
(228.6 × 152.4 cm)
1989.15

Frank Lloyd Wright
(American, 1867–1959)

**Skylight from the Francis
W. Little House, Wayzata,
Minnesota.** (c. 1913)
Leaded glass
35½ × 22½ × 2⅛"
(90.2 × 57.2 × 5.4 cm)
1984.49

Christopher Wool
(American, born 1955)

Untitled. (1990)
Alkyd on rice paper
74 × 37½"
(188 × 95.3 cm)
1990.38

Robert Yarber
(American, born 1948)

Palace. 1985
Oil and acrylic on canvas
72 × 132"
(182.9 × 335.3 cm)
1985.39

Robert Yarber
(American, born 1948)

Falling Shopper. 1985
Pastel on paper, two sheets
39½ × 55½" overall
(100.3 × 141 cm)
1985.40

Michael Young
(American, born 1952)

Untitled. 1986
Sand and acrylic on wood
20 × 20 × 4"
(50.8 × 50.8 × 10.2 cm)
1986.43

Michele Zalopany
(American, born 1955)

City of the Gods. (1986)
Charcoal and pastel on
paper in artist's frame
71¼ × 97¾"
(181 × 248.3 cm)
1992.25

Joe Zucker
(American, born 1941)

Reconstruction. 1976
Acrylic and cotton on
canvas
64 × 80"
(162.6 × 203.2 cm)
1976.5

Prints

Twenty-two monotypes from
Scenes and Sequences.
Peter Blum Edition. 1986
Monotypes
Stroll (March 1, 1986)
a. *Untitled (1)* 15½ × 22 (39.4 × 55.8)
b. *Untitled (3)* 14¾ × 22½ (37.5 × 57.2)
c. *Untitled (5)* 15½ × 22½ (39.4 × 57.2)
d. *Untitled (7)* 15⅛ × 22½ (38.4 × 57.2)
e. *Untitled (8)* 15⅛ × 22½ (38.4 × 57.2)
Voodoo (March 11, 1986)
f. *Untitled (2)* 15⅛ × 22½ (38.4 × 57.2)
g. *Untitled (4)* 15⅛ × 22½ (38.4 × 57.2)
h. *Untitled (5)* 15⅛ × 22½ (38.4 × 57.2)
i. *Untitled (9)* 15⅛ × 22½ (38.4 × 57.2)
j. *Untitled (10)* 15⅛ × 22½ (38.4 × 57.2)
Dance (November 21, 1986)
k. *Untitled (1)* 14½ × 20¼ (36.8 × 51.4)
l. *Untitled (2)* 14⅝ × 20⅜ (37.1 × 51.8)
m. *Untitled (3)* 14½ × 20¼ (36.8 × 51.4)
Companion (November 13, 1986)
n. *Untitled (2)* 15⅛ × 22½ (38.4 × 57.2)
Specter (November 13, 1986)
o. *Untitled (5)* 16 × 20½ (40.6 × 52.1)
p. *Untitled (8)* 18½ × 28 (47.0 × 71.1)
Dream (March 19, 1986)
q. *Untitled (8)* 22½ × 25¼ (57.2 × 64.1)
r. *Untitled (10)* 22½ × 25¼ (57.2 × 64.1)
Backyard (December 10, 1986)
s. *Untitled (10)* 20 × 21½ (50.8 × 54.6)
t. *Untitled (12)* 20¼ × 22⅛ (51.4 × 56.2)
u. *Untitled (20)* 20⅛ × 22 (51.1 × 55.9)
Man (April 12, 1986)
v. *Untitled (5)* 25⅛ × 22½ (63.8 × 57.2)
1988.33a–v

Günther Förg
(German, born 1952)
Krefeld Suite.
Edition Julie Sylvester. 1987
One bronze relief and four lithographs printed in color, 9/12
relief: 30½ × 19½ × 2 (77 × 49 × 5), each sheet 27½ × 21 (69 × 53); various composition dimensions as follows:
I. 19 11/16 × 13⅜ (50 × 34)
II. 19⅝ × 13½ (49.9 × 34.3)
III. 19 13/16 × 13 7/16 (50.4 × 34.2)
IV. 19⅝ × 13¼ (49.9 × 33.7)
1989.16a–e

Sam Francis
(American, born 1923)
Yunan.
Gemini G.E.L. (1971)
Lithograph printed in color, 23/66
28½ × 42 (72.4 × 106.7)
(Lembark 134)
1971.6

Untitled.
Gemini G.E.L. 1978 [1976–79]
Lithograph printed in color, 3/15
60 × 60 (152.4 × 152.4)
(Lembark 233)
1978.68

Lucian Freud
(British, born Germany 1922)
Lawrence Gowing.
James Kirkman and Anthony d'Offay. (1982)
Etching, 2/10
6⅞ × 5⅞ (17.5 × 15)
13 × 10¼ (33 × 26)
1989.13

Head of Girl I.
James Kirkman and Anthony d'Offay. (1982)
Etching, 12/16
4⅜ × 4½ (11.2 × 11.5)
10¾ × 8¼ (27.3 × 21)
1989.12

Head of Girl II.
James Kirkman and Anthony d'Offay. (1982)
Etching, A.P. IV/VII
6⅜ × 5⅛ (16.2 × 13)
13⅝ × 11⅛ (34.5 × 28.3)
1989.22

Head on a Pillow.
James Kirkman and Anthony d'Offay. (1982)
Etching, 10/14
4 × 5 (10.2 × 12.7)
9 × 9½ (22.8 × 24.1)
1990.39

A Couple.
James Kirkman and Anthony d'Offay. (1982)
Etching, 22/25
4½ × 4½ (11.5 × 11.5)
10¾ × 8¼ (27.3 × 21)
1989.23

Bella.
James Kirkman and Anthony d'Offay. (1982)
Etching, A.P. II/X
5¾ × 5¼ (14.5 × 13.3)
10¾ × 8¼ (27.3 × 21)
1989.40

The Painter's Mother.
James Kirkman and Anthony d'Offay. (1982)
Etching, A.P. VII/X
7 × 6 (17.8 × 15.2)
15 × 25¼ (38.1 × 63.7)
1989.14

Head and Shoulders.
James Kirkman and Anthony d'Offay. (1982)
Etching, A.P. VI/VIII
9⅝ × 11¾ (24.5 × 30)
15 × 16⅜ (38 × 41.5)
1989.24

Head of a Woman.
James Kirkman and Anthony d'Offay. (1982)
Etching, A.P.
5 × 5 (12.7 × 12.7)
10¾ × 8¼ (27.3 × 21)
1993.41

Ib.
James Kirkman and Brooke Alexander Inc. (1984)
Etching, 37/50
11½ × 9½ (29 × 24)
22½ × 20¾ (57 × 53)
1989.4

Head of Bruce Bernard.
James Kirkman and Brooke Alexander Inc. (1985)
Etching, 46/50
11⅝ × 11¾ (29.5 × 30)
20 × 18½ (50.8 × 47)
1987.24

Blond Girl I.
James Kirkman and Brooke Alexander Inc. (1985)
Etching, 25/50
27¼ × 21⅜ (69 × 54.2)
35 × 28⅜ (89 × 72)
1989.37

Girl Holding Her Foot.
James Kirkman and Brooke Alexander Inc. (1985)
Etching, 26/50
27⅛ × 21¼ (69 × 54)
35 × 29½ (89 × 75)
1989.34

Man Posing.
James Kirkman and Brooke Alexander Inc. (1985)
Etching, 21/50
27½ × 21⅝ (70 × 55)
35 × 29⅛ (89 × 74)
1989.35

Thistle.
James Kirkman and Brooke Alexander Inc. (1985)
Etching, A.P. V/VIII
6¾ × 5⅜ (17 × 13.5)
12¼ × 9¾ (31 × 25)
1989.9

Bella.
James Kirkman and Brooke Alexander Inc. (1987)
Etching, 45/50
16⅝ × 13¾ (42.2 × 34.8)
27¼ × 22⅜ (69.3 × 57)
1989.6

Girl Sitting.
James Kirkman and Brooke Alexander. (1987)
Etching, 45/50
19¾ × 17¼ (50.2 × 44)
20⅞ × 27¾ (53 × 70.5)
1989.36

Lord Goodman in His Yellow Pyjamas.
James Kirkman and Brooke Alexander Inc. (1987)
Etching with yellow, A.P. IV/X
12¼ × 15⅞ (31.1 × 43.3)
18⅞ × 22¼ (48 × 56.1)
1989.8

Head of A Man.
James Kirkman and Brooke Alexander Inc. (1987)
Etching, A.P. III/X
8⅞ × 7¼ (22.6 × 18.3)
19¾ × 17¼ (50.2 × 44)
1989.10

Naked Man on a Bed.
James Kirkman and Brooke Alexander Inc. (1987)
Etching, 5/10
11¾ × 11¾ (29.8 × 29.8)
23 × 22½ (58.5 × 57)
1989.20

Head of Ib.
James Kirkman and Brooke Alexander Inc. (1988)
Etching, 17/40
8¼ × 5¾ (21 × 14.6)
14¼ × 11 (36.2 × 28)
1989.5

Man Resting.
James Kirkman and Brooke Alexander Inc. (1988)
Etching, 17/30
14½ × 16⅛ (36.9 × 41)
18½ × 19¾ (47 × 50.2)
1989.7

Pluto.
James Kirkman and Brooke Alexander Inc. (1988)
Etching, A.P. IV/X
12⅝ × 23⅝ (32.1 × 60)
16½ × 27 (42 × 68.6)
1989.11

Two Men in the Studio.
James Kirkman and
Brooke Alexander Inc. (1989)
Etching, 6/25
9 × 8 (22.9 × 20.3)
16 × 14¼ (40.7 × 36.2)
1989.19

Naked Man on a Bed.
James Kirkman and
Brooke Alexander Inc. (1990)
Etching, 12/40
11¾ × 11¾ (29.8 × 29.8)
23 × 22½ (58.5 × 57)
1990.26

Head and Shoulders of a Girl.
James Kirkman and
Brooke Alexander Inc. (1990)
Etching, 34/50
27⅜ × 21½ (69.5 × 54.5)
30¾ × 25 (78 × 63.5)
1991.27

Esther.
James Kirkman and
Brooke Alexander Inc. (1991)
Etching, 6/25
8⅝ × 8 (22 × 20.2)
17¼ × 15½ (44 × 39.3)
1991.28

Four Figures.
James Kirkman and
Brooke Alexander Inc. (1991)
Etching, 8/30
23½ × 33⅝ (59.5 × 85.5)
27 × 37¼ (68.5 × 94.5)
1991.29

Kai.
James Kirkman and
Matthew Marks Gallery. (1992)
[1991–92]
Etching, 22/40
27½ × 21⅝ (69.8 × 54.6)
31¼ × 25 (79.4 × 63.5)
1992.16

Woman on a Bed.
James Kirkman and
Matthew Marks Gallery. (1992)
[1991–92]
Etching, 22/30
9⅜ × 8⅛ (24.1 × 20.4)
17½ × 15½ (44.4 × 38.6)
1992.17

Head of a Man.
Matthew Marks Gallery. (1992)
Etching, 6/20
8½ × 8 (21.6 × 20.3)
16⅝ × 16 (42.1 × 40.6)
1992.36

Large Head.
Matthew Marks Gallery. (1993)
Etching, 11/40
27 5/16 × 21 5/16 (69.4 × 55.7)
32½ × 26⅛ (82.6 × 66.4)
1993.53

Landscape.
Matthew Marks Gallery. (1993)
Etching, 11/30
5⅞ × 7¾ (15.5 × 19.7)
14 × 15½ (35.6 × 39.4)
1993.54

Hamish Fulton
(British, born 1946)
Humming Heart.
Waddington Graphics. (1983)
Three-part photogravure
with letterpress, 30/60
Three sheets, each 24 × 18¾
(61 × 47.6)
1985.7a–c

Jedd Garet
(American, born 1955)
Nice Sky.
Cirrus Editions. (1982)
Lithograph printed in color,
30/45
21½ × 40 (54.6 × 101.6)
1983.2

Blood.
Cirrus Editions. (1982)
Lithograph printed in color,
a) 34/45, b) 35/45
Two sheets, each 21½ × 40
(54.6 × 101.6)
1983.3a–b

Joe Goode
(American, born 1937)
Untitled.
Cirrus Editions. 1971
Lithograph and silk screen
printed in color, 60/110
6 × 7 (15.2 × 17.8)
8½ × 9½ (21.6 × 24)
1971.7

Adolf Gottlieb
(American, 1903–1971)
Black Splash.
Marlborough Graphics. 1967
Silk screen printed in color, 46/75
30¼ × 22 (76.8 × 55.8)
1971.1

Nancy Graves
(American, born 1940)
Extracten.
Skowhegan. 1982
Intaglio printed in color, 30/30
15 × 14⅞ (38.1 × 37.8)
22 × 30 (55.8 × 76.2)
1983.20

Philip Guston
(American, born Canada,
1913–1980)
East Side.
Gemini G.E.L. 1980
Lithograph, 26/50
32¾ × 42½ (82.5 × 108)
1989.50

Summer.
Gemini G.E.L. 1980
Lithograph, 6/50
20⅜ × 31 (51.7 × 78.7)
1989.51

Remains from the portfolio
*8 Lithographs to Benefit the
Foundation for Contemporary
Performance Arts Inc.*
Gemini G.E.L. (1981)
Lithograph, 48/50
19⅝ × 29 13/16
(49.8 × 75.9) irreg.
19 11/16 × 29 13/16 (50 × 75.7)
1989.52

Pile-up.
Gemini G.E.L. (1981)
Lithograph, 37/50
20 × 29¾ (50.8 × 75.6)
1989.53

Painter.
Gemini G.E.L. (1983)
Lithograph, A.P. 11/11
32 × 42½ (81.3 × 107.6)
1989.54

Jane Hammond
(American, born 1950)
Full House.
U.L.A.E. (1992–93)
Intaglio printed in color, 10/32
78½ × 51 (199.4 × 129.5) irreg.
1993.51

Auguste Herbin
(French, 1882–1960)
Untitled.
Guilde internationale de
la sérigraphie. (1957)
Silk screen printed in color,
102/150
20 × 26½ (50.8 × 67.3)
1971.2

David Hockney
(British, born 1937)
Pembroke Studio Interior.
Tyler Graphics. 1984
Lithograph printed in color in
hand-painted frame, 57/70
40½ × 49½ (102.9 × 125.7);
frame 46⅛ × 55⅛
(117.2 × 140)
1985.35

Caribbean Tea Time.
Tyler Graphics. (1987)
Two-sided, four-panel folding
screen: front, offset lithograph
printed in color with hand
coloring and collage; back, silk
screen printed in color on four
white-lacquered wood panels in
artist's frame, 26/36
83¾ × 136½ (212.7 × 346.7)
1987.28

*Luncheon at the British Embassy
(Tokyo, February 1983).*
Tyler Graphics. 1983
138 color photographs mounted
on paper, 18/20
46 × 83 (116.8 × 210.8)
1986.3

Jörg Immendorff
(German, born 1945)
Nachtcafe #5.
Maximilian Verlag-Sabine Knust.
1983
Linoleum cut printed in color,
4/10
61½ × 80¼ (156.2 × 203.9)
71 × 90 (177.8 × 228.6)
1983.26

*Atelier Deutschland
(Ich liebe mein land).*
The artist. 1983
Linoleum cut with hand-
painting, unique
61¾ × 80¾ (156.8 × 204.1)
irreg.; 70½ × 89 (179.1 × 226.1)
1983.22

Bill Jensen
(American, born 1945)
Endless.
U.L.A.E. (1985) [1983–85]
Portfolio of eleven etchings,
some with aquatint, drypoint,
solvent lift, open-bite, roulette,
scraping, burnishing, sugar
lift, and photogravure, 8/38
10 sheets each 7 × 5 (17.8 ×
12.7); 20 × 15 (50.8 × 38.1)
1 sheet, 5 × 7 (12.7 × 17.8);
15 × 20 (38.1 × 50.8)
1986.10a–k

Exit.
U.L.A.E. (1984–89)
Intaglio printed in color, 22/48
5 × 8 15/16 (12.7 × 22.8)
13 11/16 × 16⅝ (34.7 × 42.2)
1989.46

Guy and the Loon.
U.L.A.E. 1989
Intaglio printed in color, 17/55
9⅝ × 7¼ (24.3 × 18.4)
17¾ × 13¾ (45 × 34.9)
1989.47

Sled.
U.L.A.E. (1987–89)
Intaglio printed in color, 10/40
10⅛ × 7¾ (25.8 × 19.9)
18¾ × 15⅜ (47.6 × 39)
1989.48

Vanquished.
U.L.A.E. (1988–89)
Intaglio printed in color, 14/53
13⅝ × 9½ (34.5 × 24.1)
22½ × 17¾ (57 × 45.1)
1990.14

Lie-Light.
U.L.A.E. (1989–90)
Intaglio printed in color, 14/55
9½ × 14½ (24.1 × 36.8)
18¼ × 23 (46.3 × 58.4)
1990.19

For Alice Too.
U.L.A.E. 1990
Etching printed in color, 14/51
13¼ × 13¾ (33.6 × 34.9)
21 × 20¾ (53.3 × 52.7)
1991.12

For Alice.
U.L.A.E. (1990–91)
Etching printed in color, 10/45
14½ × 14½ (36.8 × 36.8)
22½ × 21 11/16 (57.2 × 55.1)
1991.41

Deadhead.
U.L.A.E. (1991–92)
Etching printed in color, 7/41
13¾ × 12½ (34.9 × 31.7)
21⅜ × 19 (54.3 × 48.3)
1992.22

Jasper Johns
(American, born 1930)
Coat Hanger #1.
U.L.A.E. 1960
Lithograph, 22/35
25½ × 21 1/16 (64.9 × 53.5)
36 × 27 (91.4 × 68.6)
(Field 2)
1978.6

False Start I.
U.L.A.E. 1962
Lithograph printed in color, A.P.
18 × 13¾ (45.7 × 34.9)
30 3/16 × 22¼ (76.7 × 56.5)
(Field 10)
1982.6

False Start II.
U.L.A.E. 1962
Lithograph printed in color, 24/30
18 × 13¾ (45.7 × 34.9)
30⅝ × 21⅞ (77.8 × 55.6)
(Field 11)
1989.60

Painting with Two Balls I.
U.L.A.E. 1962
Lithograph printed in color, A.P.
20 15/16 × 17" (53.2 × 43.2)
26 9/16 × 20⅜ (67.5 × 51.8)
(Field 8)
1983.13

0–9.
U.L.A.E. 1963 (1960–63)
Portfolio of ten lithographs with title page, 8/10
each 16 1/16 × 12 13/16 (40.8 × 31)
20½ × 15½ (52.1 × 39.4)
(Field 17-26)
1988.34a–k

Watchman.
U.L.A.E. 1967
Lithograph printed in color, 3/40
34¼ × 23⅝ (87 × 60)
36 1/16 × 24 3/16 (91.6 × 61.4)
(Field 60)
1986.30

First Etchings.
U.L.A.E. 1967 (1967–68)
Portfolio of six etchings and photo-engravings with title page (printed from two plates), 4/26
title page: 4⅞ × 8¼ (12.4 × 21); 6 × 9 5/16 (15.2 × 23.7)
a. *Flashlight,* 15 7/16 × 14 13/16 (39.2 × 37.6), 25⅜ × 19⅝ (64.5 × 49.8)
b. *Light Bulb,* 12½ × 8⅞ (31.8 × 22.5), 26 × 20⅛ (66 × 51.1)
c. *Ale Cans,* 18 7/16 × 11¼ (46.8 × 28.6), 25⅜ × 19 11/16 (64.5 × 50)
d. *Paintbrushes,* 22½ × 12 7/16 (57.1 × 31.6), 25¼ × 19½ (64.1 × 49.5)
e. *Flag,* 22⅛ × 17¾ (56.2 × 45.1), 26 × 20 1/16 (66 × 51)
f. *Numbers,* 13¼ × 16⅜ (33.7 × 41.6), 26 × 20 1/16 (66 × 51)
(Field 71–77)
1989.57a–g

Target.
Simca Print Artists and the artist. 1974
Silk screen printed in color, 61/70
34 3/16 × 25 15/16 (86.8 × 65.9)
34⅞ × 27⅜ (88.6 × 69.5)
(Field 192)
1980.2

Corpse and Mirror.
Simca Print Artists and the artist. 1976
Silk screen printed in color, 12/65
37 11/16 × 49 11/16 (95.7 × 126.2)
42¼ × 53 (107.3 × 134.6)
(Field 211)
1985.38

The Dutch Wives.
Simca Prints Artists and the artist. 1977
Silk screen printed in color, 21/70
40 11/16 × 51¼ (103.3 × 130.2)
43 × 56 1/16 (109.2 × 142.4)
1978.7

0 Through 9.
Gemini G.E.L. 1977
Lithograph printed in color, 10/60
6¼ × 5⅛ (15.9 × 13.1)
9¾ × 7¾ (24.8 × 19.7)
1978.4

0 Through 9.
Gemini G.E.L. 1977
Lithograph printed in color, 10/60
5⅞ × 4¾ (14.9 × 12.1)
9¾ × 7¾ (24.8 × 19.7)
1978.5

Savarin 1 (Cookie).
U.L.A.E. 1978
Lithograph, 32/42
16 5/16 × 11 3/16 (41.4 × 28.4)
25⅞ × 20⅛ (65.7 × 51.1)
1978.8

Savarin 5 (Corpse and Mirror).
U.L.A.E. 1978
Lithograph printed in color, 30/42
18⅞ × 13⅝ (47.9 × 34.6)
26 × 19 5/16 (66 × 50.6)
1978.12

Usuyuki.
U.L.A.E. 1979
Lithograph printed in color, 42/49
32⅞ × 45 15/16 (83.5 × 116.7)
34 7/16 × 50 5/16 (87.5 × 127.8)
1988.31

Usuyuki.
Simca Print Artists and the artist. 1980
Silk screen printed in color, 89/90
45 × 14 13/16 (114.3 × 37.6)
52 × 20 (132.1 × 50.8)
1980.3

Usuyuki.
U.L.A.E. 1980
Lithograph, 28/57
47 × 17 13/16 (119.4 × 45.2)
52½ × 20¼ (133.4 × 51.4)
1981.5

Usuyuki.
Simca Print Artists and the artist. 1981 [1979–81]
Silk screen printed in color, 44/85
28 5/16 × 45⅜ (71.9 × 115.3)
29½ × 47¼ (74.9 × 120)
1981.10

Voice 2.
U.L.A.E. (1982)
Lithograph printed in color, 19/54
Three sheets:
a) 34 × 23½ (86.4 × 59.7);
b) 34 7/16 × 23 5/16 (87.5 × 59.2);
c) 34⅝ × 23⅜ (87.9 × 59.4);
each sheet 36 × 24⅝ (91.4 × 62.5)
1983.6

Voice 2.
U.L.A.E. 1982
Lithograph printed in color, 4/38
8¾ × 18½ (22.2 × 47)
19 13/16 × 25 7/16 (50.3 × 64.6)
1983.28

Voice 2.
U.L.A.E. 1983
Lithograph printed in color, 28/36
8¾ × 18 11/16 (22.2 × 47.5)
19 11/16 × 25⅞ (50 × 65.7)
1983.29

Ventriloquist.
U.L.A.E. 1985
Lithograph printed in color, 37/67
33 7/16 × 23⅛ (85 × 58.7)
41½ × 27 15/16 (105.4 × 71)
1985.23

Ventriloquist II.
U.L.A.E. 1986
Lithograph, 62/69
36 13/16 × 24¾ (93.5 × 62.9)
41⅝ × 29 5/16 (105.8 × 74.5)
1986.29

Winter.
U.L.A.E. 1986
Aquatint, etching, and open-bite, 22/34
9 3/16 × 6 9/16 (24.9 × 16.7)
16⅛ × 11 15/16 (41 × 30.4)
1987.3

The Seasons.
U.L.A.E. 1987
Set of four etchings with aquatint, sugar lift, and spit-bite, printed in color, 57/73
each 19⅜ × 12¾ (49.2 × 32.4)
26¼ × 19¼ (66.7 × 48.9)
1988.21a–d

The Seasons.
U.L.A.E. 1989
Intaglio, 20/59
38¼ × 25½ (97.1 × 64.7)
46¾ × 32½ (118.7 × 82.5)
1989.45

Winter.
U.L.A.E. 1986–89
Lithograph, 20/34
9½ × 6⅜ (24.1 × 16.2)
15 × 11¼ (38.1 × 28.6)
1989.64

The Seasons.
U.L.A.E. 1990
Intaglio, 22/50
43 × 38½ (109.2 × 97.8)
50¼ × 44½ (127.6 × 113)
1990.30

Summer (Blue).
U.L.A.E. 1985–91
Lithograph printed in color, 143/225
16¼ × 11¼ (41.3 × 28.6)
1991.50

Green Angel.
U.L.A.E. 1991
Etching and aquatint printed in color, 20/46
25½ × 18 (64.7 × 45.7)
31 × 22½ (78.7 × 57.1)
1991.26

Untitled.
U.L.A.E. 1991
Intaglio, 20/38
34 × 72¼ (86.4 × 183.5)
42½ × 78 (107.9 × 198.1)
1991.39

Untitled.
U.L.A.E. 1992
Aquatint and etching, 20/50
35⅝ × 45½ (90.4 × 115.6)
43½ × 52½ (110.5 × 133.3)
1992.23

After Holbein.
U.L.A.E. 1993
Lithograph printed in color, 10/48
16 × 13⅛ (40.6 × 33.3)
25¾ × 18⅝ (65.4 × 47.3)
1993.46

After Holbein.
U.L.A.E. 1993
Lithograph printed in color, 10/48
15¾ × 15¾ (40 × 40)
23½ × 22¼ (59.7 × 56.5) irreg.
1993.49

Alex Katz
(American, born 1927)
The Red Band.
Simca Print Artists. (1979)
Screenprint printed in color, 22/60
54¾ × 36¼ (139 × 92)
(Maravelle 116)
1979.5

Red Coat.
Simca Print Artists. (1983)
Serigraph printed in color, 27/73
58 × 29 (147.3 × 73.7)
1983.24

The Green Cap.
Crown Point Press. (1985)
Woodcut printed in color, 77/200
12³⁄₁₆ × 17¹⁵⁄₁₆ (31.0 × 45.5)
17¾ × 24¼ (45.1 × 61.6)
1985.28

A Tremor in the Morning.
Peter Blum Edition. (1986)
Portfolio of ten woodcuts printed in color, 33/45
each 12 × 12 (30.5 × 30.5)
20½ × 19⅞ (52.1 × 50.5)
Accompanied by a book with eleven linoleum cuts printed in color by Alex Katz and ten poems by Vincent Katz
1986.36a–j

Ellsworth Kelly
(American, born 1923)
Red Curve (Radius of 8').
Gemini G.E.L. (1975) [1973–75]
Lithograph printed in color with embossing, 41/50
33¼ × 24 (81.9 × 61)
43 × 34 (109.2 × 86.3)
(Axsom 106)
1975.5

Light Blue with Orange.
Maeght Editeur. (1964) [1964–65]
Lithograph printed in color, 19/75
18¾ × 15 (47.6 × 38)
34¼ × 23⅝ (87 × 60)
(Axsom 14)
1971.3

Dark Gray and White.
Tyler Graphics. (1979) [1977–79]
Screenprint and collage, 26/41
30 × 42 (76.2 × 106.7)
(Axsom 180)
1979.1

Julian Lethbridge
(American, born 1947)
Untitled.
U.L.A.E. 1990
Lithograph, 10/58
22¾ × 17 (57.8 × 43.2)
1990.47

Untitled.
U.L.A.E. 1991
Lithograph, 10/49
22¹³⁄₁₆ × 17¼ (57.9 × 43.9)
1991.13

Untitled.
U.L.A.E. 1991
Transfer lithograph, 10/57
23⅞ × 17¹¹⁄₁₆ (60.7 × 45)
29⁷⁄₁₆ × 22½ (74.8 × 57.1)
1991.42

Access.
U.L.A.E. 1992
Lithograph and silk screen, 20/50
25 × 18¼ (63.5 × 46.3)
1992.24

Untitled.
U.L.A.E. 1991
Intaglio, 10/18
14½ × 10½ (36.8 × 26.7)
21½ × 17 (54.6 × 43.2)
1992.34

Sherrie Levine
(American, born 1947)
Meltdown.
Peter Blum Edition. (1989)
Suite of four woodblock prints, 25/35
24 × 18 (61 × 45.7)
36½ × 25½ (92.5 × 64.7)
1990.6

Roy Lichtenstein
(American, born 1923)
Sweet Dreams, Baby!
from the portfolio *11 Pop Artists Volume II.*
Original Editions. (1965)
Serigraph, 77/200
35⅝ × 25⁹⁄₁₆ (90.5 × 64.9)
37⅝ × 27⁹⁄₁₆ (95.6 × 70)
1976.1

The Melody Haunts My Reverie
from the portfolio *11 Pop Artists Volume II.*
Original Editions. (1965)
Serigraph, 175/200
27⅛ × 22¹⁵⁄₁₆ (68.9 × 58.2)
30⅛ × 24 (76.5 × 60.9)
1976.4

Peace Through Chemistry I.
Gemini G.E.L. 1970
Lithograph printed in color, 30/32
31¾ × 57⅜ (80.6 × 145.7)
37¾ × 63½ (95.9 × 161.3)
1989.61

Peace Through Chemistry II.
Gemini G.E.L. 1970
Lithograph printed in color, 2/43
31¾ × 57¼ (80.6 × 145.4)
37¼ × 63 (94.6 × 160)
1986.13

Mirror No. 6.
Gemini G.E.L. 1972
Lithograph and silk screen printed in color, A.P./IX
40¾ × 52¹⁵⁄₁₆
(103.5 × 134.5)
1978.13

Bull Profile Series.
Gemini G.E.L. 1973
Suite of six linoleum cuts printed in color, 26/100
each 20⅛ × 29⅝ (51.1 × 75.2)
27 × 35 (68.6 × 88.9)
1973.9a–f

Still Life with Portrait.
Castelli Graphics. 1974
Lithograph with silk screen, 58/100
38⅛ × 28½ (96.8 × 72.4)
39¼ × 29⅜ (99.7 × 74.6)
1974.6

At the Beach.
Gemini G.E.L. 1978
Lithograph printed in color, 30/38
17⅝ × 33⅞ (44.8 × 86)
26 × 42 (66 × 106.7)
1978.9

Head from the series *Expressionist Woodcuts.*
Gemini G.E.L. 1980
Woodcut and embossing printed in color, 42/50
33⁵⁄₁₆ × 27¹⁄₁₆
(84.7 × 68.8) irreg.
40 × 33¾ (101.7 × 85.7)
1981.3

I Love Liberty.
La Paloma Press. 1982
Lithograph printed in color, 20/250
32¼ × 21 (81.9 × 53.3)
38¼ × 27 (97.2 × 68.6)
1983.5

Two Paintings: Sleeping Muse.
Gemini G.E.L. 1984
Woodcut and lithograph printed in color, 28/60
34¾ × 45⅞ (88.3 × 116.5)
37¾ × 48⅞ (95.9 × 124.2)
1984.10

The Sower.
Gemini G.E.L. 1985
Lithograph and woodcut printed in color, 35/60
38 × 52¼ (96.5 × 132.7)
41¼ × 55⅜ (104.8 × 140.7)
1986.4

View from the Window.
Gemini G.E.L. 1985
Lithograph and woodcut printed in color, 14/60
76½ × 30½ (194.3 × 77.5)
79⁹⁄₁₆ × 33⁹⁄₁₆ (202.1 × 85.3)
1986.5

Brushstroke Figures: Nude.
Graphicstudio and Waddington Graphics. 1989 [1987–89]
Color waxtype, lithograph, woodcut, and screenprint, 7/60
57¹³⁄₁₆ × 37⅜ (146.9 × 94.9)
1988.6

Brushstroke Figures: Blonde.
Graphicstudio and Waddington Graphics. 1989 [1987–89]
Color waxtype, lithograph, woodcut, and screenprint, 7/60
57 13/16 × 37 3/8 (146.9 × 94.9)
1988.7

Brushstroke Figures: The Mask.
Graphicstudio and Waddington Graphics. 1989 [1987–89]
Color waxtype, lithograph, woodcut, screenprint, and collage, 7/60
46 1/8 × 31 1/4 (117 × 79.4)
1988.8

Brushstroke Figures: Blue Face.
Graphicstudio and Waddington Graphics. 1989 [1987–89]
Color waxtype, lithograph, woodcut, screenprint, and collage, 7/60
54 × 33 1/2 (137.2 × 85.1)
1988.9

Brushstroke Figures: Grandpa.
Graphicstudio and Waddington Graphics. 1989 [1987–89]
Color waxtype, lithograph, woodcut, and screenprint, 7/60
57 × 41 1/8 (144.8 × 104.4)
1988.10

Brushstroke Figures: Green Face.
Graphicstudio and Waddington Graphics. 1989 [1987–89]
Color waxtype, lithograph, woodcut, and screenprint, 7/60
58 7/8 × 41 (149.5 × 104.1)
1988.11

Brushstroke Figures: Portrait.
Graphicstudio and Waddington Graphics. 1989 [1987–89]
Color waxtype, lithograph, woodcut, and screenprint, 7/60
52 9/16 × 34 1/4 (133.5 × 87)
1988.12

Robert Longo
(American, born 1953)
Gretchen, Jules, Mark.
Brooke Alexander Inc. 1983 [1982–83]
A set of three lithographs with embossing, printed in color, 2/45
each 29 15/16 × 15 (76 × 38.1)
irreg.; 36 1/2 × 21 (92.7 × 53.3)
1983.14a–c

Suzanne McClelland
(American, born 1959)
Then.
U.L.A.E. 1993
Lithograph printed in color, 10/55
22 3/8 × 30 (56.8 × 76.2) irreg.
1993.39

Brice Marden
(American, born 1938)
Five Threes.
Parasol Press, Ltd. (1977) 1976–77
Portfolio of five etchings with aquatint, 20/25
a. 21 × 29 7/8 (53.3 × 75.8)
33 × 40 (83.8 × 101.5)
b. 21 × 29 3/4 (53.2 × 75.6)
33 × 40 (83.8 × 101.5)
c. 21 × 29 3/4 (53.3 × 75.5)
33 × 40 (83.8 × 101.5)
d. 21 × 29 3/4 (53.3 × 75.5)
33 × 39 3/4 (83.8 × 100.8)
e. 21 × 29 5/8 (53.3 × 75.4)
33 × 39 9/16 (83.8 × 100.2)
(Lewison 28)
1989.58a–e

Etchings to Rexroth.
Peter Blum Edition. 1986
Portfolio of twenty-five etchings with sugar lift, aquatint, scraping, burnishing, and drypoint, 38/45
each 8 × 7 (20.3 × 17.8)
19 5/8 × 16 (49.7 × 40.8)
(Lewison 40)
1987.20a–y

Cold Mountain Series, Zen Studies 1–6.
The artist. 1991
Series of six etchings and aquatint, 3/35
each 20 5/8 × 27 (52.5 × 68.6)
27 1/4 × 35 1/4 (69.5 × 89.5)
(Lewison 43)
1991.49a–f

Robert Motherwell
(American, 1915–1991)
Gauloises Bleues (Raw Umber Edge).
U.L.A.E. (1971)
Aquatint and linoleum cut printed in color, 16/38
11 5/8 × 6 9/16 (29.5 × 16.7)
22 15/16 × 15 1/2 (58.3 × 39.3)
(Belknap 70)
1971.4

Gauloises Bleues (Yellow with Black Square).
U.L.A.E. (1971)
Aquatint printed in color, 15/35
11 5/8 × 6 1/2 (29.5 × 16.5)
22 3/4 × 15 7/16 (57.8 × 39.2)
(Belknap 71)
1971.5

America-La France Variations II.
Tyler Graphics. (1984)
Lithograph printed in color with collage, 25/70
41 3/4 × 26 (106 × 66)
45 1/2 × 29 (115.5 × 73.7)
(Belknap 298)
1984.21

America-La France Variations III.
Tyler Graphics. (1984)
Lithograph printed in color with collage, 22/70
48 × 30 3/4 (122 × 78.1)
(Belknap 299)
1984.22

America-La France Variations IV.
Tyler Graphics. (1984)
Lithograph printed in color with collage, 24/68
41 1/8 × 26 1/4 (104.6 × 66.7)
46 1/2 × 32 1/8 (118 × 81.5)
(Belknap 300)
1984.23

America-La France Variations V.
Tyler Graphics. (1984)
Lithograph printed in color with collage, 23/60
46 × 31 1/2 (116.8 × 80)
(Belknap 301)
1984.24

America-La France Variations VII.
Tyler Graphics. (1984)
Lithograph printed in color with collage, 30/68
48 3/4 × 32 (123.8 × 81.3)
52 1/4 × 36 (132.7 × 91.4)
(Belknap 302)
1984.25

America-La France Variations VIII.
Tyler Graphics. (1984)
Lithograph printed in color with collage, 38/69
43 1/2 × 15 1/2 (110.5 × 39.4)
50 × 21 1/2 (127 × 54.7)
(Belknap 304)
1984.26

Black Sounds.
Tyler Graphics. (1984) (1983–84)
Lithograph printed in color with collage, 58/60
39 × 25 (99 × 63.5)
(Belknap 306)
1984.27

Water's Edge
Tyler Graphics. (1984)
Lithograph printed in color with collage, 54/62
28 × 23 (71.1 × 58.4) irreg.
33 × 26 1/2 (83.8 × 67.4)
(Belknap 307)
1984.28

The Persian II.
Tyler Graphics. (1984)
Etching and aquatint printed in color, 11/70
19 3/4 × 15 5/8 (50.2 × 39.7)
25 3/4 × 22 (65.4 × 55.8)
(Belknap 323)
1984.51

La Casa de la Mancha
Tyler Graphics. (1984)
Etching and aquatint printed in color, 8/70
17 3/4 × 23 5/8 (45.1 × 60)
24 × 30 3/4 (65.4 × 55.8)
(Belknap 319)
1984.52

Mexican Night II.
Tyler Graphics. (1984)
Etching and aquatint printed in color, 32/70
17 3/4 × 17 9/16 (45.1 × 44.6)
24 × 24 (61 × 61)
1984.53

Bistre Signs.
Tyler Graphics. (1984)
Aquatint printed in color, 20/24
21 3/4 × 27 1/2 (55.2 × 69.9)
27 1/2 × 33 (69.8 × 83.8)
1984.54

Blackened Sun.
Tyler Graphics. (1984)
Etching and aquatint printed in color, 11/30
33 3/4 × 22 3/4 (86.7 × 58.2)
40 3/4 × 29 (103.5 × 73.7)
(Belknap 313)
1984.55

Glass Garden.
Tyler Graphics. (1984)
Etching and aquatint printed in color, 36/59
9 3/4 × 22 1/2 (24.9 × 57.2)
18 1/4 × 31 (46.4 × 78.7)
(Belknap 312)
1984.56

Naples Yellow Open.
Tyler Graphics. (1984)
Etching and aquatint printed in color, 8/62
11 3/4 × 17 5/8 (29.8 × 44.8)
19 3/8 × 25 (49.2 × 63.5)
(Belknap 311)
1984.57

Australia.
Tyler Graphics. (1984)
Etching and aquatint printed in color, 9/25
17 3/4 × 23 1/2 (45.1 × 59.7)
25 × 30 (63.5 × 76.2)
(Belknap 296)
1984.58

Redness of Red.
Tyler Graphics. (1985)
Lithograph printed in color with collage, 89/100
24 × 16 (61 × 40.6)
(Belknap 326)
1985.10

Elizabeth Murray
(American, born 1940)
Quartet.
U.L.A.E. 1989–90
Suite of four etchings printed in color, 15/59
8 × 6½ (20.3 × 16.5) each
18 × 14 (45.7 × 35.6)
1990.31a–d

Undoing.
U.L.A.E. 1989–90
Lithograph, aquatint, and drypoint printed in color, 19/60
29 × 23 (73.6 × 58.4) irreg.
1991.15

Birds.
U.L.A.E. 1991
Monotype over etching printed in color, 12/21
7½ × 4¾ (19 × 12)
13½ × 10¼ (34.3 × 26)
1991.43

Hat.
U.L.A.E. 1991
Monotype over etching printed in color, 12/23
7½ × 4¾ (19 × 12)
13½ × 10¼ (34.3 × 26)
1991.44

Wiggle Manhattan.
U.L.A.E. (1992)
Lithograph printed in color, 19/47
58¾ × 29 (149.2 × 73.6) irreg.
1992.20

Her Story.
U.L.A.E. 1988–90
Illustrated book with text by Anne Waldman
Letterpress, lithograph, etching, and aquatint, 41/74
11 × 17½ (27.9 × 44.4)
1991.1

Bulb.
U.L.A.E. 1993
Mezzotint printed in color, 10/40
7⅝ × 4¾ (19.4 × 12.1)
17⅛ × 12¾ (43.5 × 32.4)
1993.40

Shoe String.
U.L.A.E. 1993
Lithograph printed in color with collage, 10/70
40¾ × 33¾ × 5 (103.5 × 85.7 × 12.7)
1993.45

Barnett Newman
(American, 1905–1970)
Canto XIV from the portfolio *18 Cantos*
U.L.A.E. 1964. [1963–64]
Lithograph printed in color, 3/18
14½ × 12¼ (36.8 × 31.1)
16¼ × 13¾ (41.3 × 34.9)
1992.30

Kenneth Noland
(American, born 1924)
Circle II from the *Handmade Paper Project.*
Tyler Graphics. 1978
Five layers of colored pulp with lithographic monoprinting
21 × 32 (53.3 × 81.3)
1978.10

Claes Oldenburg
(American, born Sweden 1929)
Profile Airflow.
Gemini G.E.L. 1969
Molded polyurethane over lithograph, 63/75
33½ × 65½ (85.1 × 166.4)
1986.47

Tilting Neon Cocktail.
Brooke Alexander and The New Museum of Contemporary Art. 1983
Stainless steel, plastic, and wood, 27/50
18¾ × 10 × 7⅝
(47.6 × 25.4 × 19.4)
1983.27

Nam June Paik
(Korean, born 1932)
V-Idea.
Carl Solway Gallery and Galerie Watari. (1984)
Portfolio of title page and ten etchings, some with aquatint, printed in color, 33/58
each 12 × 15 (30.5 × 38.1) irreg.
18⅝ × 21¾ (47.3 × 55.8)
1988.47a–k

A. R. Penck
(German, born 1939)
Me in the West.
Sabine Knust. (1985)
Etching and aquatint, A.P. III/X
35 × 64½ (88.9 × 163.8)
44½ × 72 (113 × 182.8)
1985.34

Robert Rauschenberg
(American, born 1925)
Glacial Decoy Series (IV).
U.L.A.E. 1980
Lithograph printed in color, 2/25
51¼ × 40 (130.2 × 101.6)
66 × 40 (167.6 × 101.6)
1981.4

5:29 Bay Shore.
U.L.A.E. 1981
Lithograph and collage, 5/30
42⁹⁄₁₆ × 88⅛ (108.1 × 223.8)
45³⁄₁₆ × 93³⁄₁₆
(114.8 × 236.7)
1981.16

Truth #11
Gemini G.E.L. 1982
Handmade paper with fabric and paper collage, unique
43 × 31 (109.2 × 78.7)
1982.7

Soviet/American Array I.
U.L.A.E. 1988–89
Intaglio printed in color with collage, 10/55
88½ × 53½ (224.8 × 135.9)
1989.49

Soviet/American Array II.
U.L.A.E. 1988–90
Intaglio printed in color with collage, 10/55
87¾ × 52¼ (222.8 × 132.7)
1990.20

Soviet/American Array III.
U.L.A.E. 1989–90
Intaglio printed in color, 10/57
87¾ × 52¼ (222.8 × 132.7)
1990.41

Soviet/American Array IV.
U.L.A.E. 1988–90
Intaglio printed in color, 10/58
88½ × 52 (224.8 × 132.1)
1990.48

Soviet/American Array V.
U.L.A.E. 1988–90
Intaglio printed in color, 10/55
88½ × 53½ (224.8 × 135.9)
1991.8

Soviet/American Array VI.
U.L.A.E. 1988–90
Intaglio printed in color, 10/59
88½ × 53¼ (224.8 × 135.3)
1991.23

Soviet/American Array VII.
U.L.A.E. 1988–91
Intaglio printed in color, 10/55
79 × 51¼ (200.6 × 130.2)
1991.38

Street Sounds.
U.L.A.E. 1992
Intaglio printed in color, 10/38
42⅞ × 49¾ (108.9 × 126.4)
45⅞ × 54⅞ (116.5 × 139.4)
1992.37

Street Sounds West.
U.L.A.E. 1993
Intaglio printed in color, 10/32
56½ × 34¼ (143.5 × 87)
1993.52

Gerhard Richter
(German, born 1932)
Mao.
Edition H. Haseke. 1968
Photo lithograph, 10/22
33⅛ × 23½ (84.1 × 59.7)
1991.9

Larry Rivers
(American, born 1923)
French Money.
U.L.A.E. 1963
Lithograph printed in color, 31/32
19¹⁄₁₆ × 29¾ (48.5 × 75.6)
22⁷⁄₁₆ × 31½ (57 × 80)
1979.4

Diane Raised I.
U.L.A.E. 1970
Lithograph printed in color, 2/20
17¾ × 23¾ (45.1 × 60.3)
22¼ × 30 (61.6 × 76.2)
1971.8

Dorothea Rockburne
(American, born Canada 1929)
Radiance.
Gemini G.E.L. 1982
Lithograph printed in color, 19/37
40 × 32 (101.6 × 81.3)
1983.23

James Rosenquist
(American, born 1933)
Expo '67 Mural—Firepole 33' x 17'
U.L.A.E. 1967
Lithograph printed in color, 41/41
33¹⁄₁₆ × 17 (84 × 43.2)
33¹⁵⁄₁₆ × 18⅝ (86.2 × 47.8)
1972.3

Star, Towel, Weather Vane.
Gemini G.E.L. 1977
Lithograph printed in color with collage, 27/42
22⅛ × 44⅛ (56.2 × 112.1)
1978.1

House of Fire.
Tyler Graphics. 1989
Colored and pressed paper pulp, lithograph, collage, 48/54
54½ × 119¾ (138.4 × 304.2)
1990.7

Space Dust.
Tyler Graphics. 1989
Colored and pressed paper pulp, lithograph, collage, 39/56
66½ × 105¼ (168.9 × 267.3) irreg.
1990.8

Susan Rothenberg
(American, born 1945)
Listening Bamboo.
U.L.A.E. 1989–90
Etching and woodcut, 22/23
42 1/4 × 65 3/4 (107.3 × 167)
54 1/4 × 83 1/2 (137.8 × 212.1)
1990.40

Mezzo Fist #1.
U.L.A.E. 1990
Mezzotint, 10/49
19 7/16 × 19 1/2 (49.4 × 49.6)
31 7/8 × 22 1/4 (70 × 56.5)
1990.21

Mezzo Fist #2.
U.L.A.E. 1990
Mezzotint, 10/48
17 13/16 × 13 5/8 (45.3 × 34.6)
24 5/8 × 19 3/4 (62.5 × 50.2) irreg.
1990.22

Red Bamboo.
U.L.A.E. 1991
Woodcut, 10/39
37 3/4 × 24 (95.9 × 61)
45 3/4 × 32 1/4 (116.2 × 81.9)
1991.45

Edward Ruscha
(American, born 1937)
Hollywood in the Rain.
Tamarind Workshop. 1969
Lithograph printed in color, 7/8
2 1/8 × 8 1/4 (5.4 × 21)
7 × 12 (17.8 × 30.5)
1973.14

Crackers.
Graphicstudio. 1970
Lithograph, 21/30
8 1/2 × 11 1/2 (21.6 × 29.2)
16 × 20 (40.6 × 50.8)
1972.4

Pepto-Caviar Hollywood.
Cirrus Editions. 1970
Organic silk screen, 45/50
15 × 42 1/2 (38 × 107.9)
1972.1

Twenty-Six Gasoline Stations.
Graphicstudio. 1970
Lithograph printed in color, 20/30
8 1/2 × 12 1/2 (21.6 × 31.7)
16 × 20 (40.6 × 50.8)
1972.5

News, Mews, Pews, Brews, Stews, Dues.
Editions Alecto. 1970
Portfolio of six organic silk screens, 8/125
each 25 × 31 (63.5 × 78.7)
1993.47

Blue Suds.
Edizioni O. 1971
Silk screen printed in color, 8/100
18 × 24 (45.7 × 61)
1973.4

Green Suds.
Edizioni O. 1971
Silk screen printed in color, 50/100
18 × 24 (45.7 × 61)
1972.2

Grey Suds.
Edizioni O. 1971
Silk screen printed in color, 8/100
18 × 24 (45.7 × 61)
1973.3

Dish.
Neighbors of Watts. 1973
Lithograph, 231/250
3 1/2 × 7 7/8 (8.9 × 20)
10 × 13 1/2 (25.4 × 34.3)
1973.16

Evil.
Cirrus Editions. (1973)
Silk screen on wood grain veneer, perfumed with "Cabochard" de Grés, 22/30
19 7/8 × 30 1/8 (50.5 × 76)
1973.10

Spooning.
Brooke Alexander and Cirrus Editions. 1973
Lithograph hand-colored with lipstick, A.P. 1
6 1/4 × 9 3/4 (15.9 × 25)
12 3/16 × 25 5/8 (31.2 × 64.8)
1973.12

Cameo Cuts Suite.
Edition Julie Sylvester. 1992
Six lithographs printed in color, 9/28
each 4 5/8 × 7 5/8 (11.6 × 19.2)
12 × 12 (30.5 × 30.5)
1992.9

Alan Shields
(American, born 1944)
Odd-Job.
Tyler Graphics. 1984
Woodcut, etching, relief, stitching, and collage, 14/46
41 × 41 (104.1 × 104.1)
1984.29

Bull-Pen.
Tyler Graphics. 1984
Woodcut, etching, aquatint, and collage, 12/46
40 1/4 × 41 3/4 (102.2 × 106)
1984.30

Milan-Fog.
Tyler Graphics. 1984
Woodcut, etching, aquatint, stitching, and collage, 19/46
39 1/2 × 31 1/2 (100.3 × 80)
1984.31

Gas-Up.
Tyler Graphics. (1984)
Woodcut, etching, aquatint, relief, knotting, and collage, 10/46
56 1/2 × 40 1/2 (143.5 × 102.9)
1984.32

Kiki Smith
(American, born Germany 1954)
Untitled.
U.L.A.E. 1990
Lithograph, 15/54
36 × 36 (91.4 × 91.4)
1990.32

Banshee Pearls.
U.L.A.E. (1991)
Suite of twelve lithographs with aluminum leaf, 14/51
22 3/4 × 30 5/8 each (57.8 × 77.8)
1991.46a–l

Untitled.
U.L.A.E. 1992
Etching and collage, 12/50
42 × 62 (106.7 × 157.5)
1992.21

Sueño.
U.L.A.E. 1992
Etching, 10/33
41 1/4 × 71 1/4 (104.7 × 181)
41 1/4 × 76 3/4 (104.7 × 194.9)
1992.33

Kiki Smith 1993.
U.L.A.E. 1993
Intaglio, 10/33
73 × 36 1/2 (185.4 × 92.7)
1993.48

Frank Stella
(American, born 1936)
Star of Persia I.
Gemini G.E.L. 1967
Lithograph printed in color, 18/92
22 1/2 × 25 15/16 (57.1 × 65.9)
25 15/16 × 31 15/16 (65.9 × 81.1)
(Axsom 1)
1986.25

V Series.
Gemini G.E.L. 1968
Set of eight lithographs, printed in color with varnish, 42/100.
a. Ifafa I, 11 1/8 × 19 5/16 (28.2 × 49.1), 16 1/4 × 22 3/8 (41.2 × 56.8)
b. Ifafa II, 11 3/16 × 19 3/8 (28.4 × 49.2), 16 1/4 × 22 3/8 (41.2 × 56.8)
c. Itata, 11 3/16 × 19 3/8 (28.4 × 49.2), 16 1/4 × 22 3/8 (41.2 × 56.8)
d. Black Adder, 11 1/8 × 25 11/16 (28.3 × 65.3), 16 1/4 × 22 3/8 (41.2 × 56.8)
e. Quathlamba I, 11 1/16 × 25 7/8 (28.1 × 65.7), 16 1/4 × 28 7/8 (41.3 × 73.3)
f. Quathlamba II, 11 1/8 × 25 3/4 (28.2 × 65.4), 16 1/4 × 28 7/8 (41.3 × 73.3)
g. Empress of India I, 11 1/8 × 32 5/16 (28.3 × 82.1), 16 1/4 × 35 3/8 (41 × 89.8)
h. Empress of India II, 11 1/8 × 32 1/4 (28.3 × 82), 16 1/4 × 35 3/8 (41 × 89.8)
(Axsom 25)
1986.26a–h

Port aux Basques from the *Newfoundland Series.*
Gemini G.E.L. 1971
Lithograph and silk screen printed in color, T.P. IV
32 1/8 × 63 15/16 (81.6 × 162.5)
37 15/16 × 69 15/16 (96.5 × 177.7)
(Axsom 54)
1992.40

Swan Engraving Circle I/State I.
Tyler Graphics. 1983 [1981–84]
Etching, engraving and woodcut printed in color, 3/5
52 diameter (132.1)
1984.3

Swan Engraving Circle II/State IV.
Tyler Graphics. 1983 [1981–84]
Etching and woodcut printed in color, 4/5
52 diameter (132.1)
1984.4

Imola Five II, State I from the *Circuits Series.*
Tyler Graphics. (1983)
Relief, screenprint, and woodcut printed in color, 7/10
66 × 49 (167.6 × 124.5)
(Axsom 166a)
1984.5

Yellow Journal, State I.
Tyler Graphics. 1982
Lithograph printed in color, 4/16
52 1/2 × 38 1/2 (133.5 × 97.8)
(Axsom 162a)
1984.6

Playskool Chair.
Tyler Graphics. 1983
Patinated cast bronze, fabricated aluminum, copper, wood dowels, etched magnesium, honeycomb aluminum, hand coloring, 3/5
30 × 30 × 13 (76.2 × 76.2 × 33)
1984.2

Imola Three II from the *Circuits Series.*
Tyler Graphics. (1984)
Relief and woodcut printed in color, 20/30
66 × 52 (167.6 × 132.1)
(Axsom 164)
1984.33

Imola Three II, State I from the
Circuits Series.
Tyler Graphics. (1984)
Relief, woodcut, stencil, and
screenprint, printed in color, 6/10
66 × 52 (167.6 × 132.1)
(Axsom 164a)
1984.34

Imola Three IV from the
Circuits Series.
Tyler Graphics. 1984
Relief and screenprint printed
in color, 28/30
66 × 52 (167.6 × 132.1)
(Axsom 165)
1984.35

Pergusa Three Double.
Tyler Graphics. 1984
Relief, screenprint, woodcut,
and engraving, printed
in color, 12/30
two sheets 52 × 66 (132.1 ×
167.6) each, hinged together
102 × 66 (259.1 × 167.6) overall
(Axsom 167)
1984.44

Then Came a Dog & Bit the Cat
from the portfolio *Illustrations
After El Lissitzky's Had Gadya.*
Waddington Graphics. 1984
[1982–84]
Lithograph, linoleum cut, silk
screen, and rubber relief printed
in color with hand coloring and
collage, 27/60
53½ × 51⅝ (135.9 × 131.1)
1984.36

Back Cover from the portfolio
*Illustrations After El Lissitzky's
Had Gadya.*
Waddington Graphics. 1984
[1982–84]
Lithograph, linoleum cut, silk
screen, and rubber relief, printed
in color with hand coloring
and collage, 57/60
60¼ × 53⅛ (153 × 134.9)
1984.37

Wayne Thiebaud
(American, born 1920)
Candy Apples.
Crown Point Press. 1987
Woodcut printed in color,
109/200
15¼ × 16½ (38.7 × 41.9)
23½ × 24¼ (59.7 × 61.6)
1987.12

Hill Street.
Crown Point Press. 1987
Woodcut printed in color,
189/200
30¼ × 20¼ (76.2 × 61.4)
37 × 24½ (95.4 × 61.3)
1988.27

Eight Lipsticks.
Crown Point Press. 1988
Drypoint and etching
printed in color, 34/60
7 × 6 (17.8 × 15.2)
14 × 12 (35.6 × 30.5)
1988.28
Steep Street.
Crown Point Press. 1989
Spitbite, aquatint
printed in color, 17/50
29½ × 21¾ (74.9 × 55.2)
38¾ × 30½ (98.4 × 77.5)
1989.42

James Torlakson
(American, born 1951)
14829 East 14th.
The artist. (1973)
Etching and aquatint, A.P.
9¾ × 14½ (24.8 × 36.8)
1973.14

Henri de Toulouse-Lautrec
(French, 1804–1901)
Aristide Bruant dans son cabaret.
Charles Verneau. (1893)
Brush and spatter lithograph,
printed in color, first state of two
55⅛ × 38⅞ (140 × 98.8)
(Adhemar 15, Delteil 348,
Wittrock 9)
1984.20

James Turrell
(American, born 1943)
Series "D" from First Light.
Peter Blum Edition. (1990)
[1989–90]
Suite of four aquatints, 16/30
39 × 27¼ (99.1 × 69.2) each
42¼ × 29¾ (107.3 × 75.6) each
1990.36a–d

Andy Warhol
(American, 1928–1987)
Campbell's Soup I.
Factory Editions. (1968)
Portfolio of ten silk screens
printed in color, 250/250
31⅞ × 18¾ (81 × 47.6) each
35 × 23 (88.9 × 58.4)
1989.39

Joseph Beuys.
Editions Schellman and Klüser.
(1980–83)
Silk screen printed in color
with rayon flock, 95/150
39¹³⁄₁₆ × 32 (101.2 × 81.3)
39¹⁵⁄₁₆ × 32 (101.4 × 81.3)
1985.5

Terry Winters
(American, born 1949)
Folio.
U.L.A.E. 1985–86
Portfolio of eleven lithographs
printed in color, including title
page and colophon, 18/39
30 × 22½ (76.2 × 57.2) each
1986.32a–m

Fourteen Etchings.
U.L.A.E. 1989
Portfolio of fourteen etchings
with collage, including
title page and colophon, 14/65
18⅝ × 14⅛ each
(47.3 × 35.9)
1990.15a–p

Novalis.
U.L.A.E. 1983–89
Etching, 14/50
42½ × 31 (107.9 × 78.8)
1990.23

Section.
U.L.A.E. 1991
Lithograph, 10/68
59½ × 40 (151.1 × 101.6)
1991.47

Theorem.
U.L.A.E. 1992
Lithograph, 10/41
31⅝ × 47⅞ (80.2 × 121.6)
1992.27

Locus.
U.L.A.E. 1993
Lithograph printed in color,
10/49
24⅞ × 35⅞ (63.2 × 91.1)
1993.44

List of **Illustrations**

John Ahearn
Margie (1980–81)
Clyde (Black and White), (1982)

Richard Artschwager
Seated Group (1962)

Frank Auerbach
Study for *Primrose Hill, High Summer,* 1959
J.Y.M. Seated, 1981

Jo Baer
Untitled (Korean), 1962

John Baldessari
If This Then That (1988)

Stephan Balkenhol
Figurensäule Mann {Column Figure Man}, (1993)
Figurensäule Frau {Column Figure Woman}, (1993)

Jennifer Bartlett
In the Garden #105 (1980)

Georg Baselitz
Peitschenfrau {Whip Woman}, 1964
Untitled (Hero), 1966
Untitled, 12.VI.87, 1987
Untitled, 2.V.89, 1989
Fünfmal Meise {Five Times Titmouse}, 1988–89
Die Wendin [from the series *Die Dresdner Frauen*
  {The Women of Dresden}], 1990
Untitled, 29.I.91, 1991
Untitled, 19. X. 91, 1991

Jean-Michel Basquiat
Tobacco versus Red Chief, 1981

Lothar Baumgarten
El Dorado (1985)

Glen Baxter
The Pleasure Seekers, 1987

Billy Al Bengston
Ventana Dracula (1972)

Jake Berthot
Nick's Door 1985–86

Joseph Beuys
Hirschkuh (c. 1950)
Gold Sculpture (1956)

Domenico Bianchi
Untitled, 1984

Ashley Bickerton
Catalog: Terra Firma Nineteen
  Hundred Eighty Nine #2, 1989

Jonathan Borofsky
Splithead at 2,783,798 (1974)–1982

Richard Bosman
Assassin (1981)

Louise Bourgeois
Untitled (1949)

Troy Brauntuch
Untitled, 1981

Roger Brown
Swamp Rose Mallow a View from Afar (1980)

Michael Byron
Water (1983)
Judas Goat Boy of Love, 1986

Miriam Cahn
Schiff {Boat}, 1982

Anthony Caro
Odalisque, 1985

Bruno Ceccobelli
Virginia, 1985

Vija Celmins
Galaxy #1 (Coma Berenices), 1973
Galaxy #4 (Coma Berenices), 1974
Galaxy #2 (Coma Berenices), 1974–75
Drawing Saturn, 1982
Night Sky #5, 1992

Louisa Chase
Mist in Mountains, 1982
Saint Joan, 1983–84

Sandro Chia
Free Elaboration (1981)
Three Boys on a Raft, 1983

Francesco Clemente
Non Androgino (1979)
Perseverance (1982)
Earth (from the series *The Four Elements*) (1982)
Self-Portrait (1984)
Salvation, 1987

Chuck Close
Large Mark Pastel, 1978
Self-Portrait, 1991

Greg Colson
El Paso, 1990

Bruce Conner
Untitled Drawing, 1972
Sampler, 1991

Alan Cote
Approaching, 1983–84

Tony Cragg
Grey Moon (1985)

Gregory Crane
Circular Valley near Big Pink, (1984)

Enzo Cucchi
Leone dei Mari Mediterranea
  {Lion of the Mediterranean Sea}, 1979–80
Untitled, 1983
Vitebsk-Harar (1984)
Untitled, 1986

Walter Dahn
Untitled, 1985
Untitled, 1985
Untitled, 1986
Untitled, 1988

John Davies
Man with Two Poles, 1975

Willem de Kooning
Untitled (c. 1950)
Untitled III (1982)

Gianni Dessi
Canto Profondo, 1984
Misura, 1985

David Deutsch
Square Pond (1984–85)

Jane Dickson
Witness (J.A.), 1991

Richard Diebenkorn
Table and Chair, 1964
Two Nudes Standing, 1965
Untitled (Ocean Park #13), 1983
Untitled, 1985

Jean Dubuffet
Memoration XX, 1978

Carroll Dunham
Purple and Blue, 1986
Large Shape with Bands, 1989

300

*This section is
arranged alpha-
betically by
artist and
chronologically
for the works of
each artist.
Dates or portions
of dates not
inscribed on the
work by the
artist appear in
parentheses.*

Barbara Ess
Untitled, 1988

William Fares
Circular Ruins, 1974
Untitled (study for Circular Ruins) 1974

Eric Fischl
Coney Island, 1981
Untitled, 1984
Untitled #8 and *Untitled #10*, 1986
The Chester's Gambit, 1991

Janet Fish
Chinoiserie, 1984

Joel Fisher
Untitled (Drawing No. 12), (c. 1982)
Untitled (Drawing No. 1), (1988–89)
Untitled (Drawing No. 26), (1988–89)

Dan Flavin
"monument" 1 for V. Tatlin, (1964)

Günther Förg
Pinakothek, München (1983–86)
Untitled, 1987
Lead Painting, 1988

Helen Frankenthaler
Untitled, 1961

Lucian Freud
Self-Portrait (1974)
Double Portrait (1988–90)
Cerith (1989)
Kai (1992)

Giuseppe Gallo
Caino e Abele {Cain and Abel}, (1985)

Jedd Garet
Black Figures #1, 1979
Picture, 1981
Breathing Water, 1982

Gilbert & George
Sad, 1980
Mad Garden, 1982
Winter Heads, 1982

Frances Cohen Gillespie
Lapis Lazuli, 1983

Lawrence Gipe
Study #7 (Fin de Siècle), 1990

Robert Gober
Untitled #5, 1984

Joe Goode
Bed, 1967

Philip Guston
Midnight, 1953
Untitled, 1953
Artist in His Studio, 1969
In the Studio, 1975

Richard Hamilton
People Again, 1969

Jane Hammond
Untitled (254, 164, 151, 80, 5, 21,
39, 193, 264, 44), 1989

Edward Henderson
Untitled, 1984
Untitled, 1985
Untitled, 1985
Untitled, 1985

Damien Hirst
Albumin, Human, Glycated (1992)

David Hockney
To Queens, New York, 1961
House behind Château Marmont, 1976

Howard Hodgkin
In Bed in Venice, 1984–88

Roni Horn
Distant Double 2.26x and 2.26y, 1989

Bryan Hunt
Sister Ship, (1976)
Cloak of Lorenzo, 1981

Yvonne Jacquette
Ferry near Battery Park (Dusk), 1981
Maine Yankee Nuclear Plant V, 1983
Tokyo Billboards II, 1985

Bill Jensen
December 1976, 1976
Chord, 1982–83
Untitled XVII, 1991

Jasper Johns
0–9, 1960–63
Untitled, 1981
Untitled, 1990

Roberto Juarez
Three Birds (1984)
Rattle, 1984

Donald Judd
Untitled, 1967

R. L. Kaplan
Summit I, 1983

Alex Katz
Good Morning I, 1974

Jon Kessler
Under Venice, 1987

Anselm Kiefer
Wege der Weltweisheit: Die Hermannsschlacht
{Ways of Worldly Wisdom: Arminius's Battle}, 1978
Dem unbekannten Maler {To the Unknown Painter}, 1982
A.D. (1989)

Martin Kippenberger
Untitled, 1989
Untitled, 1989

R. B. Kitaj
The Poet Writing (1982)
Notre Dame de Paris, 1984–86

Franz Kline
Study for *Black and White #1* (c. 1952)

Jannis Kounellis
Untitled (1980)

Guillermo Kuitca
Children's Corner, 1990
Nordrhein, 1992

Christopher LeBrun
Prow, 1983
Bay, 1988–89

Mark Lere
You Are the Space That You Occupy, 1982

Barry Le Va
Centers and Sections, 1975

Roy Lichtenstein
Mirror #10, 1970
Final Study for *Landscape with*
Figures and Sun, 1980
Archaic Head VI, 1988
Post Visual, 1993

Thomas Locher
1–11 (1987)

Richard Long
Untitled, 1987

Robert Longo
Untitled, 1981

Andrew Lord
Curves (from the series *Jug and Dish in the Afternoon*) 1984

Markus Lüpertz
Untitled (Mann in Anzug {Man in Suit}), 1976
Untitled (1979–80)

Mark Luyten
Intermezzo, (1987)

Allan McCollum
Five Surrogate Paintings, 1980–81

John McLaughlin
Untitled #20 (1966)

Robert Mangold
Study for Four Color Frame Painting #4 (B), 1984

302

Brice Marden
Untitled, 1971
Study II, 1981
Untitled, 1991

Agnes Martin
The Field, 1966

Louisa Matthiasdottir
Sheep with Pink House (1984)

Meuser
Untitled, 1986
Untitled, 1987
Untitled, 1987

Melissa Miller
Territory, 1983

Gerry Morehead
Above Eight Rivers, 1990

Yasumasa Morimura
Daughter of Art History: Princess B, 1990
Angels Descending Staircase, 1991

Malcolm Morley
Kite (1984)

Jill Moser
Trace (1986)

Robert Moskowitz
Eddystone, 1984

Robert Motherwell
Untitled, 1958

Matt Mullican
Untitled, 1986–87

Elizabeth Murray
Southern California, 1976

James Nares
Untitled, 1986
Untitled, 1986
Untitled, 1986
Untitled, 1986
Untitled, 1986

Bruce Nauman
Read/Reap, 1983

Harry Nickelson
John Tunnard, 1985
Ignace Paderewski, 1985
Untitled, 1985
Quahna Parker, 1986

Claes Oldenburg
A Sock and Fifteen Cents (Studies for Store Objects) (1961), dated 1962
Proposed Colossal Monument to Replace the Nelson Column in Trafalgar Square—Gearshift in Motion, 1966
Proposed Events for Il Corso del Coltello, 1984

Tom Otterness
Frieze Installation of The Battle of the Sexes *and* Hermit Philosopher, 1983–85
Creation Myth, 1986

Mimmo Paladino
Tre Comete {Three Comets}, 1983
Untitled, 1983

Blinky Palermo
Untitled, 1968

A. R. Penck
Venedig {Venice}, 1980
Untitled, 1981

Sigmar Polke
Untitled, 1985

Katherine Porter
To Victor Jara, 1980
Spring, 1984
Untitled, 1984

Harvey Quaytman
Nuncio, 1986

Ed Rainey
Successful Farming No. 6, 1985

Robert Rauschenberg
Untitled, 1958
Sleeping Sweeper, 1988

Edda Renouf
New York Sound Drawing #1, 1977
Visible Sound III, 1978

Sam Reveles
Skull Rack (Spanish), 1991

Gerhard Richter
Helen, 1963
Confus, 1986
18. Okt. 92, 1992
22. Okt. 92, 1992

James Rosenquist
Sketch for House of Fire, 1981

Susan Rothenberg
Untitled, 1976
Untitled, 1979
Biker, 1985
1, 2, 3, 4, 5, 6, 1988
1, 2, 3, 4, 5, 6, 1988
Dogs Killing a Rabbit, 1991–92

Edward Ruscha
Museum on Fire, 1968
Accordion Fold with Vaseline Stains, 1972
Fine Wires, 1972
Positive, 1972
Vanish, 1972
Very, 1973
Coiled Paper, 1973
Year after Year, 1973
Now Then As I Was About to Say (1973)
Jinx, 1973–74
Brother, Sister, 1987
Palette with Hot Colors, 1988
The End, 1991

Robert Ryman
Untitled, 1976

David Salle
My Subjectivity, (1981)
Untitled, 1983
Untitled, 1983
Innocent, (1990)

Julian Schnabel
Olatz IV, (1991)

Sean Scully
Us, 1988
Untitled, 1989

Carole Seborovski
Landscape Diptych, 1986

Richard Serra
No Mandatory Patriotism (1989)

Jim Shaw
Study for *Sin of Pride* (1988)
Study for *Snakes and Ladders* (1990)

Cindy Sherman
Untitled #96, 1981
Untitled #122A, 1983
Untitled #209, 1989
Untitled #228, 1990

José Maria Sicilia
Red Flower XII, 1986

Lorna Simpson
Untitled (1992)

Michael Singer
First Gate Ritual Series 1/30/76, 1976

Alexis Smith
Seven Wonders (1988)

David Smith
Untitled (1952)

Kiki Smith
Identical Twins (1990)

Ray Smith
Aves de Rapiña {Birds of Prey}, 1990

Frank Stella
Untitled, (c. 1971)
The Blanket (IRS #8, 1.875X), 1988
The Blanket (IRS #8, 1X), 1988
The Wheelbarrow (B #3, 1X), 1988
The Wheelbarrow (B #3, 2X), 1988

Donald Sultan
Forest Fire, February 27, 1984 (1984)
Domino, Feb. 2, 1990, 1990
Dominoes, Aug. 20, 1990, (1990)

Volker Tannert
Brot und Spiele {Bread and Circuses}, 1984

Mark Tansey
Discarding the Frame, 1993

Wayne Thiebaud
Desserts, 1961
Sacramento Riverscape, 1965–66
Color Study for *Neighborhood Ridge*, 1984

James Torlakson
RT Tanker, 1973

Ernst Trawoeger
Untitled (1984)
Untitled, 1984

Rosemarie Trockel
Untitled, 1983
Untitled, 1986
Untitled, 1986

William Tucker
Untitled (Study for Sculpture), 1988

Cy Twombly
Landscape, (1951), dated 1952
Untitled, 1971–72
Untitled, 1972
Untitled (1981)

Meyer Vaisman
Jugs, 1989

John Walker
Untitled, 1981
Untitled, 1983–84
Untitled, 1989

Andy Warhol
Cagney (1962)
Mao, 1973

William Wegman
Art Medal, 1983

Margaret Wharton
Family, 1981

Christopher Wilmarth
Long Given, 1974

Robin Winters
Only the Lonely, 1985
Ghent Drawings, 1986

Terry Winters
Schema (74), 1986
Conjugation, 1986
#8, 1989

Paul Wonner
*Still Life on Drawing Table with
   Flowers and Clock*, 1979

Christopher Wool
Untitled, 1988
Untitled, 1989
Untitled (1988)
Untitled (1990)

Frank Lloyd Wright
Window from the Ward W. Willis House,
   Highland Park, Illinois (c. 1901)
Windows from the Francis W.
   Little House, Wayzata, Minnesota (c. 1913)
Skylight from the Francis W. Little House,
   Wayzata, Minnesota (c. 1913)

Robert Yarber
Palace, 1985
Falling Shopper, 1985

Michael Young
Untitled, 1986

Michele Zalopany
City of the Gods (1986)

Joe Zucker
Reconstruction, 1976

Acknowledgments

This is the first publication to provide a comprehensive look at the development of the PaineWebber Art Collection over its twenty-five-year history. Although it was not possible to reproduce every item in the collection, 100 works are reproduced in color and are discussed in detailed catalogue entries, and an additional 175 works are illustrated in black and white, thereby forming a complete visual record of all acquisitions with the exception of prints and multiples, recorded in a complete catalogue listing.

The formation of the collection and the preparation of this volume have benefited from the participation of many individuals, both at PaineWebber and elsewhere, to whom we are greatly indebted.

The two outside contributors to the book, art historian Jack Flam and artist Louise Lawler, have brought their considerable experience of looking at art to their observations of the collection. Jack Flam has provided a thoughtful essay that traces the philosophical and critical evolution of the collection and the part it plays in corporate life. Louise Lawler, who first visited the collection in 1982, has contributed a remarkable series of previously published and new photographs that examine the installation of works from the collection in the PaineWebber offices.

The preparation of this catalogue required making many new photographs of works in the collection; particular thanks are due to Bill Orcutt, Ilonka Van Der Putten, and Dorothy Zeidman as well as Michael Stern and Jim Thomas, who ably assisted in this task. At PaineWebber, collection photography was coordinated by Samantha Dunham, who also assisted with all phases of the publication. Her dedication and consistently optimistic outlook were greatly appreciated. Others who deserve recognition for their roles in the care and administration of the collection throughout its development include Wanda Billington, Cheryl Bishop, Viviane Dabbah Breithart, and Susan Brundage. At PaineWebber, Gerald Blitstein, Elaine Conte, Kingsley Day, Monika Dillon, Paul Guenther, Suzanne Gyorgy, John Lynch, Kristin Mannion, Alexandra Muse, Kelly Smith, and Mark Vassallo have provided invaluable assistance.

In the initial stages of this publication Emily Braun, Kynaston McShine, and Lawrence Weschler generously shared their insights and wisdom. Connie Butler and Sheila Schwartz also provided crucial editorial advice. Allison Greene and Peter Marzio of The Museum of Fine Arts, Houston, offered much-appreciated support and encouragement. Research on work in the collection was greatly facilitated by the staff and resources of the libraries at the Tate Gallery, London, and The Museum of Modern Art, New York.

At Rizzoli, Charles Miers's expertise and enthusiasm for this project have sustained it from the beginning. Under much pressure from a busy schedule, he has coped admirably with all phases of development and production. Jen Bilik, Victoria Ellison, Rose Scarpetis, James Schulman, and Elizabeth White also provided important production and editorial assistance.

The handsome design of this volume represents the collaboration of Brenna Garratt and Woody Pirtle and John Klotnia of Pentagram Design. Their efforts in producing a clear and elegant form from the raw materials of text and photographs are gratefully acknowledged.

The artists represented in the collection, whose work we celebrate in this book, are also to be thanked for their cooperation in this project. We hope they are as pleased with the result as we are.

Finally and most importantly, we wish to express deep appreciation to Donald B. Marron and the Board of Directors of PaineWebber for their long-standing support. Their commitment to contemporary art and dedication to excellence have been the inspiration for the collection documented here.

—Monique Beudert and Jennifer Wells

Photography Credits: All photographs not otherwise credited are by Orcutt Van Der Putten. Pages 24, 276b–277a: Adam Reich. Pages 25, 116: McKee Gallery. Pages 26, 59: Bill Jacobson Studio. Pages 27, 31, 74, 76, 98, 148, 162, 236, 252, 264c, 266g–h, 271c, 276a, 280c, 281f, 283e, 285d: Zindman/Fremont. Pages 28, 106: James Kirkman Ltd. Pages 30 (top and bottom), 90, 93: M. Knoedler and Co. Pages 43, 48, 50, 54, 56, 68, 79, 84, 86, 136, 150, 158, 164, 170, 180, 182, 188, 190, 196, 202–4, 206–7, 220, 232–33, 235, 277c: Dorothy Zeidman. Pages 35, 134, 178: Sotheby's, Inc. Pages 36, 66: Sonnabend Gallery. Pages 44, 212: Glenn Steigelman. Page 60: Jack Tilton Gallery. Pages 64, 139, 156, 264a: Prudence Cuming Associates Ltd. Page 70: Robert Miller Gallery. Page 72: Scott Bowron, McKee Gallery. Page 80: The Pace Gallery. Pages 88, 120, 152, 242: Gagosian Gallery. Pages 94, 142: Christie's. Pages 100, 132, 184, 210, 270e: The Museum of Modern Art, New York. Pages 102, 166: Luhring Augustine Gallery. Pages 110, 126: Vivian Horan Gallery. Page 118: Alex Hartley. Pages 122, 280b–281a: Ken Cohen Photography. Page 124: Douglas M. Parker. Page 130: Gamma One Conversions. Page 140: Marlborough Gallery. Page 172: Michael Klein Gallery, Inc. Page 186: Michael Werner Gallery. Page 193: Friedrich Rosenstiel. Pages 194, 218, 278a: Leo Castelli Gallery. Page 198: Charles Harrison. Page 214: Ellen Page Wilson, The Pace Gallery. Page 216: Sarah Wells. Page 222: Michael Tropea. Page 250: Peter Muscato, Michael Klein Gallery, Inc. Page 260h: Acquavella Galleries. Page 261b, c, e: Richard Nicol. Page 262a: Margo Leavin Gallery. Page 269b: Jon Abbott. Page 270d: Ivan Dala Tana. Pages 274f, 275h: Tom Gabrinetti.

a	e
b	f
c	g
d	h

The above chart represents the order of illustrations in Additional Works.